A Party with Socialists in It

'A welcome corrective. This book astutely appraises British politics' most frustrating but important dissident tradition.'
—*Guardian*

'Admirably clear-sighted.'
—*New Statesman*

'At a very crucial time in British politics, this book helps us to fill in important gaps in our knowledge.'
—David Coates, author of *Prolonged Labour: The Slow Birth of New Labour in Britain*

'A well-timed explanation of the class contradictions at the root of the Labour Party from its creation to the present day.'
—*Labour Briefing*

A Party with Socialists in It

A History of the Labour Left

SECOND EDITION

Simon Hannah

Forewords by
Nadia Whittome and John McDonnell

First published 2018; second edition 2022 by Pluto Press
New Wing, Somerset House, Strand, London WC2R 1LA

www.plutobooks.com

British Library Cataloguing in Publication Data
A catalogue record for this book is available from the British Library

ISBN   978 0 7453 4558 1   Hardback
ISBN   978 0 7453 4557 4   Paperback
ISBN   978 0 7453 4561 1   PDF
ISBN   978 0 7453 4559 8   EPUB

Typeset by Stanford DTP Services, Northampton, England

Contents

Foreword to the Second Edition

Nadia Whittome MP

When I first got involved in the Labour Party in 2013, things were beginning to look up for the Labour left. The party's failure to meaningfully oppose Tory austerity policy was a disappointment to many, but it was around this period that the ground began to shift, as we started to move on from the leaderships of Blair and Brown. The left won a clutch of parliamentary selections, and you could feel the tightly controlled atmosphere of the New Labour era begin to lift. The following year would see the introduction of the system for leadership elections – ironically one that was first proposed by the 'gang of four' in the early 1980s – that would enable Jeremy Corbyn to win the leadership.

For four years after 2015, it felt like there was a real space for the left in the mainstream of British politics. Corbyn's election as Labour leader blew open Westminster, and posed a genuine alternative to the neoliberal consensus that had persisted in both main parties since Blair took over Labour in 1994. We went from being the party of PFI and the Iraq War to being the party of the National Investment Bank and free education. After decades of hollowing-out and over-professionalisation, Labour once again became the home of mass politics, as the movements that cleared the way for Corbyn's leadership came into the party.

Reading this book, you realise what an anomaly that era was. At pretty much every other moment in Labour's history, the left has been either a junior coalition partner to more centrist political forces, or an isolated and ridiculed minority. This was certainly the case in the period immediately before I joined the party during the New Labour years, but it was also the case during the post-war period and in the 1980s when the left was, in terms of organisation and links to a militant labour movement, much stronger than it was in 2015. The unlikely and momentary success of the Corbyn project produced a window of opportunity for the left's ideas, and its people. The fact that I'm an MP is in essence the product of that narrow window.

Simon Hannah's history of the Labour left is a vivid account of more than a hundred years of heroism, defeat, and mass movements which changed the course of British politics. It is a must-read for everyone now involved in the Labour left, if only because it distils a series of awkward strategic dilemmas with which we must all now grapple, and poses the question of whether the Labour left is a dead end. Regardless of what you think about that question, the story it tells is compelling.

Corbynism failed as a project in large part because it failed to learn the lessons of the history that this book contains. If the 'transformative' wing of the party was ever going to succeed, democratising the party was always going to have to be a priority. To make our project sustainable, we would have to turn outwards and rebuild the trade union movement and social movements. But instead, external pressures meant that we looked inwards, focusing on the day-to-day battle for survival and the standard electoral cycle. Despite the best efforts of many activists, nothing much changed in terms of the accountability of the parliamentary party or the party machine. The result is that we are now marginalised once again. Like the Labour left in decades past, we are back in the position of passing conference motions – on wages, energy nationalisation and the anti-union laws – which are openly flouted by the leadership.

One of the problems with the Labour left's relationship with its own history is that it very often takes the form of nostalgia, or of personal adulation for people like Jeremy Corbyn and Tony Benn. Benn and Corbyn are inspiring figures, but, especially given the strategic crisis that we now face, it is inadequate to talk about standing on the shoulders of giants and then to carry on as usual. As much as anything, it would do a disservice to the giants, who must by now be quite bored of all the adulation and frustrated with the left's lack of progress in recent years. What we need is a strategy for the future that is capable of bringing about transformational change.

What that strategy might look like is too big a question to try to deal with in this foreword, but we can say for certain that it will be answered by a movement that is much wider than a narrow circle of politicians, or even the Labour left as a whole. If we have learned anything from the Labour left's history, it is that it has never risen alone. The coming years will see mass movements around the cost-of-living crisis, climate change and racial justice, and our future will to a great extent be determined by how successful these movements are in having a political impact and developing a political expression. I see my job as being an ally to these movements, and to the project of building a re-energised and militant labour movement.

Labour remains a critical battleground for socialists in Britain. In order to confront the climate crisis with anything like the urgency that is required, we will need the state to act, and Labour is, under our current electoral system, the only means we have to form a progressive government. What its policies are, and who populates the parliamentary Labour party, is something we cannot leave uncontested, however frustrating and arduous the process of contesting it might be. The defining question for socialists today is not 'in or out of the Labour Party', but how we can bring together an ecology of different strategies and movements towards a socialist politics that has pluralism and genuine democracy at its heart.

Things change quickly. When I joined Labour in 2013, no one (least of all Jeremy Corbyn) had any idea what would happen just two years later. I come from a generation – and this generation is the future of Labour as well as the future of the electorate – that overwhelmingly rejects the economics of neoliberalism and the politics of border-building and hate. Labour held a 43-point lead among voters under the age of 25 at the last election. When polled, more than half of young people in the United States, in the beating heart of global capital, hold negative views of capitalism. Deep underground things are changing, and while 'mainstream' politics continues to be dominated by unhinged nationalist ideologues and dull professionals in suits, that process of change will shift politics in ways we cannot entirely predict.

We must learn from history, but that does not mean abandoning hope, or assuming that events now will simply be an action replay of those in the past. The strategic impasse that socialists now face, which Simon Hannah eloquently sets out, could yet be washed away by events much faster than any of us dare to dream.

Foreword to the First Edition

John McDonnell MP

What is the Labour Party for? This has been the question at the centre of the party's history since the first trade unionists and progressives came together to discuss whether an independent political party to represent working people should exist at all. The question has focused on whether the Labour Party is a party of social reform aiming simply to ameliorate our existing capitalist society, or a reformist party that seeks to replace capitalism by incremental social reform, or a transformative, some would say revolutionary party, aiming at the radical replacement of the existing economic and social system.

Both those who wish to bring about change in our society and those who want to resist change have sought to understand and influence the role of the party. The various depictions of the party have both informed the decisions of people looking for a vehicle to fulfil their ambition for change and determined the reactions of those desperate to preserve the power and privileges they have secured through the existing system.

This book's incisive history of Labour illustrates that the party has been and can be at different moments in history a party of varying roles: in changing times promoting social reform or confidently advocating and launching a reformist programme and, when the political climate permits, promising realistic transformative change. Without being overly deterministic, the party's role has naturally reflected the political environment in which it has operated, which in turn has influenced the internal balance of political forces within the party.

Nevertheless, contingency has played its part as well. By that I mean, for example, that sometimes it's down to having the right people in the right place at the right time. After Labour was near fatally wounded by the defection of its charismatic leader Ramsay McDonald in the early

1930s, nobody could have predicted that the party would be in power in the following decade with a massive parliamentary majority under the quiet, almost bureaucratic leadership of Clement Attlee.

Clearly the brutal hardships imposed upon working people as a result of the economic crash in 1929 and the subsequent Great Depression, followed by the sacrifices endured in the Second World War, embedded in society an underlying, often unnoticed, but determined demand for change. The lessons learnt from the results of the bombastic 'great man, great leader' dependency syndrome that brought about Hitler and Mussolini also produced an appreciation of the need for a different type of leader. The result was an increasing acknowledgment that another kind of leadership could be just as effective as the great orator style. This was the quieter, everyday, getting-on-with-the-job style that Attlee portrayed.

Although possibly not fully recognised at the time, Attlee was the right person in the right place at the right time. So historical contingency played its part. Nevertheless, the conditions of the 1930s and the wartime years had also delivered up a Labour Party leadership and party membership that had been hewn out of the harsh and precarious political and economic conditions they had had to face for years in order to survive.

The Labour Party at that time set itself up firmly as a party of radical transformation. Many members of the post-war government advocated a programme that went beyond ameliorative reform, and in their articles, books and speeches they set out a vision of systemic change. If that government had survived longer and had been replenished by a new generation in power it may well have had the opportunity to demonstrate how radical transformation could be achieved.

The economic conditions largely determined that a serious opportunity for radical transformation would not fall to a Labour government again until 1997. By then, however, the character of the Labour leadership had changed significantly. Gone were most of those whose desire for transformative change had come from their experience of the harshness of our economic system. The experience of years of relative economic boom had largely eradicated from memory the inherent crisis-ridden nature of capitalism. 'No more boom and bust' became the mantra of economic policy analysis. Labour in government became avowedly and firmly a party of social reform – neither reformist nor transformative. The crash of 2007–8 soon put paid to that. The whole organisation of our economy and society was thrown into question once again. At the bottom of a recession people are generally too busy trying to survive to challenge the system. It is usually when the solutions advocated by political leaders are demonstrably not working for them, and especially when they are told that everything is improving, that they take to demanding something different.

The history of Labour set out so stimulatingly in this book holds open the possibility that the party could move beyond social reform and become a genuinely transformative party once again. A party leadership under Jeremy Corbyn, and a mass membership shaped by the experience of the economic crash, the years of grinding austerity, and its resultant inequality and injustices, are taking their place in the history of the party.

Introduction

When the first edition of *A Party with Socialists In It* was published in 2018, the Labour left was riding high after the better-than-expected results of the 2017 general election. The first edition ended with an account of Jeremy Corbyn being greeted like a rock star by a mass crowd at the Glastonbury music festival. There was a sense that the strategy of socialists working in and through the Labour Party to form a left government was finally on the brink of success. Since then, however, the fortunes of the Labour left have been completely transformed, for the worse. The centrists have retaken control of the party, Corbyn is suspended as a Labour MP, and the radical policies of his years as party leader have been almost totally forgotten by the new leadership. Hundreds of socialists have been expelled and many thousands more have resigned from the Labour Party.

Naturally, plenty has been written about events since 2017, and on how the Labour left was defeated, so there is no need to reinvent the wheel when Owen Jones and others have produced blow-by-blow accounts.[1] However, this second edition does offer a chance to wrap up the analysis of the left of the party and to draw some conclusions. It is worth declaring honestly that while I joined the Labour Party in 2015 as a Marxist with no illusions about the contradictions, disappointments and setbacks that would inevitably come, I have nevertheless gone through the experience even more convinced that Labour is not, nor ever has been, a socialist party.

Jeremy Corbyn's leadership of the Labour Party proved hugely controversial. No other Labour leader in history was so denigrated or conspired against. Indeed, for all of the claims that Corbyn was unelectable, a considerable machine had to be set up by his opponents in the party to prevent Labour winning an election under his leadership, with his politics. At times the intensity of the opposition was so strong it seemed like Labour was two parties rather than one, trapped in a hopeless paralysing civil war. The renewal of old battles within the party – battles that most thought had been settled a generation ago – provided the opportunity for an account of the history of the Labour left. While there are many histories of the Labour Party, there was no history of the Labour left from the start of the party's existence. So the account offered here is ambitious – starting in 1893 and culminating with the end of the Corbyn project and a new purge of the Labour left under Keir Starmer. Given the constraints of space, many events have had to be passed over or dealt with only briefly. Nevertheless, the book introduces the major historical struggles of the left and explains what was at stake on each occasion.

Defining the left of the party can be a challenge. Labour has never been a socialist party, even if – in the words of Tony Benn – it has always had socialists in it. How does their ideology compare to the wider politics of Labourism? Is it defined by a commitment to nationalisation or to pacifism? Perhaps by the singing of the Red Flag? Perhaps it is simply more of a mood, an instinct rather than a consistent strategy? Certainly, historically, what is considered 'left' has been a moving target. What was deemed to be 'right-wing' in the 1950s became left policy in the 1970s; and while Corbynism was far to the left of Tony Blair's New Labour, it was not as economically radical as the Labour policy of the early '70s. Understanding these shifts and the politics behind them is crucial to our understanding of the party's internal politics.

What follows is a critical history – it examines what the left has done well and where and why it has failed. By and large, the history of the Labour left has been one of defeat, and Corbyn's fight was no different in that regard. So, writing an account of the left during a period of its dramatic rise and fall within the Labour Party may help shine a new light on old struggles. To provide a framework, this book will approach the dynamic at the core of the left–right division in terms of a struggle between *transformative* and *integrative* tendencies.[2] It gives an account of those who have fought for Labour to adopt a transformative agenda, through far-reaching economic, social, constitutional and political changes that challenge the existing power relations in society. Such people are on the left in as much as they conform to a general idea of what being on the political left means: being generally anti-capitalist and socialist-minded, seeking radical solutions to everyday problems, opposing Britain's role as an imperialist power. A variety of principles, tactics and strategies have flowed from their orientation to the Labour Party and Parliament as the primary vehicles for a radical, transformative agenda. Necessarily, this is also a history of the Labour left's battle with the other, more dominant, tendency in the party: the integrative tendency typified by those who want to weld the Labour Party to already existing state and social structures for the purpose of incorporating the interests of the labour movement into the establishment. They take society as it is but want greater representation, believing that this in itself will ensure laws that create a better quality of society.

Because the transformative tendency has sought to alter the existing state, economic and social relations, it has inevitably led to a struggle over the nature of the Labour Party itself – over its programme, the role of its MPs, the extent of its extra-parliamentary activity and so on. We will see how the transformative agenda within Labour has played out and the ways in which integrative forces have tried to co-opt or limit oppositional voices. From Bevanism, the Bennite movement and Corbynism on one side, to Ernest Bevin, the Revisionists and Progress on the other, Labour has seen several competing forces from both wings of the party. While the left has always been in a subordinate position, this book also offers an account of how that can change.

In preparing this second edition it is worth saying that the first was necessarily pitched differently as it was intervening in a living movement in which the contradictions of Labourism were as yet unresolved. The battle was on for the future of the Labour Party, but that battle is now over for the time being. Since we have seen the consequences of that struggle played out, this new edition seeks to draw some more fundamental conclusions for the struggles ahead. Some changes have been made to the original text, correcting a few errors or clarifying political points, while the new chapter nine and conclusion aim to weave together several of the threads from earlier chapters.

I have several people to thank for their contributions to this project: Andrew Berry, Liz Davies, Graham Bash, Andrew Fischer and Pete Firmin for their insights; Marc Wadsworth on Black sections; Neil Faulkner for his editorial help; and David Castle at Pluto. I must thank also Ruth, Steven and Edd for their comments and help. Also thank you to the many activists and Labour Party members I have chatted to – your views and ideas were often helpful. Any errors are of course entirely my own.

In addition to the original thank you notes I would add a special mention of Neil Faulkner, who first met with me in 2016 to have a discussion which then became this book, and who also helped me with my book on the anti-Poll Tax movement that came out in 2020. He sadly died far too young in February 2022. We will miss his energy and revolutionary enthusiasm. It is my sincere belief that people who never met Neil will read his books and be inspired to dedicate their lives to the fight against capitalism just as he did.

1

Divided Beginnings

The Labour Party was founded by socialists, but it was not a socialist party they founded. From its conception, Labour was a broad church designed to represent the entire labour movement. As such, it was a party born of contradictions.

Capitalism inevitably generated popular movements seeking to counteract the excesses of the system and to attempt to reform or even replace it. Trade unions and cooperatives were becoming increasingly common even in the early nineteenth century. Chartism was the first major political expression of the demands of working people in Britain; it was a movement that used revolutionary methods and petitions to demand political reform, until it was repressed during the 1840s.

The early cooperative movement underwent an evolution. Starting with utopian projects of building villages of cooperative producers (which had all failed), the movement turned to setting up cooperative businesses to compete with established companies on the high street. While some of these businesses initially thrived, they came into intense competition from the growing monopolies run by exploitative capitalists, a competition they would gradually lose over the next hundred years.

By the mid nineteenth century the workers' movement was dominated by guilds and craft unions made up of a privileged section of well-paid skilled workers who had gained the vote after 1867. Their strategy took the form of a Lib-Lab pact, with the workers supporting Liberals in elections to further their aims in Parliament. In fact, some of the union leaders went on to become Liberal MPs themselves. They believed firmly in a gradualist approach to politics, whereby things would slowly improve if one applied a little friendly pressure – the Whig View of History as inevitable progress.

But as capitalist growth began to slow down, the old methods proved inadequate. A decline in Britain's world trade in the 1890s, and its loss of manufacturing strength to other countries, led to bosses attacking workers over pay and the length of the working day in order to claw back profits. Many industries saw wages lowered for the mass of unskilled, precarious workers. This led to an upsurge in class struggle centred on the 'new unionism': mass unions organising on an industry-wide basis. These unions chalked up impressive victories in the fight for the eight-hour day and higher pay.

The economic slowdown meant Parliament was increasingly hostile to workers. The response to the new unionism was to ban picketing in 1896. At this point the Liberals could no longer be relied upon to advocate for workers' interests. Many Liberals were even supportive of anti-union measures, acting less as fair-weather union allies and more as representatives of Britain's industrial class. Workers began to talk about needing their own people in Parliament, representing their own interests.

In 1893 an ex-miner named Keir Hardie was elected as an independent MP for West Ham South. He was the first explicitly working-class candidate elected on a platform of supporting the workers' movement. Accompanied on his march to Parliament by a procession of cheering workers and their families, the press subsequently falsely reported that the crowd had attempted to force their way into the Commons. It seems Labour has rarely had friends in the media even at its founding. Hardie advocated independent working-class representation and called a conference in Bradford to launch a new national party to take workers' issues into Parliament. The result was the Independent Labour Party. Dismissing any alliance with the untrustworthy Liberals, the ILP's programme called for the 'collective ownership of all the means of production, distribution and exchange', alongside immediate reforms such as the eight-hour day, a welfare state and an extension of voting reform. The ILP looked to Parliament to implement its transformative agenda. This turn to parliamentary politics, alongside the cooperatives and trade unions, created the modern workers' movement.

Within a few years, the ILP had gained several thousand members, among them Ramsay MacDonald and Philip Snowden. Key women's rights activists and Irish freedom campaigners also flocked to the ILP, including James Connolly and Emmeline and Richard Pankhurst. The formation of the party was a significant step forward for the class consciousness of workers, enabling them to represent themselves independently of a wing of the capitalist class. The ambitious founders of the ILP wanted a real, *mass* party of the working class and believed that such a party needed to be based on the largest workers organisations, which in Britain meant the trade unions. Hardie called this the 'Labour Alliance': the unity of the socialists in the ILP with the industrial and financial resources of the unions. The one could not succeed without the other. With the Lib-Lab strategy failing, the unions and socialists needed to work together to create a new mass party of the workers.

However, arraigned against the ILP and others advocating for labour representation were many officials in the Trade Union Congress who were profoundly hostile to the idea of a separate class-based party. Many union leaders still saw the Liberals as their best bet for ameliorating the worst excesses of the system. These 'loyal, but disheartened Gladstonites'[1] had to be dragged kicking and screaming into the new class party. Some trade union leaders felt that a separate party would jeopardise years of collaborative work and could introduce a dangerous destabilising factor into British politics. In opposing the officials, the socialists narrowly won a motion at the TUC (546,000 to 434,000) calling for a specially convened conference to 'devise ways and means of securing an increased number of Labour members in the next parliament'. A narrow win, but enough to establish a new electoral alliance, known as the Labour Representation Committee (LRC), in 1900.

The conference that met to launch the LRC was attended by union delegates representing around 545,000 people, alongside socialist societies including the ILP (13,000 members), the Social Democratic Federation (9,000) and the Fabian Society (861). As the conference delegates gathered to found the LRC, they knew that by taking steps towards the creation of a party of the working class they were raising the stakes considerably. Despite its parliamentary character and the clear intention of most of its founders to play by the rules of parliamentary democracy, it was then and remains now a scandal for the capitalist class that the workers have their own party. Having committed to establishing a party of the working class, the conference debated how to achieve material gains for that class. It is tempting to say that the history of the Labour Party is a footnote to this founding conference, since the arguments raised and the political divisions that emerged in 1900 continued to reverberate down the years as contending social forces played themselves out over motion papers and policy documents.

It was the unions, not the socialist societies, who really mattered in Labour's political and social make up. By 1900, powerful networks of full-time officials had been established across the trade unions, forming a caste who saw themselves as negotiators and mediators on behalf of their members. Even today, the structural role of trade unions and their officials in the bureaucracy mean that they are usually averse to more militant forms of action, preferring the negotiating room to the picket line. The Labour Party was from the start a product of the desire of the unions for a political extension of their negotiating power. The point of unity between the ILP and the unions was that both sought to realise their goals through Parliament – the ILP as a route to socialism, the unions as a way to secure social reforms. It is also the point of unity for the integrationist approach – the material basis of MPs and union full-timers lends itself to incorporation into the existing state structure.

In the initial constitutional arrangement there was no individual membership or branches, only affiliations from trade unions, trades councils and socialist societies. Outside the unions, the ILP made up the LRC membership on the ground, their branches acting as the local branches of the new party. Of the three socialist groups present, the political lines of difference were clear: the ILP's was the dominant line, flanked by the Marxist left and the Fabians on the pro-liberal right. The ILP brought together traditions of municipal socialism, ethical romanticism, radical trade unionism and local activism. The SDF were led by

H.N. Hyndman, an eccentric ex-banker who fancied himself a Marxist, though of a somewhat sectarian and doctrinaire sort. The Fabians attracted intellectuals (including George Bernard Shaw and Sidney and Beatrice Webb), artisans and academics. The Fabians initially remained aloof from the party, their strategy being to 'permeate' the Liberals and Tories with left-wing ideas, convincing the establishment to support the plight of the poor through rational and moral argument. Their fear was that a new party might damage that long-term goal by sowing divisions.

The debate at the founding conference was largely between the SDF and everyone else. The SDF wanted Labour to be an explicitly socialist party. Their motion to the meeting argued that 'the representatives of the working class movement in the House of Commons shall form there a distinct party ... based upon recognition of the class war, and having for its ultimate object the socialisation of the means of production, distribution, and exchange'. Keir Hardie opposed this, arguing instead that the remit should be more limited, to seek to form 'a distinct Labour group in Parliament, who shall have their own whips, and agree upon their policy, which must embrace a readiness to cooperate with any party which for the time being may be engaged in promoting legislation in the direct interests of labour'. Hardie's version was not socialist and rejected the idea of class struggle – it was just about independently 'promoting' working-class interests. This position was far more palatable to the trade union leaders and the gradualists in the Fabian society. Hardie's own view of socialism was a thoroughly gradualist one, focused on parliamentary legislation. As he explained in 1904: 'I can imagine one reform after another being won until in the end socialism itself causes no more excitement than did the extinction of landlordism in Ireland a year ago.'[2] Hardie also believed that for the Labour Party to succeed, it shouldn't look to foreign political movements like communism or even social democracy – in his view it was necessary to 'have done with every *ism* that isn't Labourism'.[3] This was a direct swipe at the Marxists in the SDF, as well as a warning shot to any other radicals inspired by wild continental politics. It was Hardie who thus stamped his own ideas on the fledgling party, backed by the majority of the ILP. The SDF, unwilling to make the same compromises as the ILP and defeated on the crucial questions at conference, declared the new party to be insufficiently socialist and left in 1901.

The early Labour Party also debated the nature of capitalism and socialism. Ramsay MacDonald had an organicist view of society: we are all part of one social body and the role of Labour should be to ensure that neither bosses nor workers became too greedy or disruptive to the smooth functioning of the economy. Both had to know their place. MacDonald preferred to agitate around how capitalism was inefficient and how Labour could improve the functioning of the economy through social ownership. Ethically minded, he despised the atrocious living and working conditions of the poor and saw legislation as the primary means for reform. Others favoured the introduction of socialism as an entirely new economic system, because exploitation was built into the very nature of capitalism.

At this stage, no one involved theorised on the nature of the British state or whether it was amenable to being used as an instrument for socialism. Most were convinced, as the Fabians had argued, that 'Parliament, with all its faults, has always governed in the interests of the class to which the majority of its members belonged … And it will govern in the interests of the people when the majority is selected from the wage-earning class.'[4] They saw no distinction between Parliament and the wider state and political-economic establishment.

Even after helping to found it, most unions remained sceptical of the LRC until the threat of the British ruling class to break the workers' movement forced them to look again at the political question. The Taff Vale judgement of 1901, which opened the door for businesses to sue striking unions for loss of earnings, meant that the ability to strike was under threat (along with the salaries of union officials). Lacking any clear support from the wavering Liberals, a number of unions switched their financial and political backing to the LRC. At the 1906 election, the number of Labour representatives in Parliament rose from two in 1900 to 29.[5] At the first gathering in Parliament the MPs met and agreed to call themselves the Labour Party.

Creative Revolutions

One of the major tests for the new party was how to respond to the growing demand for women's suffrage. The working class was split on the issue – many supported votes for women, but there was also a conservative tendency in many parts (often inspired by religious reaction) against suffrage. They feared that it might break up families or lead to social anarchy. Among the left there was disagreement with the slogans of some of the suffragettes. Did they back equal voting rights (which pre-First World War meant only middle-class women getting the vote) or universal suffrage whereby working-class men and women could vote? The women's question was also a class question. The issue was made more complicated for the Labour Party by the tactics of many radicals in the suffrage movement who turned to militant direct action as a way of forcing the issue into the national debate.

Women's suffrage leaders Sylvia and Christabel Pankhurst had joined the ILP alongside their parents. Sylvia and other campaigners demanded that Labour MPs – who in theory supported votes for women – vote against all government bills until their demands for suffrage were granted. Only Hardie and George Lansbury accepted. Lansbury circulated an appeal across the labour movement which led to criticisms from the party leadership. With little support from the other Labour MPs, he resigned his seat in 1912 and stood on a platform of women's suffrage. Despite a huge East End campaign and mass rallies, the by-election ended in a narrow defeat by just 600 votes. Lansbury was out of Parliament for another 12 years. His defeat was seized upon by some to argue against throwing support behind the women's movement, especially if it meant decent Labour men might lose seats. In some cases the MPs refused to support women's demands in Parliament. Arthur Henderson argued at the 1907 conference on the suffrage question: 'I have the strongest desire to respect the feelings of conference. I must, however, have some regard to those I directly represent in parliament.'[6] Labour didn't support universal suffrage until 1912.

The ILP supported women's suffrage but was not immune to backwards attitudes towards women: when Sylvia and Christabel's

7

father Richard Pankhurst died in 1898, the ILP in Salford raised money to build a hall in his name. Sylvia Pankhurst, a well-known artist at the time, was asked to decorate the hall, only to discover on opening night that the local branch did not want to admit women.[7] Angry at the initially cool response from the Labour Party to the cause of women's suffrage, Emmeline Pankhurst called a meeting to establish the Women's Social and Political Union. The success of organisations like the WSPU (which terrified the establishment by taking a militant turn towards street actions, including smashing windows and blowing up post boxes) undermined the peaceful constitutional approach of the mainstream of the Labour Party. Left intellectuals and some workers were horrified at the attitude of the Liberal Prime Minister Herbert Asquith when he imprisoned many suffragettes. Calls grew for a 'creative revolution' to challenge the state.[8] The militancy of the suffragettes, in particular among working-class women, opened up new possibilities for radical politics. The Labour left found inspiration from the radical actions of the women's movement.

Alongside the fight for women's suffrage, the years leading up to the First World War saw a dramatic increase in unofficial strikes and militant direct action by workers. The idea of using strikes as 'an offensive weapon in a war against class society'[9] gained traction in parts of the country. The left found themselves at the centre of a nexus of issues that could help cohere a working-class party as well as a strong transformative agenda.

Despite this space opening up, Labour's fortunes were initially poor. During this period, the most militant workers were dismissive of Labour – its parliamentary nature meant that it had little connection with the mass strikes that broke out. The strike wave between 1910 and 1914, known as the Great Unrest,[10] saw growing distrust by workers of both their union leaders and their MPs, who were often one and the same person. The official leaders of the movement looked conservative, cautious and uninspiring, which created space for more radical grassroots action. Alongside this militancy the Labour Party in Westminster was faced with a reforming Liberal government that left little space for a distinct Labourite agenda. Writing in 1913, G.D.H. Cole noted that 'the Labour Party has ceased to excite enthusiasm.'[11]

What was exciting enthusiasm was the growing numbers of strikes. In 1911 railway workers struck for higher pay; in response the employers de-recognised four rail unions. The Liberal government used the army and police to break the strike and keep a skeleton timetable of trains running, leading to pitched battles being fought between strikers and the police. Outrage spread across the labour movement concerning the political use of the military in industrial disputes by a Liberal government that had been in a formal alliance with the unions just over a decade ago. Hardie spoke at meetings of railway men and their families and helped to convene a meeting between the union leaders, Labour and the Parliamentary Committee of the TUC. They pledged their support to the strikers and condemned the use of violence – something that became even more urgent when four workers were shot dead by soldiers.[12] But not everyone agreed. Men like MacDonald and Arthur Henderson were nervous about the growing militancy; they saw lurking behind it the threat of anarchy and revolutionism.[13]

The stark difference in attitude between Hardie and Henderson exemplifies the contradictory nature of the Labour Party. Both were from working-class backgrounds, religious, and temperance campaigners. But Henderson was a union leader who rejected strikes as a means of resolving disputes. He was chair of the conciliation board established in the north-east and intervened to prevent strikes, always emphasising reconciliation between bosses and their workforce.[14] He had secured and enjoyed the patronage of powerful rich Liberals, and initially rejected the calls by the ILP and trade unionists for an independent working-class party.[15] In contrast, Hardie was a man with a feel for the rank and file. He threw himself into local strikes and actions by workers – often over the heads of party leaders. When the socialist Jim Larkin organised a strike in Dublin that turned violent, Hardie was quick to visit and pledge the solidarity of the Labour Party to the striking workers, even though he had not secured the leadership's permission. In response to the killing of the railwaymen in 1911, Hardie wrote a pamphlet accusing the Liberal government of murder. Henderson – who was sitting on the Royal Commission into the crisis and mediating the dispute – complained that 'the Hardie episode will exercise a damaging influence upon our deliberations'.[16] For conciliators, it is not the done thing to accuse a government of murder when unarmed workers have been shot dead campaigning for higher wages. Henderson went as far as to table a bill in Parliament to make strike action illegal without a 30-day notice period.

During this contradictory period one MP caused significant controversy in the Labour ranks. In 1907, Victor Grayson was elected MP for Colne Valley in West Yorkshire at the youthful age of 27. He was a relatively inexperienced outsider, but the local ILP activists valued his independent opinions. They put him forward despite a formal agreement between Labour and liberals not to stand against each other. Receiving no official endorsement from Labour, he won with a majority of only 150 votes. Grayson's mixture of revolutionary rhetoric combined with Christian socialism made for an eccentric election campaign, with local parsons working alongside militant trade unionists.

In Parliament he immediately clashed head-on with the leaders of the Parliamentary Labour Party (PLP). His speaking style was histrionic but he was a gifted mass agitator and a natural rebel. He fell out of favour with MacDonald and Hardie. MacDonald did not like Grayson's politics; Hardie was envious of his youth. In his maiden speech he attacked the imperialism of the Liberal government in India, causing some consternation among fellow MPs. A few months later he disrupted Parliament by demanding a debate on unemployment and refusing the instructions of the speaker.[17] Upon being marched out by the ushers he turned to his fellow Labour MPs and denounced them as traitors to the working class, declaring Parliament 'a house of murderers'. He wanted to use his position as an MP to challenge gradualism and to put working-class demands at the heart of Parliament, something that chafed with the party establishment who saw him as a wrecker who misused his oratorical skills. These defiant acts meant that Grayson, though shunned and isolated by the establishment, was adored by many, building up a following in the ILP even though he refused to join the party formally. However he rarely attended Parliament, preferring to tour the country speaking to large crowds. He lost his seat in 1910 and went on during the First World War to back the British imperialism he had previously vociferously denounced.[18]

Though individuals may have shifted their positions, as war loomed the battle lines within Labour were already deeply entrenched.

The Labour Left in the First World War

The prospect of war occupied the thoughts and activities of many socialists in the early twentieth century. They saw in the growing inter-imperialist rivalries an inevitable military conflict to decide who would control the world markets. Labour was a member of the Marxist-initiated Socialist International and sent delegates to its Stuttgart Congress in 1907. Ramsay MacDonald sat with socialists from around the world, including Lenin and Rosa Luxemburg, to discuss the International's position on militarism, war and women's rights. Delegates voted for a motion that committed their social democratic parties to opposing war and, if it did break out, 'to use the political and economic crisis created by the war to rouse the populace from its slumbers, and to hasten the fall of capitalist society'.[19] Despite supporting this motion, Labour never translated it into a consistent anti-war strategy. Instead the party sent out a questionnaire to its affiliated organisations asking for their opinion on how to implement such a position, but few bothered to reply.[20]

Labour and the TUC organised anti-war demonstrations in the months prior to August 1914, with Hardie taking a principled stand, but this did not amount to a strategy. As soon as war was declared, jingoism swept the country and most of the working-class movement fell into line, rallying to the cause of Britain's war machine. Considering that working-class parties with ostensibly revolutionary positions throughout Europe also joined their own national ruling classes in waging war on their comrades abroad, it is hardly surprising that the less radical Labour Party did the same. The TUC issued a public appeal for young men to join the army and many long-standing socialist leaders including Hyndman and Robert Blatchford came out in support of the war.[21] The Fabians supported the trade union leaders in their efforts.

The ILP was the only organised force in Labour still opposing the war in principle. When war was declared they issued a manifesto to the British and German working-class movement: 'out of the darkness and the depth we hail our working class comrades of every land. Across the roar of the guns, we send sympathy and greetings to the German Socialists ... They are no enemies of ours, but faithful friends.'[22] The anti-war position of the ILP was arrived at by many routes: MacDonald and Hardie believed the war was caused by a diplomatic blunder and that imperial designs were leading to Britain demanding irrational outcomes like unconditional surrender; Snowden opposed the war on the ethical grounds that violence was simply evil; and Fenner Brockway and others put the case that the war was the result of market competition spilling over into military conflict.[23] For their principled stance many ILP members were beaten up by angry soldiers, and their meetings were attacked by pro-war thugs.

The ILP also helped form the Union of Democratic Control, the largest anti-war organisation in Britain. The UDC demanded an immediate end to the fighting, autonomy for the smaller nations of Europe, and a peace without national humiliations that might cause future wars. Many of its members were arrested and imprisoned for anti-war sedition; James Maxton was arrested for speaking against the war to a crowd of 2,000 in Glasgow in 1915, and was imprisoned in 1916 for agitating in favour of a strike in the city. David Kirkwood was arrested for sedition and deported (twice!) from Glasgow to Edinburgh. ILP members were also active in the No-Conscription Fellowship; Clifford Allen and Fenner Brockway were key organisers. When the call up was issued they helped men who were charged with desertion or who were conscientious objectors. Of the 1,191 trials for conscientious objection, 805 of them were ILP men. The UDC organisation distributed a million leaflets and organised constituents to demand MPs withdraw support for the Military Service Bill. The Liberal government discussed banning the UDC for its anti-war campaigning amongst soldiers. The agitational work helped build support for a mass demonstration of nearly 100,000 people in Glasgow on May Day 1918, at which Maxton spoke, receiving huge applause.

Unlike Labour, the ILP adhered to the spirit of the Stuttgart Congress. They launched a campaign around housing rights in Glasgow, targeting parasitic landlords who charged soaring rents as workers flooded into the city to work in munitions. ILP members like Helen Crawfurd helped organise a rent strike which culminated in a 20,000 strong protest and the introduction of the Rent Restrictions Act which capped rents for the rest of the war. The ILP members on the ground threw themselves into the campaign, defying the commands of the official Labour and trade union movement. The campaign was a success, boosting local support for the ILP.

It is difficult to stand against the patriotic tide during war, and the nationalist pressure broke even some prominent members of the ILP. Due to the party's pacifist position being in conflict with the agreed position of the Labour Party, Ramsay MacDonald resigned as chair of the Parliamentary Party. However, a month later he was quoted in the *Daily Chronicle* saying: 'I want the serious men of the trade unions, the brotherhoods, and similar movements, to face their duty. To such it is sufficient to say, "England has need of you", and to say it in the right way.'[24] ILP member Manny Shinwell later wrote that MacDonald was 'a man who loathed past wars, regarded future wars with abhorrence, but carefully evaded giving his opinion on the basic question of the current one'.[25] Concerned about potential industrial unrest and keen to ensure the incorporation of the trade unions' party further into the war effort, the government offered Labour MPs places in the wartime coalition after 1915. Henderson – always a safe pair of hands for the establishment – joined the War Cabinet.

When in 1916 news came through of the Easter Uprising in Dublin, against the continued British occupation of Ireland, the Labour response in Britain was that it was a 'calamitous' act of an unrepresentative minority. And when reports came of the execution of the revolutionary leader James Connolly (an ex-ILP member) in Ireland by British troops, it was rumoured that Henderson led Parliament in a round of applause.[26] The ILP too distanced itself from the national liberation struggle, declaring that: 'We do not approve of armed rebellion or any other form of militarism and war.' The ILP's conflation of an armed rebellion by the oppressed against a military occupation with an outright imperialist war meant that it couldn't differentiate between force as a means of liberation and as a tool of oppression.

As the war dragged on, 1917 saw a revival in the fighting spirit of the masses. Although the TUC had declared itself in favour of an industrial truce at the start of the war, faced with spiralling prices, a housing shortage and back-breaking overwork, many workers were growing restless. Unofficial strikes rocketed as fights over wages and working time shook industries. Politically things also began to move. The Labour Party agreed to send delegates to an international peace conference in Stockholm, and were only prevented from doing so by pressure from the US government.

Then, in February 1917, the Russian revolution fundamentally realigned left politics across the world. When news of the revolution reached Britain, socialists organised a series of mass rallies and meetings, including 20,000 tickets sold for a rally at the Royal Albert Hall.[27] The ILP and other socialist groups called a conference in Leeds, with many from the Labour left attending in solidarity with the working-class uprising in Russia. Chaired by Robert Smillie of the Miners' Federation of Great Britain (MFGB), the meeting heard speeches hailing the February revolution and the overthrow of the Tsar and condemning Parliament ('It will do nothing for you!' thundered one delegate). It passed a motion calling for 'the constituent bodies at once to establish in every town, urban, and rural district, Councils of Workmen and Soldier's Delegates for initiating and coordinating working-class activity ... to work strenuously for a peace made by the peoples of the various countries, and for the complete political and economic emancipation of international labour' – calling, in effect, for soviets. This motion and others on international peace, defending civil liberties and supporting the democratic revolution in Russia, were all passed almost unanimously.

This alliance of different forces on the left fractured when the second, October, revolution established a soviet government in Russia. Some of the delegates at the Leeds conference condemned the actions of the Bolsheviks in what they saw as an usurpation of democracy. Those that supported Lenin and his comrades went on to form the Communist Party of Great Britain.

After 1917 the ILP reaped the reward for its anti-war work: from 499 active branches at the start of the year it registered 659 by the end of the fighting.[28] The position of the ILP in the wider party was, however, far more precarious for two reasons: its lack of patriotism made it many enemies across the movement; and its formal anti-war position meant that it had vacated the leadership of Labour, being replaced by more conservative trade unionists. This shifted the balance of power towards the right. At the TUC congress in 1917 the Dock Labourers Union put forward a motion for the ILP's expulsion from the Labour Party. That motion was defeated, but the Party leadership and the TUC conspired to keep the ILP out of consultations on war aims and found a way to exclude ILP members from leadership positions after the war – by establishing Labour as a formal party.

The 1918 Constitution

The demands of political leadership during the war proved too much for the Liberals, who split in 1916 into two parliamentary factions. As a result they suffered badly when the war came to an end, and the Labour Party secured a much larger vote in the 1918 general election, almost wiping out the Liberals in Wales. Facing the prospect of becoming the official opposition to the Tories, the party leadership needed to find ways to contain the left.

Many in the ILP had become notorious for their anti-war agitation and open backing of strikes during a time of national emergency. The impact and activities of the ILP and other socialists were untenable for the union leaders who needed to appear responsible and moderate. The ILP had to be bypassed so individual members could instead join the Labour Party directly. The intention was to fatally undermine the socialist societies, especially in the post-war period, where although there was an armistice on the continent, there was increasingly open class war in parts of Britain. The labour movement establishment looked to the post-war conference to centralise the Labour Party through a new constitution which transformed the 'Labour Alliance' of Hardie (who had died in 1915) into a genuine party. On one level, the 1918 constitution appeared to be a radically democratic step forward. Co-authored by Sidney Webb and Arthur Henderson, it recognised Constituency Labour Parties (CLPs) and the trades' councils as the basis of the party. Trade union members were considered affiliates. Labour became a membership organisation. In principle the annual conference was sovereign. The constitution introduced the famous Clause IV: 'To secure for the workers by hand or by brain the full fruits of their industry and the most equitable distribution thereof that may be possible upon the basis of the common ownership of the means of production, distribution and exchange, and the best obtainable system of popular administration and control of each industry or service.'[29] The *Manchester Guardian* commented at the time that this was 'the birth of a socialist party', adding that 'the changes of machinery are not revolutionary, but they are significant ... these principles are definitely Socialistic'.

The constitution also had another intended outcome – fostering the illusion of grassroots input to hide the reality of undemocratic practices that ensured the right of the party stayed in control. Despite enfranchising members to be delegates to conferences the reality of the trade union leaders wielding their block vote meant that the mass of members had no real power when it came to adopting policy. Each trade union delegation claimed to represent the views of many thousands of workers – even though in most cases the workers had never been consulted on the voting intentions of their representatives. These passive affiliates were described by Tom Nairn as the 'dead souls of Labourism'.[30] Giving the majority of votes to the affiliate organisations and not the actual members of the party was a happy deal made between Webb and the union leaders, who distrusted the lay members for their own reasons. The union leaders saw Labour as their property and at the same time were suspicious of an actual party with its own internal dynamics potentially beyond their control. Webb's snobbish elitism meant that he put it more bluntly: he reviled most of the members of the party, later describing the CLPs as 'frequently unrepresentative groups of nonentities dominated by fanatics, cranks and extremists'[31] Richard Crossman summarised the approach of the new constitution as follows:

> since it could not afford, like its opponents, to maintain a large army of paid party workers, the Labour Party required militants – politically conscious Socialists to do the work of organising the constituencies. But since these militants tended to be 'extremists', a constitution was needed which maintained their enthusiasm by apparently creating a full party democracy while excluding them from effective power. Hence the concession in principle of sovereign powers to the delegates at the Annual Conference and the removal in practice of most of this sovereignty through the trade union block vote on the one hand, and the complete independence of the Parliamentary Labour Party on the other.[32]

The party also adopted their first programme in 1918, *Labour and the New Social Order*. Labour's new programme outlined the principle that the party would play no role in reconstituting or defending capitalism. It committed the party to a fundamental redistribution of power from the bosses to the working class, including control of industry and production. Profit would be turned over to the public good as capitalism was gradually eradicated by a Labour government. But these weren't the politics of its authors Henderson and Webb. On one level it was a response to the Russian revolution and the international advances of socialism. As its central arguments appeared to vindicate the radical policies of the ILP, this was to some degree a sop to the left just as they were being ousted from any position of strength in the party. Behind the radical rhetoric, the intentions of the Labour leaders were really to use nationalisation to promote economic growth. For them socialism simply meant a 'scientific reorganisation of society'. The labour historian Ralph Miliband concluded that the 1918 programme 'was a Fabian blueprint for a more advanced, more regulated form of capitalism'.[33] When contrasted with the kind of struggles that workers and suffragettes had waged before the war, it was a purely parliamentary document and lacked any wider application.

The Communists and Labour

The British invasion of Russia in 1920 saw Labour unite with workers in opposition. Although Labour had been hostile to the Bolshevik revolution of October 1917, the thought of another war so soon after the last – coupled with the invasion of a sovereign country which had been a war ally until recently – was too much. Reminiscent of the radicalism of the 1917 Leeds conference, a joint meeting of the TUC and Labour leaders issued a statement condemning military action and calling a conference which established councils of action up and down the country to organise workers to defy the actions of Stanley Baldwin's Conservative government. The electric mood among workers, which was at least partly the result of sympathy with an explicitly socialist government taking power after a revolution, meant even right-wing trade union leaders like J.H. Thomas of the railway union got swept up in it.

The Daily Herald, which Lansbury had edited since losing his parliamentary seat, agitated strongly against the invasion on grounds of national self-determination and opposition to British imperial bullying. The paper published a confidential War Office Circular to officers inquiring if their regiments were up to fighting the 'reds'. The circular outlined a procedure for identifying troublemakers among the troops – for instance was there any sympathy for trade unions or would the soldiers make good strike breakers? Memories of the 1911 rail strike and of troops being sent into the Clyde in 1919 against a trade union demonstration whipped up a lot of anger among workers – the normally constitutional approach of the labour movement seemed to be at odds with the flagrant use of the army as a political weapon against working people.

Outside of the ranks of the Labour Party, the post-war wave of class struggle resulted in the gradualist vision losing some appeal, and this was reflected in new political movements. In 1920, inspired by the revolution in Russia and committed to the overthrow of capitalism by means of class struggle, the Communist Party of Great Britain (CPGB) was established. A debate about the new party's relationship to Labour inevitably occurred. Different experiences brought different attitudes; some members had been in the Labour Party and saw a use in continued work in the party of the trade unions, whereas the majority had not and were implacably hostile to it, seeing it as a party that supported imperialism during the war. Initially very reluctant to affiliate, they were finally instructed to apply to do so by Lenin himself. He argued that revolutionaries should relate to Labour in some way as it was a mass party of working people, and that was where socialists needed to be. But this was only in order to expose Labour as hopelessly compromised by its support for capitalism, not to advocate particularly positively for the policies of a Labour government. In *Left-Wing Communism: An Infantile Disorder*, Lenin famously argued:

I shall be able to explain in a popular manner, not only why the Soviets are better than a parliament and why the dictatorship of the proletariat is better than the dictatorship of Churchill (disguised with the signboard of bourgeois 'democracy'), but also that, with my vote, I want to support Henderson in the same way as the rope supports a hanged man – that the impending establishment of a government of the Hendersons will prove that I am right, will bring the masses over to my side, and will hasten the political death of the Hendersons and the Snowdens just as was the case with their kindred spirits in Russia and Germany.[34]

Reluctantly the CPGB leadership agreed. When they met with Arthur Henderson, they presented their case for entry in the frankest possible terms: the CPGB wanted 'to be inside the Labour Party in order to meet its enemies face to face and to expose in front of the rank and file of the Labour movement the political trickery'.[35] The affiliation motion was defeated, but the 1.1 million votes of the railway union only narrowly went against affiliation – a result of the respect shown to communists in that embattled sector over the previous years. Despite their rejection, many communists remained members of Labour, often as delegates from their trade unions. Their vision of a self-organised working class and strikes as a weapon directed against capitalism appealed to many on the Labour left as a welcome change from the growing conservatism of the leaders of their own party.

Despite the determination and activity of its members, the young communist movement remained small, never achieving the success or organisational strength of its sister parties in France or Italy. The pacifism of the British working class remained a strong ideological tenet, reflected by and reinforced in the Labour leaders. Figures like George Lansbury were firmly convinced that 'Great Britain is the one country in the world within which it is possible to change fundamentally the existing social and industrial order without the horrors of a bloody revolution.'[36] Although the violence of the British state when faced with the general strike of 1926 would give many Labour members pause for thought, the general preference of the left of the party was for non-violent direct action backed by what they saw as common-sense 'socialist' principles.

The East London Fight Against Poverty

Some Labour left figures became household names due to the principled stand they took. Lansbury had been voted in as the mayor of Poplar in East London two years earlier. Poplar was an incredibly poor area which was suffering in the post-war unemployment spike. Social deprivation was rampant and socialists in the Labour Party had been agitating for action to alleviate the suffering, leading to the election of a majority of socialists on the local council. They argued that there was effectively a flat tax across the London boroughs: each borough paid the same amount in precepts even though they had different social compositions and problems. Demanding equality, Lansbury proposed to withhold the payment of precepts to the Metropolitan Police and the London County Council (LCC). The Labour argument was simple – they were dealing with a social crisis not of their making, and since there was no money from Westminster to relieve the situation, they would divert their funds locally into relief programmes for the poor.

Enraged by Poplar's defiance, the LCC initiated legal proceedings to get their money. Upon being summonsed the 43 Labour councillors marched from Poplar to the law court, followed by several thousand trade unionists and local people. They were instructed by the judge to hand over the money or face prison. Lansbury was adamant that no money would be paid, and 30 members of the Labour group were sent to prison. Massive demonstrations of support were organised and the incarcerated local politicians became a *cause célèbre* for the workers' movement. Prime Minister Lloyd George sent emissaries to meet the prisoners to attempt to broker a deal, but there was no change of heart from the Poplar rebels. Lansbury continued editing *The Daily Herald* from Brixton Prison, and the councillors there still met to conduct some council business, and made speeches to the crowds outside the prison windows. After a couple of months the LCC backed down, the councillors were released and a fund was set up that all boroughs would pay into to redistribute money to areas that needed it the most – a triumph for popular resistance.

It was no surprise that, after activism like this, the 1922 general election saw Labour establish itself as the primary opposition. The Liberals collapsed, hopelessly split and unable to relate to the pressing concerns of working people. The turn to Labour was not an automatic process – it took time and political argument to win the workers over to Labourism. But it was often transformative, radical struggles like Lansbury's that encouraged them to flock to Labour. This explosion of class consciousness was rarely reflected in the upper echelons of the PLP, but, with established branches across the country, the party was becoming a more active participant in the lives of working-class communities.

The Consolidation of the Left and Right

The main radical tendency in the party was still the ILP, which remained a heterogeneous organisation, including everyone from revolutionaries to Christian socialists. It had both radical and gradualist wings as well as a sizeable passive membership that met in ILP halls and was active in social pursuits like playing whist and hiking. Many ILP members were also part of the temperance movement and were attracted to the idea of socialism creating the 'new man': ethical, rational and community spirited. Members organised book clubs, hiking holidays and bicycle rides. The introduction of Labour Party branches in the 1918 constitution changed the political composition of the ILP. Moderately inclined members could join Labour directly, rather than affiliate through the ILP. As the membership became self-selecting it generally moved left. The ILP increasingly saw itself as the principled socialist wing of Labour pitted against a timid gradualist leadership.

The leftward drift of the ILP was accelerated in 1922 by the election to Parliament of the 'wild men' from the Red Clyde. Glasgow had seen an exciting campaign of class-struggle actions, including mass strikes, demonstrations of 90,000 waving red flags, and pitched battles with the police. Eventually the government sent 10,000 English soldiers to the city, fearing a revolution and doubting the loyalty of some of the Glaswegian soldiers who might be thinking of joining their brothers and sisters on the streets. The ILP continued to grow and leading militants James Maxton, John Wheatley and Manny Shinwell (who had been sent to prison for leading the 1919 strike for the 40-hour week) became MPs.[37] These rough men with thick Glaswegian accents who planned to take the class struggle into Westminster were a shock to the establishment. The left generally welcomed disruptive, morally intransigent MPs, but MacDonald baulked at the sight of the new Members singing the Red Flag outside Parliament.

Despite the gains in Scotland, elsewhere the right sought to isolate the left. After the backlash following the defeats of the three largest trade unions in 1921,[38] they seized the opportunity to launch a vicious counter-revolution in the party. As Labour was reorganised after the war into an integrative party fit for the establishment, the need to drive the radical left out of the movement grew ever more urgent. Frank Hodges, the General Secretary of the MFGB, whipped up xenophobia when he argued that the CPGB were 'the international slaves of Moscow – taking orders from the Asiatic mind'.[39]

The communists however, were only a minority. The main problem facing the right was the growing socialist anti-capitalism of the Labour left. They were determined to control their more radical comrades. For his part, MacDonald boasted to various Tories of his role in 'bringing the wild socialist Labour members to heel'.[40] The right, many of whom were still formally ILP members, would brook no talk of radicalism. The idea of Labour being 'the party of the working class' became less and less prominent the closer it got towards power. Brockway later summed up the effect of Westminster on his fellow MPs: 'I have spent three years in prison and three years in Parliament and I saw character deteriorate in Parliament more than in prison.'[41]

MacDonald and John Clynes went to great lengths to downplay the class nature of Labour's mass support and to promote the party as a trustworthy and reliable instrument of the status quo. Clynes declared that 'Labour, if entrusted with the power of government, will not be influenced by any consideration other than that of national well-being. No class or sect or party could govern the British nation on narrow class lines.'[42] Who determined the 'national well-being' would not become entirely clear to Labour members until the second MacDonald government, which we shall deal with in due course.

But it was not just from within Labour that the wild ones had to be tamed. In several ways the wider establishment too sought to incorporate the radical left from Clyde into the respectable company of civilised Westminster society.[43] Many Labour MPs were seduced by the glamour of parliamentary life and the society occasions organised by the rich wives of powerful men. This institutional seduction was played on by the Lords and the gentlemen from the well-to-do backgrounds who patronised the working-class Labour MPs. Men like MacDonald, the illegitimate son of a domestic servant, were susceptible to the charms and flattery of those who specialised in corruption. When he first met King George, MacDonald described how 'overwhelmed he was by the king's gracious attitude'.[44] Understandably, many marvelled at the fact that they were in such grand places at all. Clynes summed up the feeling in 1924:

> As we stood waiting for His Majesty, amid the gold and crimson magnificence of the Palace, I could not help marvelling at the strange turn of Fortune's wheel, which had brought MacDonald the starveling clerk, Thomas the engine driver, Henderson the foundry labourer and Clynes the mill-hand to the pinnacle beside the man whose forebears had been kings for so many splendid generations.[45]

The result was the sight of Labour MPs getting drunk – often literally – on the culture and amenities provided for the political representatives of the exploiting class. Beatrice Webb referred to this as the 'aristocratic embrace' and mocked Wheatley, the strike-leading Red Clydesman, as a 'revolutionary – going down on both knees and actually kissing the King's hand'.[46] Webb must have been pleased that the planned permeation of socialism into the establishment was a two-way street.

The First Labour Government

The 1923 election produced a shock result – a hung parliament. Neither the Conservatives nor the Liberals wanted power under such circumstances, so it fell to Labour with its 191 MPs to form its first government. As the Tory and media propaganda insisted they would prove to be a disaster, the core of MPs around MacDonald convinced themselves that they had to be moderate to be respectable. Symbolically, MacDonald's ministers wore traditional formal dress to the opening of Parliament. With governmental power, the need to restrain the radical left became even more acute. The right's strategy required appeasement of establishment powers who held the reins of economic or social influence, including the civil service, the City of London, the media barons and trade union leaders. This approach was clearly articulated by Philip Snowden, writing about the gathering of 'reliable' Labour MPs who met to discuss their conduct in government. His description is worth quoting in full because it exemplifies the fear the Labour right had of the Labour left, a fear that has hung over the party ever since:

The conversation turned upon what we might be able to do in the first session. There would be two courses open to us. We might use the opportunity for a demonstration and introduce some bold socialist measures, knowing, of course, that we should be defeated upon them. Then we could go to the country with this illustration of what we could do if we had a socialist majority. This was a course which had been urged by the extreme wing of the party, but it was not a policy that commended itself to reasonable opinion. I urged very strongly to this meeting that we should not adopt an extreme policy but we should confine legislative proposals to measures that we were likely to be able to carry ... It was no use getting swelled heads and imagining that we were omnipotent. We must remember that we were less than one-third of the House of Commons. *We must show the country that we were not under the domination of the wild men.*[47]

Quite what this could mean was demonstrated by the ministerial leadership of J.H. Thomas, who had been put in charge of 'the colonies'. On his first day in the Colonial Office he demonstrated the reflex reactionary views of the Labour right concerning Britain's imperial role when he declared to his assembled civil servants: 'I am here to make sure there is no mucking about with the British Empire.' Continuing the RAF bombing of unruly tribesmen in Northern Iraq was an unequivocal sign of his commitment to Rule Britannia.

Faced with this slide to the right, the ILP saw itself as fighting to hold the line on party policy. Its programme at this stage was for a minimum standard of living secured through higher wages and increased welfare provision, alongside the nationalisation of 'the pivots of capitalism' – not so different from the 1918 Labour programme.[48] The question was how to overcome the inherent conservatism of the party leaders and hold them to the party's socialist goals. Brockway put the case for the increasingly radical perspective of the ILP, which advocated that a minority Labour government should implement 'a socialist programme' and 'stand or fall by it':

The party should concentrate at first on the more urgent needs of the workers and win their support ... [then] the bankers would also begin the game of sabotage. Good: Then would come the moment for challenging capitalism itself by a measure to nationalise banking and finance: a better opportunity for raising the slogan: 'The People versus the Bankers'.[49]

The ILP left anticipated reaction from the entrenched powers-that-be to undermine the democratic mandate, and urged Labour to stand firm. Brockway argued such a course of action would doubtless lead to the ousting of a minority administration, but it would allow Labour to present itself to the working class as being uncompromisingly on their side. The alternative was clear – it was to do only those things 'which the Tories and Liberals would allow us to do, to go from compromise to compromise, and finally to face humiliation in a defeat which would thrust the Party into the political wilderness for a decade, while the membership recovered from disappointment and disillusionment'.[50]

There was a debate in the ILP over how best to get its perspective across. ILP Chairman Clifford Allen favoured a friendly engagement with MacDonald, believing he could make him see the logic in the ILP's approach. Allen would have weekly lunches with MacDonald in the hope of influencing the Prime Minister. However, Brockway recorded that Allen was upset when MacDonald thunderously denounced the ILP programme, incredulous as to why MacDonald seemed immune to reason.

When Maxton effectively manoeuvred Allen out as chairman, it represented a significant shift left for the ILP, and set it on a course that would inevitably lead to a decisive clash with the Labour leadership. The ILP was not revolutionary but it increasingly looked to class-struggle politics, to direct action by workers, and to bold socialist policies that were anathema to the 'respectable' Labour men. Although they did not succeed in winning leading positions in the Labour Party during this time, they did record one major success: John Wheatley – in his capacity as minster for housing in the first government – introduced an ambitious house-building programme, securing homes for cheap rent by threatening to commandeer the builders' materials if they did not comply.

The first Labour government proved to be a false dawn. It lasted only nine months and was terminally undermined by being a parliamentary minority, beholden to the votes of Liberals. Other than Wheatley's houses, the MacDonald government's legislative programme was stillborn. Labour limped along until it was brought down by an establishment offensive designed to raise a red-baiting panic. MacDonald had begun a prosecution against John Campbell, the editor of the communist *Workers' Weekly*, for publishing an article in which he urged soldiers to disobey orders if they were told to shoot striking workers. In solidarity, trade union activists protested against the prosecution. George Lansbury spoke at a 10,000 strong rally at Albert Hall and read out the offending article, calling on the police to arrest him for breaking the same law. The pressure grew to the point where MacDonald dropped the prosecution, which left him open to attacks by the Tories and Liberals for being 'weak' and undermining the army. After losing a vote of confidence in Parliament, MacDonald called an election to try and prop up his support. Then a 'leaked' – and fake – letter appeared in the press, allegedly written by the head of the Communist International Gregory Zinoviev, instructing British communists on how to take over the Labour Party and use it for the cause of revolution. Every expert and Labour MP declared it to be a fake, but MacDonald took the precaution of writing a public letter of complaint to Zinoviev, which in the eyes of many seemed to confirm that the original letter represented a genuine threat. The reaction of the Labour leaders demonstrated to the British establishment how fragile a working-class party was in the face of determined red-baiting. It galvanised the Tories and Labour lost the election convincingly.

The PLP leadership didn't follow Brockway's advice to go down fighting, they merely collapsed. But the brief period of governance was a litmus test for the capacity of the ILP to perform the role it had set itself – as the conscience of the party and the natural home of those with the clearest appreciation of socialist politics. The only conclusion can be that the ILP failed in its task. It went into government with 129 out of 192 MPs as formal members of its group, including five Cabinet ministers and the Prime Minister himself. It launched repeated attempts to influence the Cabinet and MacDonald, but all were frustrated, rebuffed or ignored. The complete lack of discipline or loyalty to the ILP displayed by its MPs was breath-taking. They were using the ILP to secure their nominations, but once elected they entirely ignored the organisation's policies and calls for a socialist backbone. Was this merely a case of cowardice and careerism, or did it reveal a deeper malaise within the party, something that was eating away at it from inside?

The General Strike of 1926

In 1925 the MFGB, backed by other unions, forced the mine owners to increase miners' wages. As the months passed, it became clear that the bosses would launch a counter-attack to reduce the miners' pay and conditions. The attack came on May Day 1926, when the bosses locked out the miners. The union leaders, apart from A.J. Cook (an ILP sympathiser) and Herbert Smith of the MFGB, desperately wanted to avoid a strike and sought a compromise. None was forthcoming – the Tory government had refused to intervene any further to subsidise the miners' wages. The TUC was ready to accept longer working hours in exchange for higher pay, but the miners were intransigently opposed. It was now an all-out fight and the TUC had to be seen to do something. They called a general strike of three million workers in solidarity with the locked-out miners.

Despite the warning signs of an impending almighty clash with the mine owners and the government, the TUC had done nothing to prepare for it, even though there was considerable sympathy for the miners across the union movement. Tellingly, when faced with the first general strike in British history, the response from the Parliamentary Labour Party was muted. MacDonald sympathised with the poverty of the miners but repeated his long held opposition to strikes, arguing 'I don't like General Strikes. I haven't changed my opinion ... I don't like it; honestly I don't like it; but honestly, what can be done?'[51] Hardly a ringing endorsement from the leader of the party of the trade unions about to go into battle against their bosses.

The Labour right's fear of the strike was not just due to their dogmatic focus on Parliament. When faced with an actual general strike by industrial workers, it was clear that the question of social power would be posed: namely, 'who runs the country?' That question had already been raised only a few years earlier in 1919, when a huge transport strike gripped the country and the Triple Alliance of miners, railway and transport workers' unions brought the country to a standstill. The government was hopelessly on the back foot until Lloyd George summoned the union leaders to Downing Street and frankly explained to them what was at stake:

> Gentlemen, you have fashioned, in the Triple Alliance of the unions represented by you, a most powerful instrument. I feel bound to tell you that in our opinion we are at your mercy. The Army is disaffected and cannot be relied upon. Trouble has occurred already in a number of camps ... In these circumstances, if you carry out your threat and strike, then you will defeat us. But if you do so have you weighed the consequences? The strike will be in defiance of the government of the country and by its very success will precipitate a constitutional crisis of the first importance. For, if a force arises in the state, which is stronger than the state itself, then it must be ready to take on the functions of the state, or withdraw and accept the authority of the state. Gentlemen have you considered, and if you have, are you ready?[52]

With the logic of the class struggle and their understanding of their own power laid out before them, the union leaders realised the implications of the general strike. Robert Smillie, the leader of the miners' federation present at that meeting, grimly concluded that 'from that moment on we were beaten and we knew we were.'[53] Mass, independent action posed a threat to the union leaders' own existence as mediators of class struggle – they became afraid of their own members. The 1919 movement collapsed and the government triumphed because the inherent transformative dynamic of a general strike posed too great a threat to the position of the union leaders and their bureaucracies, fearing that 'behind every strike lurks the hydra of revolution'.[54] Had anything changed by 1926?

The Tories, keenly sensitive to the demands of ruling-class interests, were certainly aware of the implications of a general strike themselves. As Baldwin commented on the eve of his own clash with the most powerful unions: 'The General Strike is a challenge to parliament and is the road to anarchy and ruin.' Tellingly, the TUC's modest reply – that 'The General Council does not challenge the constitution'[55] – exposed the limitations that the trade union leaders imposed on themselves, limitations that the government would have no hesitation in ruthlessly exploiting.

Despite the ill-preparedness of the General Council and the wider labour movement, when the strike was declared at midnight on 3 May workers took it into their own hands. Huge assemblies and protests happened in every major city, many attended by Labour Party members with their branch banners. Mass pickets shut down workplaces and brought other workers out in solidarity. Councils of Action were set up to coordinate activities and build the strike – in many parts of the country work stopped completely and the Council of Action or strike committee became the de facto authority in the area. Because the press was shut down, local strike bulletins appeared, communists working alongside ILP members and others to produce and distribute them. The various ILP halls across the country became staging grounds for organising distribution. As such they were frequently raided by police. Vic Featherstone, who went on to become General Secretary of the TUC, narrowly avoided arrest at an ILP hall in Shipley by hiding in a cupboard.[56] The ILP also provided couriers, canteens and entertainment, throwing their entire organisation into solidarity to support the strikers and their families.

Many Labour MPs concurred with the equivocal attitude of MacDonald, concluding that the strike was a tragic event that should be brought to a swift end. They were nervous of the potential power of three million workers on strike, of how they might shift the balance of forces in Britain towards ordinary workers and the poor. The transformative nature of the struggle terrified them as it disrupted their carefully cultivated gradualist parliamentary strategy. While the socialists threw themselves into solidarity work, the official Labour Party structures remained paralysed in the face of the strike. The ILP wrote to the TUC to offer them the use of their entire staff and headquarters in London to help support the strike. The TUC took three days to respond.[57]

Meanwhile, in Tredegar in Wales, a young miner by the name of Aneurin Bevan was put in charge of organising the local Council of Action. After shutting down production in the valley, the only work that took place there was under the instruction of Bevan in his role as chair of the committee. Locals referred to him as the 'King of Tredegar'. His quasi-royal ascension was no accident; from a young age Nye Bevan had been brought up on radical ideas and literature by his father, a miner, and his mother, a dressmaker. The hard work of the mining community and the suffering it wrought on the people left an indelible mark on him, and he was inspired by his father to want to change things for the better. He attended school but didn't like it, leaving to go down the pit at 14 with his father. Making regular trips to the Tredegar working men's library, he read the works of Karl Marx, Daniel DeLeon, Eugene Debbs and Lenin, falling in love with the cut and thrust of socialist debate.[58] During the First World War he refused to be conscripted, arguing 'It's their bloody war not ours.' He joined the ILP and became a trade union activist before standing for the local council in 1922. He was widely respected in the area, a leading spokesperson for the Labour Party, his union and his class. Bevan was compelled by his situation – he knew the tragedies that befell the working people in his part of the world. Shortly before the general strike, his father had choked to death in his arms, a victim of pneumoconiosis – also known as miner's lung.[59] When Bevan eventually became active in the Labour Party on a national level, he saw a chance to right the wrong inflicted on working people by an uncaring elite.

The ninth day of the general strike had more strikers out than on any previous day. Pickets clashed with the government-run Supply and Transport Organisation, a strike-breaking mobilisation of middle-class students and the well-to-do. Faced with the obstinate approach of the bosses and the Baldwin government, the strike leaders could either push the logic of the class struggle further into a fight to win – or surrender. They chose the latter and the TUC called off the strike, abandoning the MFGB. Brockway, who was in Manchester editing a northern daily strike paper, read out the TUCs telegram to the assembled newspaper staff. They responded in anger, accusing him of lying or being in the pay of the bosses. Another ILP member in Scotland recollected:

> I was in the thick of the General Strike ... I was the only Socialist Town Councillor in Montrose ... and we had the whole area sewn up. One of my most poignant memories was of how, when the news of the great betrayal came through, I was addressing a packed meeting mainly of railwaymen. When I told them the terrible news most of them burst into tears – and I am not ashamed to say I did too.[60]

Socialists were left numbed by the retreat of the TUC, knowing that the miners would be left to battle on alone.

The ILPs involvement in the strike had been limited, hamstrung by the conservatism of the TUC and the wider party, but over the following months as the miners' continued to fight the lock-out, the ILP did considerable work. Their most significant contribution was the joint production alongside the MFGB of the bulletin *The Miner*, which had a distribution of 100,000 copies. In some parts of the country, when miners were starved into submission and began to return to work, ILP activists were dispatched with money and food and took miners' children in for the duration of the lock-out.[61] After nine months the miners were starved into submission and forced back to work. The ILP excoriated the union leaders for failing their members, prompting Ernest Bevin, head of the powerful Transport and General Workers' Union, to condemn the 'superior class attitude [from] people in your category in the movement' shown towards the 'trade union leader who comes from the rank and file'.[62] Not for the first time working-class leaders who had led a struggle to defeat lashed out at the supposedly middle-class left. That these 'middle-class socialists' had led huge strikes on the Clyde and gone to prison for the cause was lost on a bureaucrat like Bevin.

The trade union movement sunk into malaise after the defeat; strikes dropped to one-tenth of their previous level. Walter Citrine – 'the very soul of moderation and conciliation'[63] – was elected as General Secretary of the TUC. Concessions and a 'new deal' between industry and the unions was the order of the day for the union leaders. The TUC embarked on a new conciliatory turn which saw them working with captain of industry Sir Alfred Mond on ways to reorganise the economy and improve productivity and profitability. The demoralisation of the wider movement made it hard for the left to mount a serious political challenge to this retreat. Amid the disillusionment, moves to isolate the left gathered pace, involving the usual strategy of co-option where possible and expulsion where necessary. In the post-strike atmosphere in which radicals and communists were blamed for 'stirring up the workers', the moderates in Labour were desperate not to be associated with communism or revolutionary activity.

The party leadership went into overdrive to purge Labour of reds. An edict was passed requiring local branches to expel known communists. When branches refused they were expelled wholesale, 23 in 1926–7. As the number of expelled branches grew, attempts were made by communist sympathisers to organise themselves into what became known as the National Left Wing Movement (NLWM). Coordinated around the *Sunday Worker* – a CPGB-funded paper 'open' to the wider movement and which by 1926 had a circulation of 100,000 copies – the NLWM argued that it was not an alternative to Labour, and was trying to be supportive, but it wanted to move the party 'nearer to the heart's desire of the rank and file'.[64] Radical figures like A.J. Cook from the MFGB backed them, and nearly 100 Labour organisations and local parties supported the 1925 NLWM conference.

Many grassroots Labour members were sympathetic to the communist movement, either through general sympathy with Marxist politics, support for the Soviet Union as a workers' state or because of regular collaboration with CPGB activists in the practical work of the unions. A considerable number of members shared the revolutionary left's criticism of the actions of the party leaders in the general strike. At the NLWM conference in 1926, the call to 'cleanse the Labour Party of the agents of capitalism' was well received.[65] Inevitably the Labour right were utterly hostile. To stifle the left mood a strategy of co-option was adopted. MacDonald and R.H. Tawney produced a new programme for the party, *Labour and the Nation*, which committed Labour to fight for 'transforming capitalism into socialism'. The hope was that a clearer socialist statement of intent would accommodate the desires of the restive left-wing, frustrated and appalled by the defeat of the general strike and looking for a clearer commitment from their party and leaders to fundamentally change the world, not tinker around at the edges of the economy. The programme was a solid piece of Labour socialist rhetoric, but like other such statements it would not survive contact with government. It was, however, enough to project a left turn, which abated some of the criticism. That was the carrot – the stick was the disaffilia-tion of CLPs that backed communist candidates in elections or on trades councils, isolating the radical left and scaring left sympathisers into line.

However, it was not the Labour right but the communists themselves who finally sundered their connections with the Labour left. The rise of Stalinism in Russia, a consciously anti-revolutionary force that bureaucratised and killed the revolution, saw a new orientation for the CPGB. As the Stalinist influence spread across the Communist Inter-national, the CPGB was instructed to break all ties with the Labour left and denounce them as 'social fascists' – in essence as bad as Hitler in Germany because they were not consistently anti-capitalist enough. The CPGB began a campaign of vilification and even violence against Labour activists, ending any sympathy they may have had within the party. This was a godsend for the Labour leadership, who no longer had to worry about the influence of communists in their ranks. The editorial board of the *Sunday Worker* suddenly declared that the NLWM was being shut down and that its members should join the CPGB or face the consequences, causing a tidal wave of protest from activists across the movement.[66]

The new political line from Stalin (known as the Third Period) equated the Labour Party with fascism because they both propped up capitalism; they were essentially 'two sides of the same coin'. The Labour left were considered even worse, since like a Pied Piper they lulled radical workers into the orbit of fascistic social democracy. Some within the communist movement, including followers of exiled revolutionary leader Leon Trotsky, sought to oppose the Stalinist policy of socialism in one country and the Third Period, but they were in a minority internationally.

In 1928 the Labour Party moved into its famous headquarters at the newly built Transport House – the offices of Bevin's TGWU. Bevin had travelled a long way from his younger days, when he had addressed the Leeds Soviet conference in 1917 and made a speech for revolution and the independence of the colonies.[67] Now, from his plush office, he saw himself as the lynchpin between the political and industrial establishments of the labour movement. Bevin was a living example of what Marx referred to as 'social being determining consciousness' – the more he was embedded in the machinery of the labour movement the less radical his outlook on the world.[68] At Transport House, Labour had a floor dedicated to its administrative operations, providing meeting spaces for the NEC and other relevant bodies. It was also a venue for the TUC to meet. Bevin appreciated being able to keep the centre of the party – indeed the labour movement – close to his union. But it was not just organisational control he craved, he also consolidated his ideological grip through his chairmanship of the board of *The Daily Herald*, for which he secured a deal to improve its printing presses and increase its circulation to over a million. Transport House came to represent not just the unity of the industrial and political wings of the movement, but also the growing power of the bureaucracy over party management, control and discipline.

First Time as Tragedy...

The failure of the first Labour government led to serious soul-searching among the left. Starting in 1926, the ILP had been developing a deeper criticism of the gradualism of Labour, culminating in their manifesto *Socialism in our Time*. The ILP left was already in open opposition to what they saw as the timid nature of the party leadership and their lack of a radical perspective. Their response was to double down on key principles and objectives after the defeat of the miners and the counter-revolutionary backlash of the Trade Union Disputes Act.[69] *Socialism in our Time* made the case for a living wage, arguing that the working masses had the primary claim on the nation's wealth. The policy was radically redistributive and aimed at ending poverty. If employers would not pay the living wage then they would be forcibly nationalised. The big industries – coal, banking, rail and electricity – would be nationalised directly, others such as engineering and agriculture would be aggregated and run under state direction. The entire thrust was markedly different to the 1918 programme *The New Order*, which had called for state direction to rebuild the economy on the assumption that a mixed, state-led system could revitalise capitalism.

At the 1928 Labour conference the motion for a living wage was diluted into a motion calling only for a commission of inquiry into the *possibility* of such a policy. By the time this had worked its way through the conference machine it had established an inquiry to look solely into the issue of family allowances, dropping the living wage policy entirely. The demand for the living wage was not helped by the almost universal hostility of the unions, licking their wounds after 1926 and afraid to raise 'extreme' demands in the face of a Tory government that had already broken their organisations once. The union leaders also rejected the idea that Labour should interfere in the wage question in such a way as to reduce their own central role as negotiators in industrial matters. The ILP were predictably furious with the union bureaucrats for sabotaging their central policy.

Understandably frustrated, some ILP leaders took matters into their own hands. Without consultation, James Maxton launched a joint manifesto with the miners' leader A.J. Cook and began a speaking tour around the country. Others in the ILP were outraged – the manifesto had been agreed behind closed doors with no wider consultation, in a very undemocratic act move by Maxton.[70] Others were more sanguine, appreciating it as a bold, ambitious and provocative move from the left. The Cook-Maxton manifesto differed quite considerably from the *Socialism in our Time* strategy. In opposition to the moral and political collapse of the TUC after 1926, Cook-Maxton offered a more radical class-struggle outlook, advocating militant trade union action, uniting with the unemployed and creating cooperative societies, nationalising the banks, land, railways and mines without compensation, and getting rid of the monarchy. Maxton had concluded that the defeat of the general strike by state repression would radicalise the workers, 'making revolution inevitable'.[71] However, the accompanying speaker's tour attracted only limited numbers, and mid-way through it the CPGB's new Third Period 'social fascist' line led to their members denouncing the manifesto as the work of a 'pseudo-left'.[72]

2

Second Time as Disaster

'The myth has grown that in our society the state is neutral. It is not, and never has been. Therefore its apparatus must be democratised and made more responsive to the needs of a democratic society.'

Eric Heffer

The defeat of the unions in 1926 saw workers turn to the Labour Party to defend them from the rapacious Tories. By the time of the 1929 general election they all had the vote – every adult over 21 could now vote and 8 million voted Labour. The result was Labour's best yet, with more MPs returned than ever before. The ILP retained a significant presence in Parliament: of the 287 Labour MPs, 140 were aligned with the ILP, although only 37 had been directly funded with ILP money in their election campaigns. Labour had the most MPs, though not a majority, pulling the party back into the familiar strategic debate about how to get legislation passed with Liberal support. The second MacDonald administration was seen by many in the ILP as a chance to undo past mistakes and show working people what Labour could achieve. Moreover, Maxton had won a motion at the 1929 conference that gave the PLP, not the Prime Minister, the right to nominate the Cabinet. The hope this time from the left was that a stronger representation of genuine socialists might ensue. Worryingly, MacDonald displayed contempt for party democracy by ignoring the conference decision and selecting his own Cabinet.

Six months after the election the Wall Street Crash ripped the heart out of the world economy. The left's fears about the inadequate political strategy of the Labour leaders were tragically realised in the catastrophe that was the 1929–31 government. Faced with an economic crisis at the very heart of capitalism, and with millions of workers looking to them for protection, the Labour government spectacularly failed to meet the challenge. They failed to identify the causes of the wider problems: that, alongside the Great Depression, the British Empire was staring into the abyss and British industry was being crushed by both commercial and financial foreign competition. Britain's economic strength and the resulting power of its working class had always been predicated on its role as a global power – which also formed the material basis for the jingoism and nationalism in the workers' movement. The MacDonald government had no serious answers to the unravelling of British imperial power and the ensuing economic decline, despite being elected by the mass of enfranchised working men and women to deliver real change. If ever there was a time to deliver on the pledge to implement whatever they could of their programme, and 'go down fighting' rather than capitulate to the self-preservation of the capitalist elites, it was now. But the tragedy of the first Labour government was repeated, only this time with far more damaging results.

The lack of a specific socialist policy meant that Snowden at the Treasury fell back on the tried, tested and failed methods of the Liberals and Tories. Snowden proved a disastrous choice for Chancellor because he refused to deviate from the old liberal policies: he was a zealous supporter of both free trade and maintaining the gold standard. Ignoring the trade unions and his own party members, he leaned heavily on the civil service and the Treasury for advice. Defiant in the face of what would later become Keynesian orthodoxy, Snowden opposed deficit spending to boost the economy and create jobs. Instead he oversaw an austerity regime which only made the economic crisis far worse for working people. Inevitably, MacDonald and Snowden faced opposition from within the party from the earliest days of the government. ILP members, including Maxton and Wheatley, proposed an amendment to the King's Speech which would commit the government to nation-alising key industries and an income sufficient for workers to sustain their families.[1] The amendment was defeated in the PLP and some MPs became increasingly exasperated at the vocal antics of what they saw as a recalcitrant left minority.[2]

The central problem facing the Labour government was that of keeping its pledge to reduce spiralling unemployment. Despite election promises, unemployment actually doubled under the two-year administration, reaching 2.7 million. MacDonald's handling of the crisis was denounced weekly in the ILP press. The lines of contention were clear: 'The issue is whether in this economic situation the Labour Movement is to make futile attempts to rebuild capitalism or whether it is to accept the challenge of the failure of capitalism by boldly determining to lay the foundation for a new social order.'[3] The ILP demanded that the issue of unemployment be tackled to ensure that workers' lives were not destroyed by a crisis they had not created. Unemployment laws limited payments to only those people that were 'genuinely looking for work', which was being used to arbitrarily throw people off welfare. The ILP tried to get these onerous parts of the law removed but were defeated in the Commons by the Tories and Labour right. As the crisis ground on, Labour retreated from even mild social reforms and welfarism, instead launching an attack on the living standards of working people as a way of trying to save British capitalism. In 1918 the party had pledged to 'lend no hand' to the revival of capitalism and to see it buried. Now the leadership was scrabbling around desperately looking for cuts to prop up the economy – for which it took some merciless criticism from the ILP.

The Labour right in the PLP were very hostile to the activities of the ILP, seeing their MPs as wreckers who were undermining the party in a fragile situation. Wheatley was unrepentant however, pointing out that all the ILP MPs were doing was implementing the party policy adopted at conference: 'No rebel has yet cast a vote in Parliament except for something which was the declared policy of the Party. We are not in rebellion against the Labour Party, but we are in rebellion against anybody who will try to lead it away from its great historic mission. That mission was the abolition of poverty. Until that task is accomplished every Labour man and woman ought to be a rebel.'[4] At their 1930 conference the ILP declared that they were a 'separate socialist organisation' and were not beholden to the right-wing policies of the government.[5]

As the class war intensified, people had to choose sides. Confronted by financial speculators launching an attack on the pound, thereby plunging the British economy further into stagnation, the option was either to make bold inroads into wealth and property to rebuild the economy on a socialistic basis, or make the poor pay for the crisis. The ILP leadership wrote to its parliamentary group requesting that each MP publicly sign up to the principles of *Socialism in our Time* or leave the ILP. Faced with this choice many ILPs parliamentarians abandoned the party *en masse*, shrinking its membership in the Commons from 140 to just 18. Confronted with the economic crisis gripping the country, the pressure of Parliament and the rightward shift by Labour, most of the left MPs opted for the gradualist approach of MacDonald.

In August 1931 MacDonald decided that his allegiance lay with the bankers and employers – he concluded that it was the workers' intransigence that was really preventing the sacrifices necessary to get the economy healthy again. In his diary he wrote: 'If we yield now to the TUC we shall never be able to call our bodies or souls or intelligences our own.'[6] He was, however, happy to yield his body, soul and intelligence to the demands of the government's creditors. In the perennial battle of any Labour leader, that between class and country, MacDonald finally sided with a view of the national good 'defined by British bankers in a crisis made by international speculators'.[7]

The financiers did not prescribe specific cuts but they did demand a balanced budget to 'restore confidence'. Looking for cuts that all parties could support, eyes turned to the May Committee of Inquiry, which recommended £97 million worth of cuts and the gutting of welfare and unemployment benefits, a policy that would hit the poorest hardest. Backed by the Conservatives, MacDonald proposed to implement the welfare reforms to balance the budget. This was too much even for many on the Labour right. The fall-out and subsequent retreat in Parliament led to a split in the Cabinet, with eight Ministers refusing to agree to the 20 per cent cut in unemployment benefit. Faced with a concerted attack on the pound and an ultimatum from the Bank of England that if cuts weren't made then the credit supply would dry up, MacDonald submitted the resignation of his government to the king, only to re-emerge afterwards as Prime Minister in a coalition government with the Tories.

MacDonald declared an election in 1931 that split Labour in two. MacDonald, Snowden and Thomas declared themselves members of National Labour and supporters of an emergency coalition government with the Tories to 'ensure national stability'. They stood for election on the basis that if a 'National Government' was not returned then people's savings would be decimated and hyper-inflation would grip the country. Snowden made the most treacherous attack on his old party, describing Labour policy as 'Bolshevism run mad'.[8]

Due to the combined efforts of the Tories, the now ex-Labour leaders and the fear tactics of the media, Labour was routed at the 1932 election losing 225 MPs. Only 52 Labour MPs were elected (three ILP MPs were elected separately), leaving a vacuum in the PLP leadership after nearly every Cabinet member lost their seat. After a few months the government agreed to leave the gold standard without any serious fuss from the City of London, even though the previous Labour government had been warned not to do so by the same bankers.[9] MacDonald led the most integrationist wing of his party into an uneasy alliance with the class enemy, ending up distrusted by the Tories and hated by his fellow socialists. This was the culmination of the Fabian strategy writ large on the pages of history, just at a time when the working class was looking to Labour to secure its welfare and living standards and needed a bold and audacious party fighting for their interests. MacDonald's remaining time in Parliament was a shambolic end to a disastrous career as Prime Minister. In his last rambling, tearful speech to Parliament, Maxton famously interrupted him: 'Sit down man! You're a bloody tragedy.'

The Labour rank and file considered the MacDonald strategy a betrayal of their party and of the workers' movement. Even Clement Attlee, normally quite a temperate Labour MP, described it some years later as the 'greatest betrayal in the political history of this country'.[10] It was easy for the remaining Labour members to blame MacDonald, Thomas and Snowden individually, but others offered a more radical critique. Jennie Lee for instance, a left-wing ILP member from Scotland, attacked the notion that the great betrayal was an 'isolated and infamous act', arguing that it was the logical end point of the entire political philosophy of the old party leadership, reared as it was on a diet of liberalism and Fabianism.[11] The mistake was the result of the strategy that had been adopted in 1900, not of the actions of a few misguided individuals.

As the most senior surviving MP, Lansbury was the only eligible candidate for the leadership position, taking over after Henderson lost his seat. This offered a rare moment in the party's history for a left-wing leader. Lansbury commanded respect and was much loved by Labour members and workers across the country, but his pacifist principles sat dangerously outside the prevailing militarist mood of the time. With the collapse of the PLP, the balance of power in Labour shifted decisively towards the union leaders. Men like Bevin, Citrine and Henderson met to organise a 'council of war' with the intention of making Labour electable again and acting as a bulwark against any turn to the left. They could not tolerate Lansbury as leader for long, and set about making plans in motion to oust him.

Adieu, ILP

Once again, the failure of a Labour government led to a radicalisation of the Labour left. Some more moderate Labour thinkers even began to talk openly about the problems with the 'gradualist' approach; Tawney is often quoted as saying that when it came to reforming capitalism into socialism 'onions can be peeled leaf by leaf, but you cannot skin a live tiger claw by claw'. It is the tiger after all, that usually does the killing. Attlee boldly declared at the 1932 party conference: 'no further progress can be made in seeking to get crumbs from the rich man's table ... they cannot get socialism without tears, that whenever we try to do anything we will be opposed by every vested interest, financial, political and social'.[12] The left turn that the ILP had been taking for a decade accelerated and deepened, heading towards a more radical reformism and away from the ethical socialism they had initially counterposed to Fabianism.[13]

Both Labour and the ILP had to find a way of dealing with the fallout from the MacDonald disaster. The two organisations, one a constituent of the other, had come to different conclusions. The ILP was increasingly critical of the gradualism of the party leadership; the failure of the Labour government on top of the defeat of the miners was too much for ILP members. The Labour right, for its part, was intent on forcing the ILP to either surrender or leave the party. The ILP had been on a tight leash since 1929 when the PLP changed its standing orders to prevent the ILP left from voting against the government. This silencing of dissent fell very hard on the more radical MPs and some refused to sign the new standing orders. As punishment, the NEC refused to endorse the 19 ILP candidates who stood in the 1931 election. With only 52 MPs left, Labour demanded complete unity in votes in the commons. The ILP rejected this, arguing that the problem with the Labour government had been political, not organisational. If they were not free to speak their mind then how could they explain to the working class and Labour voters what the problems were? The ILP demanded that the socialist measures in the Labour manifesto be implemented, but with the PLP autonomous of the democratic structures of the party it was simply not possible to push a clear socialist line. Amid the growing rancour, the calls for outright disaffiliation became cacophonous. Brockway went to visit Lansbury to broker peace, but the latter refused to countenance going back to the federal model of pre-1918, which the ILP believed was the only way to save Labour from a split.[14]

The ILP National Council was totally divided on the question of disaffiliation, so gave no recommendation to the 1932 conference in Blackpool. The ILP debate split three ways: disaffiliation, continued affiliation or continued negotiations. Brockway, Maxton and others met with representatives from the Labour Party to try to reach an agreement. They proposed that MPs should be able to vote against the PLP line but would then have to face being reported to their CLPs where local members would decide what to do with them – either endorse their actions or censure them in some way. The Labour Party representatives were uninterested, demanding acceptance of the PLP standing orders as the only basis for continued negotiation.

The ILP convened a second conference in Bradford in a tense atmosphere. The local ILP paper – the *Bradford Pioneer* – printed an open letter to the conference delegates headlined: 'The ILP was born in Bradford. Have you come to bury it?' The appeal had only limited resonance; the ILP delegates voted by 241 to 142 to leave Labour, an act described by one historian as 'suicide during a fit of insanity'.[15] Brockway supported disaffiliation, though later agreed that the decision had been a mistake. The hard-line tendency argued that the split meant a 'clean break' in which ILP members cut off all ties with Labour, no longer even associating with it through their trade union affiliations. The decision to not pay the union political levy proved particularly disastrous: many ILP union activists were now treated as pariahs; in many union branches they weren't allowed to take part in political discussions as branch chairs loyal to Labour had them removed from the meeting. Leaving Labour in the way they did meant being exorcised from the political wing of the movement, cut off from the many thousands of workers and socialists still affiliated.

The split tore apart comradeships that had been built up over many years. For ILP members like Jennie Lee, a miner's daughter brought up on radical socialist traditions, it was clear that Labour's entire strategy up till that point had failed. She sided with Maxton, later writing that 'the British working class movement was in no mood to accommodate me. It had split into warring factions ... I had to choose.'[16] Nye Bevan was furious with her: 'Why don't you get into a nunnery and be done with it? ... I tell you, it is the Labour Party or nothing ... I know all its faults, all its dangers. But it is the Party that we have taught millions of working people to look to and regard as their own.'[17] Despite Bevan's thunderous criticisms, Lee would not be budged, she believed leaving was the only logical course of action left open to principled socialists. For many radicals the ill-fated attempt to unite liberals and socialists had reached its logical conclusion – the broad church of integrationist, liberal Fabians and transformative radicals of various stripes was finished, broken by the cold reality of the MacDonald government.

The split was indeed a disaster for the ILP. Despite the Great Recession and mass unemployment, being outside of Labour proved to be a barren place. A rigorous campaign of activism didn't stop the ILP's membership collapsing – many had been paper members only or had viewed it more as a social club. It is tempting to look at the trajectory of the ILP and conclude that they behaved in a sectarian or destructive manner and that remaining in Labour would have been preferable, as Bevan argued at the time. But being locked into a party led by people who detested them, the grass definitely looked greener outside. If there had been more internal democracy in the Labour Party then the ILP might have fared much better, but the consensus between the NEC, the PLP and the TUC meant that pursuing constitutional reform was simply not possible. The ILP believed that the rise of fascism and the crisis of capitalism was a harbinger of the final breakdown of the system and that it could therefore win mass working-class support from Labour by being independent. This perspective proved to be misjudged.

Independence did however allow some freedom of action. A majority of ILP members supported sending a brigade to Spain in the late 1930s to support the revolution. Brockway himself – who had praised Gandhi and maintained a theoretical commitment to non-violence – changed his position in the face of an actual revolution in which his friends, international collaborators and comrades were involved. The ILP sent 25 members to Spain to fight on the side of the Republicans, and would have sent more were it not for government intervention. They fought alongside the POUM,[18] and some of their battles were famously described by George Orwell in *Homage to Catalonia*.[19] It was a measure of how far the ILP had come since 1916, when they opposed the Dublin uprising on pacifist grounds.

In late 1938, feelers were put out by Stafford Cripps, acting on behalf of Attlee, to seek a meeting with the ILP to discuss reaffiliation. The meeting between the two party leaderships in one of the committee rooms of the Commons proved to be a positive affair. The Labour leaders were apparently quite keen for the ILP to rejoin on the same basis as 1931 – that is with an independent press and party structure and their own policies, but with an agreement not to vote against the PLP whips in the Commons. The ILP leadership accepted this; even Maxton who disagreed in principle but accepted it as long as the majority of the party felt that it was the right thing to do. The Labour NEC also voted to endorse the reaffiliation. But then the war broke out. Labour supported the war while the ILP opposed it, and with Labour's temporary electoral truce with the opposition parties in place, reaffiliation at that point proved impossible.

The Socialist League

When the ILP disaffiliated, some of its supporters chose to stay with Labour as they still saw it as the best hope for radical change. After the July 1932 ILP conference had voted for disaffiliation, the Socialist League emerged a month later to carry on the legacy of the ILP within the Labour Party. The League was part think tank, part grassroots activist network, part left pressure group. In the tradition of the Fabian movement it set out to publish pamphlets, essays and books on various aspects of socialist theory with the aim of intellectually preparing a future Labour government for replacing capitalism. It was bankrolled by Stafford Cripps, a popular parliamentarian who had been elected (twice!) in 1931. Although Cripps came from an aristocratic background, like many others he was radicalised during the 1920s. The experience of the second MacDonald government set him on a course towards a semi-revolutionary politics, though this was contemptuously dismissed by Hugh Dalton MP as 'an adolescent Marxist miasma'.[20]

Cripps was joined by Harold Laski, a prominent intellectual who went on to teach Ralph Miliband. Other leading figures included Nye Bevan, Barbara Betts (later Castle), William Mellor and Ellen Wilkinson. A young Michael Foot was also an active member – an ethical socialist inspired by H.G. Wells, he and Betts read Marx together in their twenties.[21] Laski helped found the Left Book Club and co-founded *Tribune* with Cripps, Bevan, George Strauss, Wilkinson and the publisher Victor Gollancz. Major Clement Attlee was also a contributor to pamphlets and lectures by the League. This was a time when the intellectual fires of the Labour left were burning with the intensity of a movement trying to find its way forward after a historic defeat.

The Socialist League in some ways represented the most advanced internal theoretical challenge to Labour's gradualist approach, and certainly reached the most radical conclusions based on their research, analysis and lived experience. It sought to win the party to a transformative strategy, and in doing so transform the party itself. The question would be how far they could go before the integrative tendencies of the party overwhelmed them. The League started off strong: within three months it had 70 branches across the country and a big presence at the 1933 and 1934 conferences. While it had little influence in Parliament, it did combine a dynamic and serious theoretical endeavour with a broad reach of support across the party. It fused with the Society for Socialist Inquiry and Propaganda, which included G.D.H. Cole, and succeeded in ousting Ernest Bevin from his position as its chair. The League's approach was thoroughly empirical and educative; it sent members out to gather data and material for its pamphlets, to ensure the arguments would be irrefutable by Tories or the bosses. The intention was to turn these facts into agitation and propaganda for socialism.

Unlike the ILP, which started life as a separate party and maintained its existence as such throughout its time in Labour, the League opted for a different approach. It initially prioritised the education of Labour members and getting left-wing policies adopted at conference. As an affiliated socialist organisation, the League had delegate rights on local bodies. In addition, because the local Labour branches were quite weak and disorganised, with few active members and a general sense of despondency after the MacDonald fiasco, League activists prioritised trying to develop a healthy intellectual party culture.

The main debates that gripped the Socialist League focused on unemployment and socialist planning, the problems of Labour as a socialist vehicle, and wider concerns about how British capitalism and imperialism prevented the success of a socialist programme. After the collapse of the great strike and then MacDonald's betrayal, people were attracted to radical theories and insights into the limits of parliamentary socialism and the trade union movement. The way the bosses had crushed the general strike through mass scabbing by the middle classes, and the Tories used the army or police to break strikes, opened up a wider discussion around the role of the state and the tenacity with which the ruling class would pursue the class struggle. Many believed that the gradualism of the Fabians and MacDonald had been exposed by the concerted sabotage of the British economy the 1929–31 government had witnessed. In his article, 'The Choice Before the Labour Party', Tawney outlined the prevailing fears on the left:

> If the privileged classes' position is seriously threatened they will use every piece on the board, political and economic, the House of Lords, the Crown, the Press, disaffection in the army, financial crises, international difficulties, and even, as newspaper attacks on the pound in 1931 showed, the émigré trick of injuring one's own country to protect one's pocket – in the honest conviction that they are saving civilisation.[22]

The League recognised the class struggle: 'We have got to decide on which side of the economic conflict we belong, and having decided, face up to the implications of that conflict', as Barbara Betts solemnly declared.[23]

Leaders like Cripps and Laski believed that it would not be possible to achieve socialism through strictly constitutional-parliamentary means; mass direct action would be needed to buttress any left Labour government once in office. Cripps ran into considerable trouble when he implied that the monarchy might sabotage an elected left government; the Labour NEC forced him to publicly retract his statement. The League turned their theory into a series of motions for the Labour conference, with proposals to abolish the House of Lords and for the introduction of an 'Emergency Powers Act' to 'takeover or regulate the financial machine, and to put into force any measures that the situation may require for the immediate control or socialisation of industry and for the safeguarding of the food supply and other necessities'.[24] The League won a vote at the 1932 conference for the nationalisation of the Joint Stock Banks to prevent capital flight.

While radical compared to the constitutionalism of the party and the conservatism of the trade union leaders, the League's approach was still a parliamentary route, though one which accepted the importance of extra-parliamentary action. In effect, their socialist programme represented a series of laws that a left Labour government could implement, with their success guaranteed by the speed of the legislative agenda – hence the need for emergency powers within days of being elected – and the active support of the wider working-class movement. The continuing domination of the right in alliance with the union block vote was not significantly addressed. The League's position also seemed to reduce the problems of the MacDonald government to a question of timing: if only they had implemented a socialist programme in the first few weeks, then any possible attempts at capital-strikes, bankers blackmail or industrial sabotage could have been be avoided.

International issues dominated the agenda in the 1930s. Labour's continued support for the British Empire caused some consternation in the ranks. Its position as a governing party administering the Empire never wavered once in either 1924 or 1929–31. By contrast, the League's members arrived at a wholly different, anti-colonial, position. Labour was formally committed by its 1933 conference to support 'socialisation and self-government' in India,[25] but in 1935 Attlee proposed an amendment that would grant India only Dominion status – far short of truly democratic independence. The prevailing view in Labour was that India was too vast and too primitive a country to administer its own affairs, as such, until their society had developed, 'the Labour Party considers that the British Government must act as trustee for the native races'.[26] Against this Western paternalism and appeal to the 'white man's burden', H.N. Brailsford published a controversial book, *India in Chains*, that linked the question of British imperial rule to the subjugation and enforced 'backwardness' of the Indian people. He argued that it was the alliance between British colonialism and the propertied classes in India that conspired to keep the mass of people down. Britain ruled India in a way that robbed the people of education and thus of the political capacity to run their own affairs – creating a vicious circle in which continued British occupation appeared necessary. The League rejected the racist category of 'backward people' and called for self-determination based on a Constituent Assembly that would ensure a full and democratic debate for the Indian people.[27]

Overall, Socialist Leaguers were dismissive of the League of Nations. Rather than focusing on the details of how the League of Nations worked, their criticism ran deeper – the imperialist context itself precluded its effectiveness as a tool for world peace. They believed that the failure of the League of Nations to intervene in Manchuria to help the Chinese fight the Japanese, and its prevarication over Mussolini's invasion of Abyssinia, were not the *result* of a lack of will – rather, the lack of will was itself an expression of the political problems of the League. Some in Labour argued that the League of Nations was effectively a product of imperialism, and although they were not in favour of withdrawing from it, they only supported its actions in as much as they could be considered progressive for the world working class.[28] This position was scandalous to the Tories, the Liberals and many Labour integrationists.

Lessons Learned?

Despite the departure of the ILP, Labour with Lansbury at its head still moved left as a consequence of the fallout from the MacDonald government. For many socialists within Labour the signs were good that lessons may have been learned and a new dawn was coming for a revived, more democratic and more clearly socialist party. The process of governmental disappointment followed by a turn to the left to rein-vigorate the demoralised membership was by now a familiar pattern. What was not yet clear was the extent to which the Labour hierarchy would tolerate, let alone encourage, debate over principles and tactics to consolidate the activist base before the 'serious work' of preparing for government arrived. The 1930s provide a textbook example of the usual 'turn to the left' process once in opposition.

At the 1932 conference, the left – led by Charles Trevelyan – won votes on nationalising the Joint Stock Banks, preventing a return of Snowden and MacDonald, and condemning gradualism as a strategy. They also won a motion at the 1933 conference to commit Labour to call a general strike in the event of war. The 1934 policy statement was just as radical on the domestic front. The party's programme *For Socialism and Peace* committed it to the nationalisation of land, banking, coal, iron and steel, transport, power and the water supply, as well as the setting up of a National Investment Board to plan industrial development. These policies only lasted until 1937, when the right won back control. The commitment to the general strike in the event of war was overturned by a joint meeting of the PLP, the NEC and the TUC at Transport House.[29] The left's labour of Sisyphus during these battles would be familiar to many subsequent generations – all the good work done at conference was undone in committee meetings and back-room deals over the following months.

In some ways the Socialist League initiated policies that became Labour mainstream thinking. For instance, as a response to mass unemployment they advocated planning and credit to boost demand – a Keynesian measure synonymous with post-war Labour policy.[30] But other ideas were more controversial, for instance workers' self-management, debated at the 1933 conference. The view of the right, led by Herbert Morrison, was that workers, bosses and the government should jointly run industry, ensuring a collaborative approach to any problems. This became known as corporatism, which the left feared would subordinate workers to their bosses.[31] Morrison advocated forms of local municipality that were supposedly based on the lessons of Lansbury in Poplar, but with one crucial component missing: Poplarism had been based on mass participatory activity, but Morrison favoured efficiency over democracy, a political machine over local participation.[32]

The Socialist League challenged the corporatist view, some of its members even associating it with creeping fascism. They wanted a greater share of control for workers in industry, linked to a planned economy. The League's notion of workers' control issued in a proposal for a National Economic Council made up of trade unionists, experts and representatives from industry.[33] The League's vision had trade unionists sitting on the boards of nationalised companies as the *representatives* of their members, not merely as management personnel.[34] The Leaguers were critical of any 'national plan' that didn't also involve moves towards the expropriation of capitalists, considering that anything less would just be a move to manage capitalism to ensure productivity. Inevitably this led to a clash with union leaders like Bevin, who regarded the League's policies as unrealistic and divisive.

Attempting to draw the lessons from the first two Labour governments, a series of proposals were made in the 1933 document *Labour and Government* to put in place measures to stop future disasters. It committed Labour to holding a special conference of the labour movement before accepting office in a minority government, as a means to secure some kind of oversight on possible policy initiatives. A Labour Prime Minister would also have to consult the PLP before deciding on a Cabinet – a mechanism for getting more critical voices heard in the formation of a government. Most importantly, it insisted that the policies of any future government had to be agreed at conference and 'embodied in the General Election manifesto'.[35] The decision of conference was quite clear – any future minority government must implement a socialist programme and stand or fall in the Commons on that programme.[36]

After its initial successes, the Socialist League rapidly ran aground, failing to amend Labour's programme at the 1934 conference. Mellor wrote in *The Socialist Leaguer* that it was a combination of the trade union block vote and the NEC's control of the Conference Arrangements Committee that had defeated the League's intervention. He concluded that the League should reach out beyond Labour. They had reached the limits of what was possible given the current constitutional and political arrangements, and should therefore turn to the wider workers' movement to fight for socialism.[37]

The League's main political campaigns were against unemployment, fascism and imperialism. Since appeals to the Labour leadership fell on deaf ears, they looked outwards to joint initiatives with the ILP and the CPGB around issues like unemployment. When the left organised a series of hunger marches and mass protests against the devastating effects of poverty and the lack of jobs in working-class communities, Socialist League, ILP and CPGB activists were centrally involved in putting pressure on the National Government to tackle the issue. The CPGB had by this stage abandoned their social-fascism argument and swung towards a Popular Front policy: that working-class parties should unite with 'progressive capitalists' to defend democracy against fascism.

When Oswald Mosley, recently returned from Italy and keen to put Mussolini's fascism into practice in Britain, organised a provocative march through London's East End to terrorise the Jewish community, more joint actions were organised. While Labour's leaders and *The Daily Herald* urged Labour members to 'Keep Away' and stay indoors, the Socialist League, ILP and CPGB organised a massive anti-fascist demonstration that confronted the fascists on Cable Street and broke up their march route, humiliating the racist Black Shirts and proving the strength and unity of the workers' movement – despite opposition from the official leadership.[38]

Debates on world events dominated the 1935–6 period, in particular the Italian invasion of Abyssinia (modern-day Ethiopia) and the fascist counter-revolution in Spain. With the Italian invasion looming, the TUC, NEC and PLP called on the League of Nations to use any means at its disposal to stop Mussolini. Lansbury opposed on strictly pacifist grounds; the Socialist League on anti-imperialist grounds. As Cripps explained: 'If war comes before the workers in Great Britain have won power, that war will be ... in the interests of British imperialism.'[39] The League called for a general strike, a policy inevitably blocked by the TUC.

The argument for non-intervention in Spain was that it would stop arms and equipment falling into the hands of Franco's fascist forces but Nazi Germany and Fascist Italy were already supplying Franco with all the material he needed to beat the Republicans and the left. In the cause of solidarity, the Socialist League supported intervention on the side of the Republic. The debate over how to respond to Spain frustrated many on the left, particularly Laski. Labour adopted a position of fundraising for non-military materials such as medical supplies. The League wanted them to go further, arguing for military support for the Republican government against the fascist rebels. The 1936 party conference was movingly addressed by two Spanish Republicans, which boosted the left's case but was not enough to overturn the union block vote backing the executive's policy of non-intervention. Laski bitterly wrote after the event: 'After a long fight those blasted trade unions decided on non-intervention though they knew this meant a sure rebel [Franco] victory in Spain ... I have never seen such blindness in a body of leaders since I began to be interested in politics ... It is just pitiable.'[40] At subsequent meetings, workers still demanded action: in the words of one union member 'we have to go to Transport house and turn it upside down.'[41]

The decision of the Labour Party not to assist the Republicans in Spain drove the Socialist League further into the arms of the CPGB. Along with the ILP and CPGB they launched a Unity Manifesto calling for a united front of all working-class organisations against fascism. Labour's leadership wanted nothing to do with it. When the League debated the Unity Campaign in January 1937, members expressed mixed opinions. The delegates voted 56 in favour, 35 against and 23 abstaining on a motion to back the Unity Manifesto, but most knew this would propel them into a headlong clash with Labour and risk disaffiliation. It also caused big ructions on the left: many in the ILP were very critical of the show trials in Moscow where well-known communists were being executed based on false charges. There was no criticism of this in the Unity Campaign. Those who were doubtful of the CPGB's intentions were right to be concerned; it was revealed after the conference that the CPGB had been secretly promoting the dissolution of the League 'in the best interests of the [Unity] campaign'. Clearly the Stalinists were concerned about a radical left emerging within Labour, and wanted it either stamped out or absorbed into the CPGB.

In response to the Unity Campaign, Labour's NEC moved to bring matters to a head. The excuse was the League's collaboration with the CPGB, but that was only the official explanation. The real goal was to kick the stool from under the left and isolate figures like Laski and Cripps. As an exasperated Hugh Dalton wrote in his diary concerning Cripps' regular outbursts: 'Cripps seems quite unable to see the argument that he is damaging the party electorally ... He has become very vain and seems to think that only he and his cronies know what Socialism is or how it should be preached.'[42] The list of left demands were seen by the NEC as damaging to the standing of the party: 'Buckingham Palace – League of Nations – "compelling" [trade] unions to declare a general strike – prolonging Parliament beyond five years ... "Seize land, finance and industry" (without compensation?) – Emergency Powers Bill in one day'.[43] All these demands were considered vote losers. Faced with a global capitalist crisis and the rush to war, the Labour hierarchy decided to close such socialist experiments down in order to triangulate towards electability.

It was Dalton who led the charge against the Socialist League, dismissing it as a 'rich man's toy ... the "so-called Unity campaign" [was] financed by two rich men who were using their private wealth in constant attacks in the policy and leadership of the Party'.[44] The fact that both Cripps and Trevelyan (a landowner) were rich made the attacks sound authentic to many rank-and-file members. But, as Transport House closed in, there were protests from others in the movement; the *New Statesman and Nation* pointedly asked in January 1937: 'do Transport House realise that a very large proportion of those who work hardest for the Labour cause up and down the country want the United Front and that a great many of them are already doing their best to operate it locally in relation to particular issues?' But the protests fell on deaf ears.

Rather than allow the right to drive their members out of the party, the League's leadership decided to disband without a fight. Betts was phlegmatic about it: 'This is not a funeral, but a deliberate political tactic'; she held out the hope the forces involved could carry on in some way. But others knew that it was over. J.T. Murphy was despairing: '[The League] decided not to face expulsion but to die'.[45] Foot later wrote: 'Many were to regret that decision in later years when the left in the party, robbed by their own act of any effective organisation, found themselves hopelessly pitted as individuals against the Executive machine'.[46] The dissolution of the Socialist League was the end of the only official 'loyal opposition' in Labour. Another would not emerge for another decade. Looking back after re-joining Labour, Brockway lamented: 'Thus ended ingloriously the Unity campaign. Its result was the destruction of the Socialist League, the loss of influence of Cripps, Bevan, Strauss and other "lefts", the strengthening of the reactionary leaders and the disillusionment of the rank and file'.[47]

When Labour published its immediate Economic Programme in 1937 it jettisoned any talk of workers' control and extolled the virtues of Morrison's corporatist socialism, the same position that had been defeated in 1933. For all their effort and intellectual work, the Socialist League's political gains were rolled back in double-quick time by Transport House.[48] Labourism reasserted itself. As Tawney argued in 1931, 'Until the Labour Party recognises that it is not socialist it is unlikely to become socialist.'[49]

The Hammering of George Lansbury

In the wake of the National Government disaster, Lansbury's leadership had helped stabilise the party and hold it together; not an inconsiderable feat considering the events. Labour made some advances, especially in London, where Morrison launched a successful campaign to win the London County Council. But the right had come to see Lansbury as a nuisance and a menace to Labour's electability, and as such he had to be defeated. His pacifism looked hopelessly out of touch in the face of fascism in Italy and Germany. Increasing pressure was being put on the party to advocate the use of force against Mussolini, or at least the use of sanctions. Lansbury wanted an international conference called by the League of Nations to resolve these issues. He knew he was isolated in the PLP; he had a small loyal following of MPs, but many left Labour MPs disagreed with his strict pacifism. In an epoch where rearmament was central to Britain's imperialist role in the world, the Labour right looked to deliver the men and guns needed. Pacifism in this context was seen by the right as irresponsible and by the left as hopeless. A key moment in the restoration of a more 'moderate' leadership and policy direction was the 1935 Labour conference, at which the right-wing wanted to ensure 'the ritual martyrdom of George Lansbury'.[50]

Lansbury's nemesis in this instance was the intractable Ernest Bevin, a bruiser of a trade union boss who delighted in contrasting his 'common-sense' approach with what he saw as the hopeless idealism of the socialists. Bevin appealed to the importance of maintaining Britain's imperial role in the world in order to ensure stability and peace internationally. After all, if the anti-imperialist aims of the Labour left were adopted then there would be a scramble by Germany, France and others to grab the ex-colonies, leading to even more wars.

Lansbury had offered to resign if the PLP or conference wished him to do so, but Bevin scolded him to fall on his sword himself: 'It is placing the executive and the movement in an absolutely false position to be taking your conscience round from body to body asking to be told what you ought to do with it.'[51] The response to this from delegates was lukewarm, some even booed, but it was a powerful message from the country's most powerful trade union leader for Lansbury to go. It was not the last time Bevin would be the executioner of the left at a conference. His speech swayed the conference to support the League of Nations, and the anti-war position was defeated by 2,168,000 to 102,000 votes. Dalton was pleased, recording in his diary that Bevin had 'hammered Lansbury to death'.[52] Feeling the ground collapse beneath him, with little support at conference and even less at the National Council of Labour, Lansbury resigned. By now in his mid seventies, he turned away from Labour and committed the last years of his life to the peace movement, dying in 1940 as the world descended into bloody slaughter.

3

The Age of Consent

The political contradictions left unresolved at the end of the First World War were bound to unravel in a destructive, terrible manner. The rise of fascism in Europe and the scramble to redivide the world between the Great Powers posed significant problems for socialists, and the destruction by fascists of mass socialist movements in Germany, Italy and Spain had seriously weakened the left internationally. On the eve of the war, the Labour left was a shadow of its former self. Key figures on the left felt the sting of the party's disciplinary whip as the lights went out over Europe once again. By late 1938, Cripps was disillusioned about the prospect of any alliance with 'progressive capitalists' and had swung back to opposing the Popular Front, calling for a campaign of left parties to oust the National Government from power. With Franco about to seize Barcelona and finish off the Republic, Cripps wrote to the NEC asking them to reopen the debate on a united front campaign of all socialist parties in Britain to support the Spanish left. Exasperated by Cripps' repeated refusal to accept defeat, the NEC wrote to him demanding a public pledge of loyalty to the agreed party line of no intervention. Cripps refused, pleading democratic imperatives, and was expelled. Now the NEC's blood was up, they cast about for other dissidents to make an example of. They did not have to look far. At a public meeting on the day of Cripps' expulsion, Bevan declared to the audience: 'if Sir Stafford Cripps is expelled ... for wanting to unite the forces of freedom and democracy they can go on expelling others. They can expel me. His crime is my crime.'[1] The NEC duly expelled Bevan less than a week later. George Strauss suffered a similar fate. Bevan at this point was despairing: 'If every organised effort to change Party policy is to be described as an organised attack on the party itself, then the rigidity imposed by party discipline will soon change into *rigor mortis*.'[2] The problem was ended when Cripps performed a volte face and ended up endorsing the National Government in order to defeat Hitler.

The wartime coalition agreement also meant that Labour would not stand against the Conservatives or Liberals in any by-elections – general elections having been suspended for the duration of the war. Labour members brought up on the horrors of the vicious Tory governments of the inter-war years had to stomach maintaining a Tory majority of 200 in the Commons. Understandably many rebelled, with the consequence that during by-elections the ILP or a new left party called The Common Wealth Party would get significant votes. A lot of local CLP activists clandestinely supported such candidates, who were putting forward anti-war arguments and demands for a socialist government after the war.[3] Jennie Lee stood as an independent in a bitterly fought by-election in Bristol in 1943, grappling with the paper shortage and no petrol for travelling around the constituency by speaking at open air rallies on car roofs. Lee's message was simple: working people needed socialist domestic policies. She openly identified with the 1942 Beveridge Report, which outlined the key areas for post-war domestic policy: 'A vote for Lee is a vote for Beveridge.'[4] Lee lost the election, but re-joined Labour shortly afterwards, saying that the conditions that had caused the split with the ILP were 'no longer a guide to her political views'.[5] Within the ranks there was concern that the party leadership would drag its heels on the implementation of Beveridge's recommendations. In her maiden speech to the 1943 party conference, Barbara Betts warned that it was 'Jam yesterday and jam tomorrow but never jam today!' Her speech ended up on the front of the *Daily Mirror*.

Within the party itself, serious opposition to the policies of the PLP was rare. Cripps had been readmitted to Labour in 1942 and entered the Coalition Cabinet, from that point ceasing to play any role on the left. A 1944 conference resolution moved by Ian Mikardo, calling for wide-scale nationalisation and workers' control of industry, was passed with very enthusiastic support from the party rank and file in opposition to the NEC and ministers. Bevan was involved in a running battle over the question of press censorship and publicly attacked Churchill and Morrison for banning the *Daily Worker* and threatening to censure the *Daily Mirror*. He also led two damaging backbench rebellions against the government, opposing Bevin's partisan handling of various miners' strikes in 1943–4 and his implementation of the notorious 1AA legislation that threatened to put striking workers in prison for five years. Bevan laid into the 'trade union bosses at the top' who had lost contact 'with the people at the bottom' (an unforgivable criticism of the TUC which left Bevan as a marked man at Transport House after the war).[6]

Laski – popular with the members but disliked by many in the party hierarchy and by trade union bureaucrats (who loved to refer to him as *Professor* Laski in a snide dig at the intelligentsia) – called for the nationalisation of land and of the Bank of England to raise morale after the retreat at Dunkirk. When he approached the Labour Party Policy Committee with this proposal he was entirely rebuffed. Dalton argued that what was needed was air-force victories and improving the means test. Afterwards he laughed that the committee had sent Laski 'away with his little tail between his little legs'.[7]

Bevan and Cripps urged support for the war effort, writing in *Tribune*: 'Every good socialist will do his utmost to assist the anti-fascist forces', adding that it was important that socialists not 'permit the war to degenerate into a simple struggle between rival imperialisms'.[8] This was essentially George Orwell's position. What the left lacked was a clear alternative to the war that escaped the abject failures of pacifism, which had been so spectacularly undermined by Chamberlain's failures to guarantee 'peace in our time'. The problem was a reflection of the complexity of the situation – this was not a simple rerun of the First World War; the threat of fascism was very real and not just based on jingoistic anti-German bluster. This was an imperialist war *and* an anti-fascist war. The left had to consider how to handle the contradictions at the heart of the international crisis. The ILP's pacifist position alienated some members like Lee, who argued that there was a marked difference between the clearly inter-imperialist nature of the 1914–18 conflict and the urgency of an international fight against fascism.[9]

A priority for many Labour was to ensure that working people came out of the war in a better position than they had been in during the 1930s – to win the war and win the peace. Labour leaders mobilised the British working class in support of the war on the basis that a fair share of the spoils would go to that same class as a reward for their sacrifice. On their side, the capitalist class could rely on loyalty from the party of the trade unions, a willing ally through difficult times. The danger for the capitalists was the increasing radicalism of the working class in the face of war, and the need to both mobilise mass forces and introduce economic planning to ensure victory. Could they rule in the same way, even if they won the war?

Socialism Without Tears

A sense of hope in the country had lifted Labour's 1945 election victory above anyone's expectations. Labour's new cohort of MPs sang The Red Flag as they stood outside Parliament, much to the concern of Attlee and the king, but there was nothing much that could be done to stop the cheers from the Labour ranks. This caused some consternation. 'These new Labour MPs are a strange looking lot – one regrets the departure of the sound old Trade Unionists and the advent of this rabble of youthful, ignorant men', complained Tory MP Sir Cuthbert Headlam.[10] Huge rallies up and down the country greeted the newly elected Labour MPs. With 393 out of 640 seats in Parliament the dramatic defeat of the 'war hero' Churchill was a sweet prize for the labour movement (added to by the crushing defeat of the Liberals, reduced to 12 MPs). The left-wing MP J.P.W. Mallalieu recalled his victory rally in Huddersfield: 'an open air meeting of 10,000 people. As I spoke, the voice of an elderly man kept coming from the crowd, repeating the age old fear of the British working class: "Don't let us down lad! Don't let us down!"'[11] Roy Jenkins noted at the time how he would be surrounded by men in the pub after election rallies, 'a sea of tired faces looking up in hope'.[12]

The historic 1945–51 Labour government cannot be understood outside the context of how British politics had changed during the war. Although 1945 is often portrayed as the high point of Labour's parliamentary-route socialism, the reality is a little more complex. It would be wrong to portray Attlee's government as simply a Labour victory over the capitalists. The economic and social changes were not Labour's alone; they enjoyed broad support across the establishment. The Beveridge report of 1942 was written by a Liberal. The Tory MP R.A. Butler had already introduced wholesale reform in school education in 1944. The sweeping state ownership of key industries needed for the war effort demonstrated that in times of crisis relying on the market to deliver efficiently was impossible, which made Labour's nationalisation agenda seem far more like common sense. Planning had been necessary to ensure that production was orchestrated in such a way as to have any hope of victory against one of the most formidable war machines ever established. Public ownership was no longer seen merely in terms of class war, but as a new form of socialism that was beneficial to both workers and capitalists – all part of the national good.[13] This consensus, known as Butskellism,[14] was what really allowed the Labour Party to manage the state effectively. The Attlee government ruled with the consent of the British ruling class, which was why Attlee, who had earlier argued that you couldn't get 'socialism without tears', now seemed to be able to introduce widespread nationalisation with no upset at all. The elites blessed Labour with their consent to manage the state, as long as certain requirements were met (which we shall come on to soon). Arguably, Attlee's government was a continuation, not a revolution.

The philosophy of the Labour government was instinctively integrationist, welding legitimate class demands onto the existing power relations of British capitalism. When President Truman visited George VI he nervously inquired about the nature of the recent Labour victory. In response to his question, 'I hear you've had a revolution?', he received the bemused reply, 'Oh no, we don't have those here.'[15] The king himself had a hand in the Cabinet, pushing for Bevin to be foreign minister instead of Attlee's preference, Hugh Dalton. Attlee acquiesced.

What was expected of the Labour government in return for its loyal integration into the state? In compensation for the nationalisation of their dilapidated and failing industries, the capitalists expected a king's ransom. The amounts handed out to the previous owners of the nationalised industries were huge: the mines cost the taxpayer £164 million, electricity £540 million, gas £265 million and the railways £1 billion.[16] Considering that a number of these had been loss making, the enormous levels of compensation were a slap in the face to working people still labouring under rationing and living in slum housing. Overall, the nationalisation programme encompassed the most unprofitable 20 per cent of the economy – the only major exceptions being steel and road haulage.[17]

Alongside the need to preserve British capitalism there was a genuine fear of a possible outbreak of revolutionary activity among demobbed working-class soldiers. In places like Egypt the army had mutinied after concern grew in the ranks over a possible continuation of war, this time against the Soviet Union. The war-weary men wanted to return to their homes, jobs and a decent life. The consensus around the need for radical measures to prevent radical dissent was best expressed by the representatives of the ruling class themselves. The Tory MP Quentin Hogg voiced their fears when he warned Parliament in 1943 that 'If you don't give the people social reform, they will give you social revolution.'[18]

As such, the 1945 Labour government can be seen as the product of the balance of forces at the time. It came to power not only because it guaranteed the continuation of capitalism, but also because of the deeply held wishes of the working class to get their reward for the sacrifices made during the war – a reward that few believed Churchill and the Tories would deliver. In the wake of the Great Depression and the war there was a real need for a socialised, collective response to the country's problems.[19] For many on the left it appeared that the years of hard work building a clear socialist programme after 1931 had paid off. The 1945 election manifesto famously announced that Labour was 'a socialist party, and proudly so' – language that seemed a far cry from the compromising rhetoric of the MacDonald era. Many were convinced of the socialist nature of the government by the extent of its nationalisation of key industries. Many workers and the Labour left generally believed that this was just the first salvo in the fight to forge a socialist commonwealth: more nationalisations would follow. Finally, it seemed that the problems of poverty and social deprivation would be resolved.

When Attlee announced his Cabinet it included names familiar from the left: Bevan, Shinwell, Cripps and Wilkinson all took positions. Other left MPs like Jennie Lee (having left the ILP) and Michael Foot were editing *Tribune*, which at that time was close to the government on most questions. Outside of the Cabinet, Harold Laski was chairman of the Labour Party. This was a strong showing of people who were not just 'Labour' but also socialists of one stripe or another.

Some on the left nevertheless expressed doubts even in those heady days of excitement at the arrival of the New Jerusalem. Some of the new left MPs had misgivings in their hearts as they entered Parliament on the first day, though their exuberance at having achieved such a monumental victory probably drowned out the doubts – initially at least. Tom Driberg, part of the 1945 intake, was concerned about the overall composition of the Cabinet: 'On the whole it is a government of the right rather than the left of the Labour movement.' Dalton at the exchequer, Bevin at the foreign ministry and Morrison as Deputy Leader and Leader of the House of Commons were a powerful faction of the right at the heart of government.

For most on the left there was no need to debate the way the Labour government nationalised industry and built the welfare state, at least not at first. The election manifesto of 1945 had clearly stated that Labour's 'ultimate purpose at home is the establishment of the Socialist Commonwealth of Great Britain – free, democratic, efficient, progressive, public-spirited, its material resources organised in the service of the British people'. In reality, however, the government could have gone further; the 'socialist commonwealth' still looked a lot like state nationalisation under a Labour government with progressive taxation on the rich – a social democratic programme, not a socialist one. There would be no 'mucking about' with the state: Attlee pursued no significant democratic reforms and constitutional arrangements were untouched; the House of Lords was left intact.

Inside Parliament, the Labour majority was simply too large for the Tories to pose a threat, and the left largely fell in line with the overall direction Attlee was taking. This created a sense of unity that had been lacking for years. But as the government wore on, debate opened up over crucial questions.

Unruly Workers

In relation to the much-vaunted nationalisation measures, there was anger on the trade union shop floor over the manner in which the reforms were carried out. Old management structures remained intact, 'jobs for the boys' at the top of the public sector replicated the old class structures of the privatised industries, bullying was rife as the tensions between workers and managers remained, and workers did not feel that they had any real say in how the companies were run. Between 1947 and 1951 there were over 8,000 unofficial strikes in the newly state-owned companies.[20] The dilapidated nature of the companies prior to nationalisation contributed to the sense that state control was inefficient and bureaucratic – an argument that Margaret Thatcher and others were to deploy successfully in the 1980s, when the post-war settlement was aggressively terminated by the Tories.

What socialists saw as a step towards the New Jerusalem, the capitalists saw as a useful crutch to maintain capitalism. Capitalists will support nationalisation if it secures a positive business environment, ensuring profit remains relatively untouched. State intervention is acceptable so long as it *increases* business and profit opportunities. This meant that in exchange for the NHS, some state ownership and improved welfare provision, the capitalists demanded a higher level of exploitation of the working class. The outcome was a 30 per cent increase in production between 1946 and 1948 with no corresponding increase in wages. In February 1948 Stafford Cripps introduced an austerity budget with a wage freeze across the economy. The TUC endorsed the freeze as a way to stop inflation. In response to Cripps' budget a Tory minister sneered that it marked 'the end of an era of socialist policy and socialist propaganda.'[21]

The formation of the NHS was one of the most essential victories of any Labour government in British history, representing a bold move based on the notion of collective and social welfare with universal accessibility. Nationalising the hospitals had not been in the manifesto – Bevan had to fight for it against opponents like Morrison and the British Medical Association, who did not want to become state employees. The notion that 'the NHS will last as long as there are folk left with the faith to fight for it' recognises that it represented the crystallisation of the balance of class forces at the time, and that such an institution could not permanently survive intact under a capitalist system. The Tory opposition to the NHS provoked some of the most militant class-based politics from Labour. Bevan's natural hatred for the Conservatives was undeniable, and their behaviour in trying to sabotage his project left him livid. At a Labour rally in 1948 he set out his forthright views: 'So far as I am concerned they are lower than vermin, they condemned millions of people to semi-starvation.' The comments were considered scandalous but Bevan was unapologetic, though he never used the phrase again.

When the government finally turned to the nationalisation of steel in 1948, it exposed the limits of consent and revealed the lengths to which the capitalists would go to defend their profitable businesses. Attlee understood the reason for the opposition: 'of all our nationalisation proposals, only iron and steel aroused much feeling, perhaps because profits were greater here than elsewhere.'[22] As a response to the move towards incorporating profit-making enterprises into the public sector, the sugar company Tate and Lyle launched the 'Mr Cube' campaign against nationalisation. Mr Cube was a cartoon character who appeared on two million sugar packages and 100,000 rationing books. As part of the campaign, material was sent to over 4,000 schools, more than 3,000 speeches were made in working men's clubs and factories, and £200,000 was spent on advertising. The opposition to nationalisation from business, the Lords and the steel industry itself was described by one minister at the time as a 'concerted action by a number of people for sabotaging an Act of Parliament'.[23]

The opposition ground down the nationalisation bill and the political will to implement it. When steel was eventually nationalised in the final phase of the Labour government in 1950, it was only a half-hearted attempt. The largest steel companies were aggregated into one umbrella corporation as a prelude to a proper state takeover that never happened. The bosses sabotaged the government's efforts when the British Iron and Steel Federation refused to acknowledge the new corporation. As such, in 1951 it was very easy for the new Conservative government to put iron and steel back into the private sector. The outcome of the fight over steel nationalisation was the Parliament Act of 1949, which limited the ability of the Lords to interfere with the Commons. A more radical government would have proposed abolishing the Lords entirely, but in true British fashion Attlee decided to only tinker around the edges.[24]

Despite the continued austerity regime on the home front, the class struggle remained muted compared to the 1920s. No doubt the links between the trade union leaders and the Labour government were a deciding factor in dampening the ardour of workers.[25] Better to suppress strikes in favour of a legislative programme that appeared to be working than to be seen to destabilise the government. When the détente between the union leaders and the Cabinet failed to stop workers taking action over wages or working conditions, the Attlee government was not averse to using the army to break strikes. They kept the wartime Order 1305 that banned strikes. In fact, between 1945 and 1951 the army was ordered on 18 separate occasions to cross picket lines and do the jobs of striking workers. The notorious strike-breaking Supply and Transport Organisation was (secretly) re-established by the civil service, with the blessing of Cripps in the Cabinet. The Attlee government's attitude to striking workers was a living example of the party's general view that strikes against a Labour government by trade unionists were unacceptable, and that it was the government's job to ensure the wheels of industry kept turning. Labour in power saw itself as defender of the national interest, not of the needs of working people.

Bevan was briefly moved from Health to the Ministry of Labour in 1950. It was during this time that the wartime anti-strike ordinance was finally removed from the statute books – but this wasn't through Nye's benevolence or forethought. In his biography, Foot claims that Bevan had been working for some time to repeal the anti-trade union

rumour was that they would be sent to 'fight the reds'. A large part of Labour's election victory was down to the belief that they could better negotiate and work with the Soviets, unlike the bellicose Churchill who favoured a confrontation. Now there was also concern that a belligerent attitude had developed in the Labour Cabinet, spearheaded by men like Bevin, who was to play a crucial role in establishing NATO as a means of counteracting the growing power of the Soviet Union.

Bevin was very happy to spend money on continuing conscription and establishing permanent army bases in Europe. His pro-militarist policies attracted criticism from many, including Emrys Hughes, editor of the left-wing *Glasgow Forward* and an MP after 1946, who asked: 'if we are going to have this millstone of a large army around our necks, where are we to find the money for housing, education, better health services and all the other things that people will expect (and rightly so) from a Labour government?'[27] Around this time, there was growing opposition in the trade unions: a communist-backed motion put to the TUC on foreign policy – which was highly critical of the Attlee government's policies, especially the 'encirclement of Russia' strategy adopted by NATO – won 2.4 million votes.[28] Unknown at the time, Attlee's cabinet had agreed in secret to build a nuclear weapon. Smarting from being talked down to by the Americans, Bevin spoke enthusiastically of wanting an atomic bomb: 'we have got to have this thing whatever it costs. We've got to have the bloody Union Jack on top of it!'[29]

It was opposition to Bevin that prompted the initial revolts in the PLP. The belief was that the foreign minister was acting against the election pledge of the party to *mediate* between Washington and Moscow. The brewing opposition, in the form of articles in *Tribune* and motions put to PLP meetings, escalated after June 1946, causing the party apparatus to threaten expulsions for outspoken critics, via an article in *The Daily Herald* in October. Not content with writing critical articles, the left agreed to push the debate out into the open. Richard Crossman sought to amend the King's Speech to call for a 'third force' (European social democracy) against both Soviet and American ideologies, but his rebellion stalled after pressure from the government. Bevan played no public role in the first serious challenge by the Labour left after the war;

being in the cabinet he did not want to make it look like there was a split on the front bench.

As a local adjunct to the debate around the Soviet Union, the CPGB attempted to affiliate to the Labour Party once again in 1946. They argued that they were keen to forge a united working-class party but their critics labelled them hostile entryists bent on creating a one-party state. Although their affiliation was never a realistic idea (Labour was generally unrelentingly hostile to communism at this stage), that didn't mean party leaders were complacent about the CPGB gaining more influence among their members again. Increasingly fed up with what they saw as an attempted hostile takeover, the Labour leaders moved to prevent the affiliation of parties like the CPGB from ever happening again. Labour was a broad church, but not that broad. Herbert Morrison moved an amendment to the party constitution which stated that any organisation 'having their own programme, principles and policy for distinctive and separate propaganda, or possessing branches in the constituencies or engaged in the promotion of Parliamentary or Local Government candidates or owing allegiance to any political organisation abroad, shall be ineligible for affiliation to the party'. The supposed growing influence of communism in the party was something that deeply concerned its chairman, Morgan Phillips. Charged with rooting out pro-communist dissidents or Trotsykists, Phillips helped organise a network of informers across the party, both in Parliament and outside, who were tasked with gathering evidence from speeches, articles or pub conversations that might single someone out as a red. The information was then sent to Transport House to be compiled in files that were referred to as 'The Lost Sheep' – a worrying echo of the McCarthyite witch-hunts brewing across the Atlantic.

Keep Left

The Keep Left organisation was born out of the winter crisis of 1946–7. Severe weather had led to a coal shortage, forcing a three-day week on industry and leaving many homes without heat or light. Keep Left emerged as a grouping out of regular meetings between left MPs,

Mikardo, Bruce, Foot, Crossman and others. They believed that more planning and strategic thought by the government could have prevented the crisis. This was not simply about the principle of pushing forward the socialist agenda, it was also born out of a serious concern that Labour would lose the next election unless more radical policies were implemented to deal with the crisis.

Keep Left were also suspicious of the emergence of the US as a superpower, and did not want Britain to become an American satellite. To the Labour left the announcement of the Truman Doctrine and the end of US isolationism was simply Washington's excuse to expand its spheres of influence to ensure profits for Wall Street. Laski and others condemned the actions of the US and NATO in countries like Greece, Japan, Turkey, Iran and Italy.[30] As the Soviets consolidated power in Eastern Europe, Keep Left advocated a third-force approach to oppose both power blocs.

They agreed to produce a *Keep Left* pamphlet and circulate it before the Labour conference as a critique of what they saw as compromises and prevarication on the part of Attlee and his allies. Published by the *New Statesman*, its main demands were for a third force in Europe led by a socialist Britain, and for a ministry of economic affairs to develop more strategic planning. Those behind Keep Left started off well, helping to organise a backbench rebellion in the Commons in March–April 1947, when 70 MPs voted against the National Service Bill, arguing that conscription should be reduced from 18 to 12 months. This act of defiance brought hell down on their heads from Bevin and his allies.

The pamphlet proved popular in the left press and among party members. The honeymoon period for the government was over and after two years it was more acceptable to be openly critical and to demand more ambitious social policies. The growing debates in the party were infuriating the hierarchy, and as their backbenchers became more rebellious the patience of the Cabinet dwindled rapidly. A backbench rebellion forcing a change in government policy to please the left was simply unacceptable, and discipline had to be reintroduced. In masterful fashion, Attlee, Dalton, Morrison and Bevin chose a combination of stick and carrot to batter the left back into irrelevance, or at least into silence, whichever was easier.

They hoped to end the fight at the 1947 conference. First Denis Healey was tasked with writing a rebuttal of Keep Left, in a pamphlet called *Cards on the Table* which was circulated to every delegate. The chair opened up the session with an attack on Russia's destabilising influence and support for US efforts to secure post-war stability. Then Bevin spoke in the hope of repeating his performance in 1935 when he had delivered the fatal blow to George Lansbury's influence in the party. Bevin spoke at length about the crucial work he had been doing, setting up NATO, establishing the UN, liaising with Washington over their plans for Marshall Aid in Europe. He referred to the actions of the parliamentary left as a 'stab in the back' and demanded 'loyalty' from them. Of the supposed middle-class intellectuals who made up the Labour left he bitterly remarked: 'I grew up in the trade union movement, you see, and have never been used to this sort of thing.'[31] After his bravura performance the left was routed and heavily defeated in the conference votes. Bevin was a past master of the standard trick used by trade union bureaucrats against their political enemies: smear them as middle-class outsiders in the workers' movement in a demagogic appeal for votes.

After the Marshall Plan announcement and the return of Crossman and others to the Labour fold, only a small minority of MPs were left to oppose the pro-American orientation of Bevin and Attlee. The retreat of the centre-left allowed the party leadership to make its move against the far left. Transport House turned on MPs Leslie Solley and Zilliacus and others who, having regularly clashed with Bevin and company over issues like NATO, were suspected reds. Facing expulsion from the party, Zilliacus was even prevented from speaking in his own defence at conference by an almost unanimous block vote of the unions.

Towards the end of the first Attlee government there were two attempts to reinvigorate the left. A follow-up Keep Left pamphlet, imaginatively titled *Keeping Left*, was published in 1950, but by this point the intellectual mood in the party had shifted considerably. Former advocates of socialism in 1945, or of a swift Emergency Powers Act, were now consoling themselves that what the British wanted was a

'Scandinavian style social democracy'.[32] *Keeping Left* did not represent much beyond its initial signatories in the PLP, and it certainly didn't inspire the kind of excitement in the left press that its predecessor had done – no doubt because in repeating the old arguments it did not break any new ground.

A more grassroots organisation was the Socialist Fellowship, launched in 1949 by Ellis Smith and Fenner Brockway, who was by now returned to Parliament as a Labour MP. The Fellowship was an attempt to rebuild something similar to the pre-war ILP or Socialist League, bringing together Trotskyists like Gerry Healy and John Lawrence (and their newspaper *Socialist Outlook*), with left MPs and some communist fellow-travellers. It achieved quite considerable success with modest resources. One useful role played by this short-lived initiative was its organising of a series of informal conferences against the looming crisis on the Korean peninsula, to argue against British involvement in any US-led war – but the debate over what position to take on Korea caused splits. A group led by Tony Cliff left to form the Socialist Review Group, arguing that it was unprincipled to choose between Washington's and Moscow's expansionist ambitions. Brockway and Smith resigned from the Fellowship after they supported a pro-war motion in Parliament, a tragic decision by Brockway who had maintained a relatively principled anti-imperialist stance throughout his political life. Despite these losses, by early 1951 *Socialist Outlook* had a circulation of nearly 10,000, and rallies around the country were addressed by leading activists such as Harry Constable from the dockworkers. This was markedly more success than had been achieved by Keep Left, which had confined itself to the chambers of Parliament – the place where the left was inevitably weakest. Momentum was growing around the Fellowship as it intersected with a developing anti-war mood and the revival of class struggle among builders and dockers, but Transport House swung the guillotine and proscribed the organisation – just as they had done with the Socialist League. The Fellowship obeyed the NEC instructions and dissolved itself, though *Socialist Outlook* continued for another three years before it too was banned by the party hierarchy.

After scraping back into power at the 1950 general election, the 1950–1 administration was not much to write home about in terms of new policies. It is something of a pattern with Labour governments that they run out of ideas after two years – this was certainly the case with Attlee's 'socialist revolution' after 1945. The Labour Party approached the 1950 election with no real strategy or many new ideas. Laski called for 'a bit of fire and inspiration, of guts and glory' in the manifesto, but none was forthcoming. Labour secured a victory and an extra 1.5 million votes, but lost 78 MPs to a resurgent Tory Party. With a wafer thin parliamentary majority of six, the pressure on the left to stay in line was formidable – rebellious talk was frowned upon even more than before.

The impact of the Labour left in the period of the most successful Labour government up to that point was limited. The 1946 ban on 'factionalism', ostensibly to stop the CPGB joining the party, also had a detrimental impact on the Labour left, which was unable to seriously coordinate its efforts from below without running the risk of attracting the attention of Transport House. The incorporation of 'Red' Ellen Wilkinson, Bevan and Cripps into the Cabinet seriously affected the ability of the left to act independently, and the moving target of the role of the Soviet Union in the world confused many socialists. But the deeper problem was that the demands of the left in the CLPs over workers' democracy and social control of industry were not taken into the PLP at any stage as the left MPs had no parliamentary strategy to speak of. The PLP left never properly challenged the top-down public ownership model of the state-run enterprises. In other words, they fell into the same trap as the Labour right in associating socialism primarily with corporatist state ownership of industry.

This is not to denigrate the tremendous achievement of the NHS – still a pinnacle of socialist policy – but it does beg the question: why more wasn't done across other sectors of the economy? Greater collective ownership of the profitable parts of the economy relates to the strategy of production for human need – the fundamental plank of socialism. By limiting themselves to the implementation of the 1945 manifesto the Labour left exposed the fact that it wasn't Attlee who was held back by timidity but them. The responsibility of managing a capitalist state seemed to produce a collective amnesia, almost as if everything the Socialist League had debated and theorised had been forgotten.

The key political problem was that the left limited itself to criticism of how much should be nationalised, rather than starting a debate over what was *meant* by collective ownership. Labour's policy during this time was essentially a state corporatist one, which the Tories fundamentally agreed with. An alternative programme that included significant changes in the state industries, workplace relations, the constitution, and Britain's role in the world would have produced a far more transformative result. Arguably the basis was there to do this; what was lacking was the political will.

If there was one political mistake the Labour left made in this period it was in believing that the Labour right had essentially the same strategy but just disagreed on the pace of change. Bevan, in his speech to the Durham Miners Gala in 1948, urged the movement to give Labour more time: 'We need twenty years of power to transfer the citadels of capitalism from the hands of a few people to the control of the nation.' The arguments around consolidation versus expansion of the public sector during the late 1940s were part of this narrative. But Attlee's government, involved in strike breaking and secretly pursuing nuclear weapons, was ripe for deeper criticism. While concerns over the slow pace of social reform in Britain rumbled on, it was the outbreak of the Korean War in 1950 that finally inspired the Labour left to break ranks. Attlee called another election in 1951 and won nearly 14 million votes, more than the Tories. But the Tories won more MPs, and Churchill became Prime Minister, cutting off the path to the New Jerusalem for over a decade.

4

The Civil War

'The Labour Party has never been a socialist party,
although there have always been socialists in it.'

Tony Benn

After the political skirmishes of the immediate post-war government,
Labour in opposition saw an outbreak of factionalism and open ideological warfare in the party. Two men became synonymous with this
struggle: Nye Bevan on the left and Hugh Gaitskell on the right. The
intensity of the conflict throughout the decade pushed the broad church
to breaking point and raised existential questions about the nature of
Labour as a party and its strategy in post-war Britain. By the early 1960s
peace had returned under the avuncular leadership of Harold Wilson,
apparently with neither side able to claim an outright victory.

The background was Bevan's rebellion in the early 1950s. The
Korean conflict had just turned the Cold War hot and President
Truman appealed to the UN, and in particular Britain, to back up the
US intervention in the south. Attlee had proposed cutting back on
social policy as a calculated sacrifice to support British militarism. The
anti-communist mood was so prevalent by this point that there was
complete unity in the Cabinet over support for the US and the South
Koreans. The main concern Bevan and others had was to ensure that the
military campaign did not detract from the social welfare programmes.
However the US demanded more and more money be spent on the war
machine. They forced Britain to spend £100 million on NATO, taking
the UK's military expenditure up to 7.5 per cent of GDP.[1] Attlee agreed
to a three-year rearmament programme that would in the end amount

to £3,600 million. Bevan was amazed 'how quickly the parsimonious treasury voted for money for arms, but nothing else'.[2]

Bevan and his handful of allies argued passionately that the scale of the military expenditure was simply unrealisable unless cuts were made to social spending. Finally he found a line he was not willing to cross. His worst fears were confirmed when Gaitskell introduced a bill that proposed taking teeth and eye treatment off the NHS. Bevan, a proud man with the NHS as his crowning achievement, threatened to resign if the bill was pursued. Attlee tried to convince him not to go, but when the bill was introduced, Bevan felt he had no choice. Along with John Freeman and Harold Wilson, he resigned his Cabinet post. He saw the cuts as a betrayal of the founding principle of the NHS: that it would provide health care 'from cradle to grave'.

There was widespread support for Bevan among the membership but his resignation provoked a tide of abuse in the media, who roundly condemned him as an egotist, a frustrated careerist and a self-isolating fool for his actions. One Labour MP derided Bevan's supporters as 'an uneasy coalition of well-meaning emotionalists, rejects, frustrates, crack pots, and fellow-travellers'.[3] Such was the official condemnation of the Bevanite movement at its birth. After their resignation, the bullish left MPs published a pamphlet called *One Way Only*. Their argument was that they were only appealing to the policies of 1945 and that it was the Attlee government that had gone back on them in recent years. The strength of this approach was that the MPs appeared to the rank and file not as insurgent disruptors but as continuators of the spirit of 1945. This was why, when the party leadership couldn't deny that the polices had not been implemented, they 'had to resort to personal vilification, bureaucratic manoeuvres and petty tyranny'.[4]

The first shots of what became regarded in Labour folklore as the 'civil war' in the party were heard in Parliament in March 1952. When a motion on rearmament was being discussed, Bevan's supporters put forward a motion condemning the expenditure. The controversy opened up running battles over the balance between welfare and warfare, with the left still urging the government to do more for the poor and working class at home instead of spending money on wars on behalf of the United states. When 57 MPs voted with Bevan against the party whips, the fires of the right were stoked. For them the rearmament debate was all about proving that Labour was a reliable political ally of Washington and could play its role in the fight against communism. To them the Bevanite rebellion smacked of irresponsible posturing, and they suspected the Bevanites of being backed by Moscow.

To many in the party outside of the hallowed chambers of Parliament the stance of the left MPs was exemplary. At the 1952 conference Bevan supporters won seven out of the eight CLP representative seats on the NEC. Bevan's popularity with the rank and file in the CLPs saw him voted top of this list. Right-wing leaders like Morrison and Dalton were unceremoniously ejected from the NEC, a slight that enraged the establishment and many of the trade union leaders. The fury against the Bevanites was also a response to the fear that they represented a genuine movement in the party and – most ominously – in the unions. The relative stability in the trade union movement – during the years where the grassroots was quiet and obedient to the bureaucracy – was unravelling as a stable economy and full employment emboldened union members. Bevanism captured a mood across the workers' movement for a new kind of politics and a return of the hopes of 1945.

What Was Bevanism?

The 1950s was a decade of increasing class struggle. Three times as many days were lost to strike action in 1955 compared to 1951. At the same time the Tories were bending over backwards to include the union leaders in their governmental decision-making – regular meetings with the TUC and heads of key unions were sought by ministers. Arguably the Tories pursued an integrationist strategy better than the Labour Party did. Although the Tories re-privatised road haulage, iron and steel, they were generally committed to social welfare and maintaining full employment.[5] As the unions grew and strengthened, some workers became suspicious of their union leaders and concerned that they were too friendly with the Conservatives. Memories of the shooting of strikers and the defeat of the general strike in the inter-war years still lingered for many militants.

It was also a time of mass migration, starting with the *Empire Windrush* in 1948 and continuing under the Tories as the rapid expansion of industry and the public sector created a labour shortage that had to be made up from abroad. However, the mass immigration quickly became a political football as reactionary forces flocked to racist and nationalist arguments, initiating the kind of racism that has come to characterise mainstream politics subsequently.

In this world, the Labour left faced an uncertain future. As the predicted Tory barbarity failed to materialise and the boom continued, the question loomed as to what kind of politics Labour would need in order to win power again. Bevan's book *In Place of Fear* set the right tone for many in the party. In his passionate but rambling style, Bevan made the case for a collective vision against individualism and for the fulfilment of the promises of 1945 – in essence, for Labour to retain the spirit of its policies from the 1930s. *In Place of Fear* describes a country divided between property and poverty, with democracy as a mediating arena of struggle; in Britain's case this meant Parliament. If 'democratic parliaments under private property, under capitalism, are the professional public mourners for private economic crimes', the key was to turn Parliament into a bastion for working-class resistance: 'the function of parliamentary democracy, under universal franchise, historically considered, is to expose wealth-privilege to the attack of the people. It is a sword pointed at the heart of property power.' Whereas the Socialist League had thought about the problems of power and how to exercise it, Bevan believed in a neutral Parliament that was there for the taking at any general election. This unproblematic view of the state meant that the problems of the post-war state-ownership model were only seen from the perspective of improving ministerial oversight and the allocation of civil servants; at no point does Bevan mention workers' control of industry or even the issue of joint ownership.[6]

Bevan's commitment to the neutrality and centrality of Parliament meant that he singularly failed to critically examine the role of the state at all, demonstrating a thoroughly ambiguous and confused attitude towards it. This is even more surprising given that he had experienced what the Socialist League in the 1930s had only theorised: that when faced with an actual encroachment into the profits and power of the capitalists by a Labour government there would be determined resistance. The combat over iron and steel nationalisation clearly confirmed the fears about ruling-class sabotage of a reforming Labour government, even if it enjoyed an unassailable parliamentary majority. But it also demonstrated something more: the true nature of power in society, and that while Parliament was considered sacrosanct by Labour, the capitalists were happy to undermine it and operate against it when they felt the need.

Nevertheless Bevanism was a powerful mood across the party, distrustful of compromise and wanting to see more resolute action – though actual policy differences were vaguer. To spread their message across the party the core left leadership operated as two 'Brain Trusts'. To broaden their reach outside of the bear pit of Parliament, their role was to tour the country speaking at CLPs and union meetings to explain the politics and the arguments of the parliamentary left. The first Brain Trust was made up of left-wing MPs, who were supported by the 'Second XI' composed of prospective parliamentary candidates. In addition the movement had support from *Tribune*, now moving in a left-wing direction, and the *New Statesman*. This linked them to well-known left-wing activists across the CLPs, tapping into 'some of the rebellious vitality of the ranks'.[7] The Bevan group on the NEC and in the PLP saw themselves, and were seen more so by their enemies, as the mouthpiece for rank-and-file discontent with the drift in policy.

Disciplining the Left

The Bevanite movement threatened the established hierarchy in a number of ways. Bevan himself was an established leader and popular with rank-and-file members. Still basking in the glory of the NHS and his principled resignation over cuts, many saw him as a staunch class fighter. The Bevanites also threatened a staple component of bureaucratic rule, since they provided alternative channels of communication across the party. The Brain Trust meetings were popular, dynamic and totally out of the control of Transport House.[8] Through Foot they had *Tribune* and through Crossman, the *New Statesman*. For the right, the real threat was that Bevanism might spread from the party and into the trade unions, challenging internal power relations and established cliques of control. The right had to act quickly to cauterise the wound. Gaitskell damned the movement, labelling it an organised conspiracy; others denounced it (unfairly) as a 'party within a party'.

But it was the success at the Morecombe conference that triggered an almighty backlash from party leadership. To stop them organising, Bevanite MPs were banned from meeting separately. At the PLP meeting in March 1952 it was agreed, for the first time since 1945, to reintroduce the standing orders that restricted the freedoms of the MPs. The allegation made by the right was that the Bevanites were 'a special group within the party, organised, secret, and with their own whips'.[9] The Bevanites denied this – they weren't that well organised! This actually spurred on the left: the re-imposition of standing orders forced the movement out into the wider party and the unions, creating a much more destabilising situation for the party establishment.

This development demonstrated one usually unspoken but cast-iron law of the labour movement: while militants are tolerated episodically in the unions or in the party, they must not be allowed to combine their efforts. Even more intolerable is that a prominent left Labourite should be seen to interfere in the internal workings of the unions against their entrenched leaderships – that was something that no union bureaucrat would accept. As a result, Bevanism, in the words of Leslie Hunter, 'came into a head-on collision with the leaders of the big trades unions'.[10]

A key battle was over the docks. Some dockers had criticised the head of the TGWU, Arthur Deakin, and left to form a new union. *Tribune* covered their strike and the new union sympathetically, which outraged the right. Backing a left union movement was simply unacceptable. Deakin moved to end the subsidy for *Tribune* from Transport House. *The Daily Herald* regularly published critical articles against Bevan and his allies. *Tribune* was rounded on by Gaitskell: 'it is time to end the attempt at mob rule by a bunch of frustrated journalists', he thundered.[11]

These attacks were both personal and demagogic, redolent with the whiff of fear from the establishment when a potential radical force emerges. In response the Bevanite MPs urged CLPs to send in letters of complaint to *The Daily Herald*.

Deakin and other right-wingers in the TUC hated Bevan but they couldn't accuse him of being middle class. After all, he was the son of a miner from the Welsh Valleys – the King of Tredegar during the 1926 strike. He had impeccable working-class credentials, whereas Gaitskell was a lecturer by trade and from a well-to-do family. But this did not stop Deakin, the General Secretary of the TGWU, from siding with Gaitskell on every major question. When Bevan stood for treasurer against Gaitskell in 1954 he was furious when he found out that the Durham miners had backed the other candidate. 'How can you support a public schoolboy from Winchester against a man born in the back streets of Tredegar?', he demanded to know of Sam Watson, the miners' leader.[12] Clearly bureaucratic ties were thicker than class loyalty. Bevan stood for the leadership after Attlee stepped down in 1955 but only 26 per cent of the PLP backed him – 58 per cent supported Gaitskell.

A central part of the right's strategy was expulsions and threats of expulsions. The union bosses worked with Transport House to root out the Bevanite 'lost sheep' from the party. During the meeting that had re-imposed standing orders on the PLP, a number of right-wing MPs demanded the heads of those who had voted against the whips. The calls for expulsion grew louder in 1954–5, culminating in the Shadow Cabinet moving to expel Bevan from the PLP after he criticised Attlee in the Commons once too often. When it became known that Labour was supporting nuclear testing, Bevan rounded on Attlee and demanded to know if he would use nuclear weapons in the event of a conventional military attack. Flustered and angry, Attlee and his allies had the whip withdrawn from Bevan. He was then summoned to Transport House for a three-hour meeting where he was forced to apologise to Attlee personally and to the party generally for his regular critical interventions in Parliament. Deakin had been quite keen to secure Bevan's expulsion, but the Tredegar socialist narrowly escaped this fate – the NEC voted to censure him but not expel him by 15 votes to 10.[13] It is a testimony to the extent of this ideological clash how far Bevan had come from being the hero of the NHS to being so reviled by his erstwhile comrades only a few years later.

Bevan was partially saved by the looming general election. Labour couldn't afford to expel such a prominent and well-liked figure just before a public holding to account of their policies and suitability for government. The leadership was concerned about the huge level of support Bevan had across the party – CLPs up and down the country rushed to his defence, passing motions and sending them to Transport House. However, the general election defeat in 1955 and the near miss of his expulsion clearly exhausted Bevan. Although he finally became treasurer of the party in 1956, he was a man looking for some kind of conciliation with the leadership, worn down by the constant tension and friction at the centre of the party.

...All its Faults, All its Dangers

Left politics in the mid to late 1950s was dominated by the Campaign for Nuclear Disarmament. Many on the Labour left at this time were active in CND, which had been formed in 1957. Despite its apparent single-issue focus, it acted more like a lightning rod for a whole range of left issues – nuclear weapons were simply seen as the most odious and dangerous development of recent times. Membership of CND was

> not simply a token of the individual's opposition to the Bomb, but a capsule statement of his position on a variety of unrelated issues which the Bomb was felt to symbolise ... the average CND supporter would be opposed ... to capital punishment, racial discrimination, the monarchy, capitalism and religion, and if religious, to the church ... None of the political parties truly catered for this form of global radicalism. While electorally the majority of CND supported the Labour Party, they made it plain that this was largely *faute de mieux* [for want of a better alternative].[14]

The debate on nuclear weapons was thus a debate about a lot more besides, and victory on that question represented for the left a step forward on all the other issues as well.

The mainstream media attacked CND as a tool of the communists and an ancillary for Moscow, dismissing it as a group of well-meaning but dangerous pacifists who would disarm Britain in the face of her enemies. Although CND was in fact very moderate in its demands, the scaremongering and attacks by the establishment gave it an aura of radicalism. Unfortunately these attacks came from the very establishment that CND hoped to influence. The wedding of the Labour right to the state and class interests of the ruling elites meant that any talk of reducing Britain's role in the world or taking the country out of NATO was anathema. The party's official position was in favour of global disarmament, but on the condition that Britain would only eliminate its nuclear weapon programme when other states did the same – multilateralism. The grassroots members, who had no wish to see nuclear war and no loyalty to US-led military alliances, felt very differently. The extent of the support for CND in the party CLPs and from the newly elected TGWU General Secretary Frank Cousins with his huge block vote was a very real threat to the multilateralist position. In addition, Victory for Socialism, a small grouping made up of pro-Soviet and pacifist thinkers in Parliament, was working to secure a unilateralist disarmament position. Faced with over 150 motions to the 1957 conference calling on Labour to adopt a position for unilateral disarmament, the NEC was very worried about losing the vote.

Then the left met an unexpected opponent at conference – Bevan. When the motion on nuclear weapons came up, he rose to the podium to speak. He explained that he was against nuclear weapons but that unilateral disarmament was impossible – nuclear weapons had to be dismantled internationally, not just in one country. Bevan was clearly concerned about Britain's role in the world – just as Bevin had been in the 1945 government. He rounded on conference delegates: would they send a foreign secretary 'naked into the conference chamber' of the UN? He described the proposal as 'not a policy but an emotional spasm'.

Bevan's siding with the leadership shocked and distressed many of his followers in the party. His powerful and passionate rhetoric in the service of the right brought many of his followers to tears as they saw their leader turn on them. As his speech reached its climax, the left-wing delegates sitting in the front rows heckled him, begging him to stop ('Don't do it Nye!'). Bevan finished and sat down to cheers from the right who saw that their *bête noir* was now on their side. Even one MP from the right of the party felt dismayed: 'When Bevan sat down, I had to get up and go away. I couldn't stand any more. I felt as if I had been present at a murder – the murder of the enthusiasm that has built the Labour movement.'[15] The motion on unilateralism was defeated by 5.8 million votes to 781,000. Even Cousins couldn't vote for it. He consulted his delegation, urging them to vote for disarmament, but was outvoted 14–16, so the TGWU cast its vote to keep Britain's nuclear weapons.

Why did Bevan do it? A number of theories abound. His old ally Tom Driberg argued that it was a 'sacrifice [of] his personal convictions for the sake of the unity of the party'.[16] One wonders when the right has made similar sacrifices. Others have concluded that Bevan supported the bomb to assist in strengthening the non-aligned (Third Force) movement, or possibly simply to defend Britain against foreign influence.[17] This is a similar conclusion to the one Ralph Miliband drew in 1961, namely that Bevan viewed unilateralism as a threat to the intricate web of foreign relations Britain was enmeshed in, and that such a policy would reduce the influence and power of a 'Socialist Foreign Minister' (Bevan was Shadow Foreign Secretary at the time) to forge multilateralism among other nations.[18] He may have wanted a return to the Third Force movement of the Keep Left days, where Britain, Yugoslavia and India could form an alliance against west and east, but this was just a dream. Bevan was a radical at home but had an integrationist Achilles Heel when it came to international relations; he couldn't break from the Labour right on this central question, and in the end this was what demobilised his movement. Britain's position as an imperial power in the world was one that cut to the core of even the radical voices on the left of Labour.

Whatever the individual motivations of their leader, the Bevanites never recovered from their leader's defection. Although Bevanism as a mood or a movement was always much larger than just one man, with implantation in the unions and across the CLPs, it had ultimately allowed itself to become defined by the whims of the King of Tredegar. The collapse of Bevanism provides one of the most salutary and essential lessons for the Labour left – never rely on a single leader, especially one with the extraordinary pressure of parliamentary politics bearing down on them. Bevan himself – as he had said to Lee about the party years earlier – demonstrated all the faults, all the dangers of Labour, a party integrated into a militarist concept of Britain as a nuclear armed power.

A Class That No Longer Exists

When Labour lost its third general election in a row in 1959, some concluded that the party simply couldn't win any more. Harold Macmillan's claim that 'you've never had it so good' reverberated around the country, fridges in kitchens and cars in driveways giving the appearance of middle-class life extending across all of society. With low unemployment, an increase in housing and a functioning welfare state, the old class antagonisms seemed temporarily ameliorated (though never eliminated). This was the spur for the 'revisionist' controversy in Labour. There followed pronouncements that the old class arguments were dead and buried, that, in the words of Douglas Jay, Labour was 'in danger of fighting under the label of a *class* which *no longer exists*'.[19]

The revisionists were led by Gaitskell, whom many people thought Bevan was probably referring to when he talked of the danger of a party leader being a 'desiccated calculating machine'. Gaitskell was certainly a calculating bureaucrat, and the first Labour leader to consciously advocate the triangulation of electoralism towards the middle classes as the party's central strategy. Previous generations had argued that compromises were a temporary pause on the long march to socialism.[20] But now they sought out a permanent electoral alliance with the middle classes through a clear moderation of their policies.

Revisionists like Tony Crosland argued that with the mixed economy, full employment and a rising standard of living, *capitalism* as it was widely understood had ceased to exist in Britain. Property was no longer the issue – the state sector already encompassed enough of the economy to leave the rest of it susceptible to Keynesian measures to end unemployment and poverty. What mattered now was equality under the rubric of social democracy, not socialism.[21] Under the post-war consensus, the shift to the left in Britain was now permanent, and the unions enjoyed more freedom and power than business did, even under a Tory government. Gone was the class-struggle rhetoric of the past, instead more nebulous values such as social justice became common currency. Bevan accurately described the differences as being 'between those who want the mainsprings of economic power transferred to the community and those who believe that private enterprise should still remain supreme but that its worst characteristics should be modified by liberal ideas of justice and equality'.[22]

One Bevanite, Richard Crossman, wanted to engage with these ideas rather than merely dismiss them. He agreed that Labour had to find a new path but disagreed that the only battles left were over social justice and wealth redistribution. Instead he argued that the rise of corporatism represented a threat to democracy and that Labour had to 'prevent the concentration of power in the hands of either industrial or state bureaucracies'.[23] His response was to place nationalised industries in the control of both Parliament and the workers themselves – a form of industrial democracy. Sadly Crossman had abandoned these ideas by the early 1960s.

Following the 1959 electoral disappointment, Gaitskell again turned on the left, blaming them and the public association of the Labour-union link for the defeat. The result was an attempt to amend Clause IV at conference.[24] The Gaitskellites misjudged the situation and overstretched themselves – the idea of social ownership encapsulated in Clause IV still held a place in the heart of the workers' movement that many were not yet ready to abandon. The unions resisted ditching Clause IV and the proposal was defeated. Even right-wing leaders who would have died in a ditch to support Gaitskell against Bevanism were not willing to compromise on Clause IV, producing a rare moment of unity between the unions and the left. Bevan, in his last speech to conference, explained why he thought Clause IV should remain: 'Are we going to send a message from this great Labour movement, which is the father and mother of modern democracy and modern socialism, that we in Blackpool in 1959 have turned our backs on our principles because of a temporary unpopularity in a temporarily affluent society?'[25]

In a sense the revisionists were just being honest – Clause IV was largely a symbolic commitment written into the 1918 constitution. Although it was successfully defended on this occasion, in the daily practice of Labour governments to come, Gaitskell was proven right. Despite the symbolic victory of saving Clause IV, it had no impact on subsequent Labour governments. The defence of the Clause by the left only slowed down the march of the revisionists, it did not stop them. The party was committed to an integrationist strategy by this time, informed as much by tradition as by choice, and the left was not sufficiently well organised or politically clear enough about an alternative. A simple defence was not enough; there was a desperate need for a sharper understanding of what socialism under Labour would look like. Nostalgia for Old Labour was becoming an emotional spasm, not a clear guide to politics.

Unilateralism Wins

Continuing the rumbling battles over foreign policy, this period saw the left–right split intensify over the continued question of unilateral disarmament. After three years of campaigning and cajoling, the movement behind unilateralism was gaining strength, helped by Frank Cousins and the might of the TGWU. There were mass annual demonstrations with thousands of people marching to the Atomic Weapons Research Establishment at Aldermaston. Many CND protestors looked to Labour as their natural political ally. At the 1959 party conference the unilateralist motion garnered over 2.7 million votes, and a growing number of labour organisations were now committed to dismantling British nuclear weapons. The 1960 conference in Scarborough was clearly going to be a historic showdown. Foot, writing in *Tribune* just before the conference, urged delegates to seize the opportunity afforded by Cousins' public backing of the left on the issue: 'Scarborough will be momentous', he concluded. 'No-one can doubt that. Either it will mark the rebirth of the party or the name will become the symbol for tragic and dismal confusion.'[26]

To the surprise of many, the conference motion in favour of unilateralism passed, against the instructions of the NEC. The mood was jubilant among the rank and file, though there was a certain naive belief that the conference vote had settled the matter. In fact, CND was unprepared for the victory and had no plans for how to follow through and ensure the conference position was adopted by the wider party. By contrast, the party's leaders knew exactly what to do. Their response was instructive for two reasons. Firstly, due to the vote taking place in a year with no general election, the change in policy had no impact at all on the message coming from most MPs after the conference. After Gaitskell lobbied hard among the union leaders (appealing to their 'common sense' – there was a general election on the horizon after all), he successfully outmanoeuvred Cousins and the decision was reversed the following year, causing no real upset for the political line or functioning of the Labour Party nationally. Secondly, Gaitskell furiously defended his right to speak publicly against the position even if it was passed. He declared that MPs would ignore the vote, defying the conference delegates: 'So what do you expect them to do: Go back on the pledges they gave the people who elected them from their constituencies? ... Do you think that we can become overnight the pacifists, unilateralists and fellow-travellers that other people are?' He announced to the assembled delegates that he and his comrades would 'fight, fight and fight again to save the party I love', which meant overturning the motion at the next conference and decisively beating the left. He admitted that the conference was essentially powerless to alter the PLP's course: 'The place to decide the leadership is not here but in the Parliamentary Labour Party.'[27] Many delegates were left wondering what the point of conference was if that was the case.

To Gaitskell's credit at least he was honest. He truly believed, as almost every other Labour leader has done, that MPs should not be bound by conference decisions. What hope did the rank and file have when the parliamentarians were so intent on maintaining their autonomy?[28] The 1960 conference became infamous for many activists. The sheer obstinacy of the parliamentarians exposed just how little the membership could hold their representatives to account. It was a difficult lesson to learn.[29]

Rebels With a Cause

After the third electoral defeat in 1959, the NEC launched a revamp of the party to appeal beyond its traditional voter base. Internal polling data had found the party significantly underperformed among newer, younger voters – the prevalence of white hair among Labour MPs did not help, and the party had not had a functioning youth organisation for several years. Some Labour branches had 'youth sections' attached to them, but there were no official national or regional structures. The insurgent feeling among many younger members led to demands for a genuine national organisation for the young people, especially as they were becoming more involved in campaigns and issues like unilateralism. Rather than lose an entire generation to CND, a new organisation was proposed – named Young Socialists (YS) – that would be run centrally but with some limited activities designed to attract younger activists. YS was partly intended to head off the groundswell of support that Keep Left, a rank-and-file publication unrelated to the old Keep Left group, was getting. Keep Left was clearly run by Trotskyists and was organising among younger members of the party, gaining a hearing for its socialist arguments. The NEC thought it was better to integrate the youth into something controllable than allow autonomy to run amok.

This was a time of shifting cultural values and challenges to the status quo. The emerging youth counter-culture of the 1950s – rock and roll, short skirts and teenage rebellion – was a factor in the revival of the radical left. Criticisms of western consumerist culture entwined with a growing mistrust of the Soviet bloc. The crushing of the Hungarian revolution by Soviet tanks in 1956 had exposed the reactionary nature of Stalinism to a whole new generation, while in Britain the sense of alienation and cultural despondency among many young people was palpable. This was the era of literature written by 'angry young men', where the vituperative play *Look Back in Anger* by John Osborne captured a mood. Mods and Rockers battled it out on Brighton beach as different youth subcultures reacted to the new economic situation in different ways, resisting or subverting the dominant values of the time. Consumer capitalism, so lauded by their parents, seemed like a cultural wasteland for many of the baby-boomer generation.

The new youth organisation was one of the few success stories coming out of Labour in the early 1960s. YS blossomed to over 700 branches within the space of a few years. Where YS groups had become active in campaigns, ranging from supporting the Glasgow Apprentices strike to campaigning against apartheid in South Africa, they reported significant gains in membership. The Wigan branch in particular achieved astounding growth, with over 300 joining in a couple of months through what was called 'Wiganisation': mixing politics with social events to attract working-class youth interested in more than just bland committee meetings.

There were also organisational concessions that allowed debate and ideological struggle to emerge in a more structured way. YS was permitted to have its own conference, though its leadership would be selected from regional delegates, accompanied by three enforcers from the NEC to ensure that things did not get out of hand. The constitution of the new organisation was fixed and unamendable, it even banned political discussion on a range of topics, but at least there was now a functioning youth section that could advise the NEC on youth matters – a step forward. The NEC also proposed a youth paper to be edited by an appointed person, though it did specify that 'the member of the Transport House staff in charge of the publication will himself be a Young Socialist'.[30] A young man named Roger Protz was assigned the job but resigned within months, claiming that Transport House was running the magazine and he was just a token figurehead. Within months of his resignation he became the editor of *Keep Left*.

Some new YS groups began to resist the control of Transport House. In 1960, as part of the move to co-opt the youth into the party mainstream, the NEC instructed two YS branches to desist from sponsoring *Keep Left*. The magazine hit back in its next issue with the headline: 'Our reply to the disrupters and witch-hunters on the NEC: we shall not shut down this paper'. Another 26 YS branches signed up as sponsors. There was a growing sense that Transport House was out of line by censoring the youth.

The first YS conference in 1961, meeting just six months after the events of the Scarborough debacle, ignored the ban on discussing certain topics and passed a range of left motions on nationalisation, leaving NATO, withdrawal of troops from the colonies, and – most con-troversially – unilateralism. They also overwhelmingly passed a motion calling on Gaitskell to resign, which infuriated the NEC. There was another showdown between Gaitskellites and socialists at the following conference where – although the Labour Party had by now backed down on its unilateralist position – the YS conference again passed motions in favour of unilateralism and calling for Gaitskell to resign. Frustration with the manoeuvrings of party bureaucrats at May Day rallies in London and Glasgow saw YS members storm the conference stage, which led to swift retaliation from the NEC. Protz was expelled and then several left-wing members of the YS National Committee were suspended. *Keep Left* was formally banned in 1962.

When the 1962 Labour Party conference backed the suspensions and the attacks on the paper, *Keep Left* responded by urging YS to fight for its autonomy and to defend free speech in the party. In contrast, when the other radical left paper – *Young Guard*, backed by Ted Grant and Tony Cliff – was turned on by the NEC, its editors capitulated under the pressure. They agreed to a series of demands, promising to 'improve the paper's tone[!], be open to all YS opinion and stop being "factional".[31] At a subsequent YS conference, *Young Guard* supporters went as far as voting against a motion calling for a fight back against the *Keep Left* expulsions. But *Keep Left* also played a part in its own downfall. It was run by a Trotskyist group led by Gerry Healy, and despite some notable campaigning work it alienated many YS members with its dogmatic predictions of impending capitalist doom and its ultra-left posturing.[32]

By 1964, with a general election looming, the Labour Party NEC had had enough. Reg Underhill was appointed to deal with the Trotskyists among the youth. *Keep Left* called a separate, independent YS conference in 1965 which took most of the branches with it. The rump 'official' YS conference that year was the last – the national party shut the organisation down shortly afterwards. The left was divided on the issue of the fight back, not least because a serious concerted campaign against Transport House would obviously lead to a split (which it did). But if *Keep Left* had simply surrendered it would have led to the neutering of any attempt to build an independent youth movement. Once again, the emphasis on defending a transformative course when the leadership demanded integration mattered when the left made its decisions.

The remaining YS branches were relaunched as the Labour Party Young Socialists (LPYS) in 1965. The struggle between the youth and the Labour leadership was not over Trotskyism as such, since most of the demands of the supposed revolutionaries were not about revolutionary strategy or tactics – they were the typical left-wing demands of the time around workers' rights, nuclear weapons and British imperialism. The fight occurred essentially because the youth sections were too critical of the leadership and too boisterous in their attitudes. Though Healy's followers had departed, in 1964 Ted Grant and his supporters in the youth sections and in Liverpool launched a new socialist newspaper, with a name that was to become familiar across the country – Militant.

The End of the Civil War

By the end of the 1950s the civil war was winding down. Bevanism had dwindled from its highpoint of the mid 1950s and the *Tribune* group in Parliament emerged as the primary left organisation. The group largely limited itself to the parliamentary struggle which left it fighting a losing battle on unfavourable terrain. For all its activity the left had failed to stop the ascendancy of the right – Labour had in reality become a revisionist party. The strength of the Bevanite movement was undermined by its limited focus on continuing the 1945 agenda. It failed to examine what had changed in British capitalism, the nature of the post-war boom, or the role of a powerful rank-and-file trade union movement. From 1947 onwards, the left's arguments were more suitable to describing the problems of *lassiez-faire* economics and counter-posing these in a rudimentary way to the planned economy of socialism. Any serious analysis would conclude that British capitalism was not really organised along these lines any more. Other issues weren't adequately dealt with, including the role of the mixed economy in sustaining capitalism, the role of Labour in disciplining the workforce for greater profitability, and the democratisation of state-run enterprises. It was this unimaginative clinging to the past that perhaps most dogged the Bevan years and left it unable to really challenge the right – despite the defeat of the Clause IV amendment in 1959.

When Labour published their economic proposals in *Industry and Society* in 1957 it encapsulated a thoroughly revisionist view of public ownership: that it should be extended to iron and road haulage but no further. Further public ownership would be examined on a case by case basis only if it was proved that the industry in question was 'failing the nation'. The principle of using nationalisation as a weapon of war against capitalism and to strengthen socialism was already lost in practice; now it was lost in theory.[33] Gaitskell died suddenly in 1963, but his legacy was eventually to triumph in later generations. In his last years of life, Bevan was deeply frustrated at the enforced silence that his Shadow Cabinet role – the reward for backing the leadership – now imposed. He had finally won the position of Deputy Leader in 1959, but by this time he was suffering from terminal cancer. His view of many of his fellow MPs was thoroughly jaded: 'I am heartily sickened by the Parliamentary Labour Party. It is rotten through and through: corrupt, full of patronage and seeking after patronage, unprincipled.' When a journalist friend asked for his views on the future of socialism in the Labour Party, he replied: 'Well what other instrument is there? Though I know that, sometimes I don't know how I could stay in the *Labour Party*. It isn't really socialist at all.'[34]

At the time, however, the end of the civil war was claimed as a victory for both sides. When Harold Wilson won the leadership the left were overjoyed. A Bevanite, the very man who had resigned in 1951 alongside Nye, was now in charge of the party. Wilson surrounded himself with Bevanites, people like Crossman and Castle. With the Tories in disarray over economic questions, a Labour government – and a left one at that – looked possible for the first time in a generation. But before long the right were even more pleased. Wilson was a changed man since his Bevanite days. With his eyes on 10 Downing Street, he was more than happy to plot a course taking revisionism as his starting point. The incoming Labour government, however, faced a problem – the affluent days were coming to an end. The post-war boom was fizzling out and major structural issues with the British economy would soon be revealed. People remember the Macmillan line 'you've never had it so good', but few know the words that followed: 'What is worrying us is "is it too good to be true?" or perhaps I should say "is it too good to last?"'

It was not going to last.

5

'Though Cowards Flinch...'

'From the 1970 onwards, the left began their slow inexorable assault. Labour's long death march had begun. The centre of gravity inside the Party was shifting decisively to the left.'

Philip Gould, New Labour strategist

The election of the new Labour government in 1964, headed by the relatively youthful Harold Wilson, finally ended 13 years in opposition. The bitter factional fighting of that time seemed to have receded into the background as minds were now sharply focused on questions of government and power. Labour faced quite a challenge concerning the economy. The virtuous circle of full employment, high wages, rising living standards and strong unions was unravelling. The Tories had been ousted precisely on the basis of people's fears about the slowing down of the economy. Now Labour had their chance to impose their own vision of political economy, led by a key ally of Bevan. While Wilson promised big things, on the key issues of the economy, jobs and wages, his government failed to deliver.

The ascendency of the revisionists ushered in a period of party unity behind a technocratic managerialism. This process was already well under way before Wilson entered 10 Downing Street – the 1961 manifesto *Signpost to the Sixties* had outlined the self-imposed limits of the incoming government, a unity deal struck between the right and the left to ensure their joint electability. It was drafted by Gaitskell and George Brown for the 'modernisers', alongside Crossman and Wilson representing the remains of the Bevanite movement which had once so terrified the press barons at Wapping.

The battleground was not ideological any more, it was no longer a question of socialism versus capitalism. The new thrust was an attack on the Tories for their lack of competence in managing capitalism. The Conservatives were depicted as stale and incompetent, whereas Labour would bring in new technicians, younger managers, more socially aware executives. Labour's vision was one of a meritocracy – the problem with the corporation's boards of directors was that they were populated by the traditional families of the upper crust, who should now make way for bright young things schooled in the latest techniques of business. It was clear that the *Signpost*'s authors had made peace with modern British capitalism. There were some socialist-sounding intentions however, in the form of plans to create a new Department of Economic Affairs and launch a National Plan for the economy.

The only mention of nationalisation was steel and iron, the old battle-ground that Attlee had failed to secure a generation earlier. But this was couched in the context of declining industries, unable to match the export capacity of other, more sprightly and dynamic economies in Japan or Germany. Unlike in the 1940s, this time the capitalists were more sympathetic to public ownership of these by now unprofitable industries; what limited 'socialistic' change did occur again only happened with the *consent* of the ruling elite.[1] This was the background to Wilson's call to use the entrepreneurial capitalist state to harness the power of science and new technology. Instead of unequivocally siding with workers, the Labour leader criticised 'bloody mindedness on both sides of industry'.[2] Labour fought the 1964 election on a popular programme to appeal to the new middle classes, explicitly rejecting much of its socialism and trade union history – a step on the road to what eventually became New Labour. Clearly, such a direction required a restriction on the rogue members and entryists who were causing problems, ushering in a period of strict centralist control by the party apparatus.

What was the state of the Labour left at this point? At a grassroots level it was reeling from a series of expulsions and reorganisations, particularly in London. The party apparatus often targeted those on the left they deemed to be Trotskyists, but it also expelled other socialists. They were dealt with using the constitutional equivalent of extreme prejudice: expulsions and entire CLP reorganisations. A journalist at the time described how Labour's national agent Sara Barker held the party by a firm hand: 'A hint of heresy, a whiff of recalcitrance, and Sara's tanks would emerge from the dead of night from the garages under Transport House and move unstoppably towards the offending parts of the country.'[3] Although the number of Trotskyists who had much influence was limited, they were seen as a clear and present danger by the party machine and the right. The Bevanite movement may have receded into the background, but the social democratic, integrationist controllers of the party were in no mood to allow any alternative oppositional voices.[4]

Wilson's Regime

Wilson had won the leadership in 1963, backed by the left who remembered him from his Bevanite days and assumed his views had not changed. Not a surprise, as having a naive faith in certain leaders was always a historic weakness of the left. But when Wilson became Prime Minister in 1964 promising to 're-kindle an authentic patriotic faith in our future', it was with a razor thin majority of only four MPs. This had a profoundly dampening effect on the ardour of the left. MPs were whipped into line to support the government and recalcitrant CLPs were advised to keep their criticisms private so as not to destabilise the government. Once again it was the left that had to make sacrifices for the sake of party unity and the preservation of the government, never a burden that fell on the right.

Wilson quickly proved to be a disappointment. Talk of peace was replaced by supporting the US invasion of Vietnam. Labour supported immigration controls for the Commonwealth for the first time, and deflationary measures were introduced that cut living standards for working families.[5] The government's partisan handling of the seamen's strike in 1966 further disillusioned members. Although prescription charges were abolished in 1965, they were reintroduced at an even higher rate in 1968.

Of course, there were also significant social changes during this time as well. The Cabinet supported backbench MPs in bills to relax or decriminalise a whole host of repressive legislation, including on divorce, abortion, homosexuality and capital punishment. But it was the right-wing of the party, people like Crosland, Shirley Williams and Roy Jenkins who took the lead in implementing these policies, not the left.[6] Tony Benn served in Wilson's Cabinet but was not a particularly left figure at this time, becoming famous for his campaign to shut down pirate radio stations operating off the coast.

With a thin majority, Wilson called another election in 1966 and successfully consolidated a much healthier majority in Parliament. He found he could do even less with it. The economy was spiralling out of control, and the Tories had removed many of the economic controls established during the Second World War. Michael Foot argued at the time that Labour 'should have re-established this apparatus, in particular the exchange controls' – instead capitalism was freer of restraint and harder to regulate.[7] The much vaunted National Plan, launched in 1965, aimed for an annual growth rate of 3.8 per cent and a 25 per cent increase in output by 1970. But the plan was toothless, indicative only, encouraging private enterprise to cooperate with the unions to increase productivity but with no means to compel recalcitrant businesses. The jobs and economic growth simply failed to materialise as the pound suffered from currency speculation and international pressure grew on Labour to make cuts to spending. Faced with a weakening economy and a historically high balance-of-payments deficit, Wilson, unwilling to take socialist measures, fell back on the old economic orthodoxies of wage restraint and public sector cuts – James Callaghan slashed £500 million from the 1966 budget. The National Plan was, in the words of one economist who worked for the government, 'conceived October 1964, born September 1965, died (possibly murdered) July 1966'.[8] The Department for Economic Affairs was similarly put out of its misery in 1969 after failing to achieve very much at all.

In such turbulent times, Wilson had to keep his party together and defuse any potential left insurgency so as to avoid a repeat of the 'civil war' of the 1950s. He was canny in his manipulation of the Labour left, and knew how to play them to get the result he wanted. A number of methods were used.

Ambiguity: Wilson hoped to maintain the balance of power by rolling back some of the arguments from the right about the essence of the party programme. Between the left's commitment to symbols like Clause IV that entailed nothing practical, and the right's insistence on their commitment to a capitalist mixed economy, Wilson never showed 'any great wish to remove the ambiguities, confusions and evasions which have surrounded so much of Labour policy'.[9] It would have been far more honest for Gaitskell to have got his way and abandon Clause IV, since nationalisation meant nothing of any real value to the Wilson government.

Incorporation: Wilson sought to stifle critical voices in the PLP, utilising the usual tactic of offering ministerial seats to MPs who might otherwise cause problems. Crossman was offered Housing, which precipitated his resignation from the leadership of CND. Two other left-wing MPs also announced that they would not be standing for re-election to the CND steering committee. Castle was given Overseas Development, then Transport and finally Employment. Jennie Lee took Minister for the Arts, establishing the Open University in 1969.

Personal relations: Wilson's approach was often like a friend or a friendly uncle. As one *Times* journalist reported: 'I am constantly astonished by the number of left-wing parliamentary critics who claim they have just had a heart to heart private exchange with Mr. Wilson.' To them the Prime Minister displayed 'a sensitive understanding of their point of view' and was 'always ready to get them on the first rung of the ministerial ladder'.[10] To the left he was conciliatory while in practice he implemented the political agenda of the right.

The cuts Wilson introduced were opposed both in the wider party and on the backbenches. Between 1966 and 1970 there were six significant backbench rebellions of around 25–40 MPs. But with a majority of 97, they did not threaten the government, especially as the MPs mostly abstained rather than vote alongside the Tories. As such the PLP regime was generally liberal, despite regular calls from the right to punish transgressors. The avuncular Wilson was himself not averse to giving a tongue lashing and issuing threats. When 62 MPs abstained on a Defence White Paper in 1966, in protest at Wilson's refusal to introduce cuts to the military budget while social welfare was being slashed, Wilson famously chided the rebels: 'All I say is watch it.

Every dog is allowed one bite, but a different view is taken of a dog that goes on biting all the time. If there are doubts that the dog is biting not because of dictates of conscience but because he is considered vicious, then things happen to that dog. He may not get his licence renewed when it falls due.'[11] Further rebellions did occur, but Wilson's Chief Whip, John Silkin, preferred a more relaxed approach that discouraged intransigence and ameliorated divisions in the PLP.

Lacking an alternative strategy and with no clear leaders, the left were sluggish to act. MPs like Eric Heffer and Barbara Castle were well regarded for their principled stands on certain matters but this never cohered into a serious challenge across the wider party. In Castle's case her most left-wing days were already behind her. But what dogged the parliamentary left more than anything was their loyalty to keeping Wilson as Prime Minister. Any accusations or claims that he was being conspired against or that he should be removed were met with thunderous denunciations in the pages of *Tribune*. If crucial votes came up in the Commons, the left would grumble but ultimately fell into line. They were faced with the unpalatable truth, that Parliament is based on an instrumental, pragmatic logic of numbers – not on principles. They did not want to be seen to bring the government down. It was painfully clear by this stage that the nature of the first-past-the-post system forced divergent political forces into one party to have any chance of winning elections. As Foot described at the time: 'The Management Committee of my [CLP] have wanted us to do everything in our power to persuade or urge the Labour Party to take a different course, but they have never wanted us to tear the Labour Party to pieces. This is the perpetual dilemma of people on the Left of the party – Aneurin Bevan experienced it in the fullest measure.'[12] Foot did however concede that the left would vote against a government even to the point of bringing it down on some issues, for instance the sending of British troops into Vietnam, but he was unendingly grateful it never came to that.[13]

The Archetype of Disillusionment

As the PLP continued to disappoint so many activists the gulf between them and the MPs grew increasingly wide. The Labour left could have focused its energies on activities outside of the stifling Westminster bubble, building links and seeking to renew itself through involvement in the growing social movements of the 1960s that came to be known as the New Left, but there was precious little evidence of this either.

Malcolm Caldwell, a dedicated Labour campaigner, voiced a feeling of disillusionment in a letter to *Tribune* on 20 August 1965:

> Socialist principles have been tossed aside with almost indecent cynicism and casualness. Racial discrimination in Britain has been condoned and strengthened. American butchery in Vietnam has been actively supported and encouraged. Social welfare and economic development in Britain have been sacrificed to carry out a reactionary economic programme at the behest of international finance capital. What of the Left leaders in Parliament? Tell them off on your fingers, comrades, and think of their words and deeds in recent months while the Labour movement has been sold down the river. It is a sad picture and I can personally neither see nor offer any excuses. Are we finished, we of the Labour Left?[14]

A young John Prescott, at that time a union official in the seamen's union, spoke out from the grassroots: 'There is a wealth of evidence we could produce to show that behind the government, in its resistance to our just demands, stand the international banks, the financial powers which really direct the government's anti-wages policy.'[15] Many thought the conclusion was obvious. Writing from a New Left perspective in 1967, John Saville confidently concluded that 'Labourism has nothing to do with socialism ... the Labour Party has never been, nor is it capable of becoming, a vehicle for socialist advance, and ... the destruction of the illusions of Labourism is a necessary step before the emergence of a socialist movement of any size and influence becomes practicable.'[16] The New Left published a May Day Manifesto the same year which excoriated the Labour Party and in particular its left-wing. They had no illusions that the Labour left would mount an anti-capitalist challenge, no matter their good intentions.

There were occasional flourishes from the leadership where a backbone appeared to form, but these were mere episodes against a backdrop of political depletion. At one point, in an act of desperation that outwardly looked like bravery, Wilson stood up to the financiers and threatened the Governor of the Bank of England that he would dissolve Parliament and run an election under the slogan of 'the people versus the bankers', promising to float the pound. The bankocracy backed down in that instance, but as the economy continued to falter Wilson was forced to borrow more money at the cost of implementing 'deflationary measures'. The growing realisation for many on the left was that Labour had transformed from being a party that was an inadequate vehicle for socialism to one that now sustained and defended capitalism against its own mass working-class base. The much talked about start of a series of socialist governments starting in 1945 was clearly off the agenda, and the National Plan had been killed by the global markets and money lenders.

More problems arose on the international arena, including one that was to become an ongoing issue for decades: Northern Ireland. There was a unanimous view among the Tories and Labour that a bipartisan approach was needed to support the UK loyalists in the Protestant community. Ken Livingstone, then a young new Labour member, described his view on the party's failures in the six counties: 'Did the Labour government intervene to ensure that Catholics got decent housing and decent jobs or to stop gerrymandering? No. Labour politicians ... sat silently and ignored the discriminations they knew existed.'[17] The sectarian discrimination festered until the mid-1960s when unrest exploded as the oppressed Catholic minority fought back against the majority Protestant unionists in the partitioned north. A mass social movement emerged demanding reforms and social justice, leading to regular clashes with the Unionists as the tensions and divisions spilled out onto the streets. A police attack on a peaceful Northern Ireland Civil Rights Association demonstration in 1968 was followed by an ambush in January 1969 by loyalists and off-duty RUC officers on the People's Democracy Long March. This ratcheting up of the conflict came to a head in 1969 when a provocative march by up to 15,000 Orange Order

Apprentice Boys led to three days of rioting and resistance from the embattled Catholic community. This 'Battle of the Bogside' was the start of the euphemistically named 'troubles'. In response, Wilson made the fateful decision to deploy the British army, until that point stationed in their barracks, to a policing role in the northern state.

The Labour left in the CLPs and Parliament began to develop an almost anti-imperialist attitude to the Northern Irish situation. As the occupation spiralled out of control, with the Bloody Sunday massacre in 1972 and the arrival of punitive 'anti-terrorist' measures during the 1970s, the left position hardened – it was one of those rare occasions where there was a general convergence of views on a profoundly divisive question between the reformist and revolutionary left.[18] Organisations like the Troops Out Movement became a mobilising force that united activists from the Republican movement with the Labour left and revolutionary socialists. The reason for this was not hard to find. There were thousands of Irish people in the Labour Party, many workers from an Irish background were fiercely Republican and they had a wide base of support in cities like Liverpool and Glasgow with large Catholic populations. When the young Republican militant Bernadette Devlin was elected to Westminster at the age of 21 – the youngest ever MP to sit in the Parliament – her abrasive and staunch views on 'the troubles' contrasted sharply with the opinions of mainstream Labour MPs, but she received loud and boisterous support from many of the Labour backbenchers during her speeches. *Tribune* was notably lukewarm on the Irish question and Tony Benn kept a steadfast public silence on the question – though admitting in his diary on numerous occasions that he favoured withdrawal of the troops.

It is worth considering here the rise of a dangerous new factor in domestic British politics – racism.[19] The Windrush generation who arrived in 1947 had grown up and new immigrants were arriving to seek jobs and build communities. Although immigration usually coincided with economic upswings when there were plenty of jobs to go around, nevertheless some right-wing politicians and newspaper editors whipped up a sense of unease, and there emerged a new mantra surrounding immigration: that it was a competition for jobs and houses.

Race riots in Notting Hill and Nottingham in 1958 had reflected a growing anti-immigrant racism, and in 1964 Labour had lost a safe seat in Smethwick in the Midlands to a Tory running on the infamous slogan 'If you want a nigger for a neighbour, vote Labour'. In 1968, Tory MP Enoch Powell delivered his infamous 'rivers of blood' speech in which he predicted race riots and a fall-of-Rome style scenario unless immigration was checked. The violent, fascist National Front was launched to agitate and (literally) fight against immigrants and the 'traitors' on the left who supported them.

Labour had initially opposed immigration controls on Commonwealth citizens and had fought Tory legislation on this issue in the early 1960s. But their electoralist instincts began to overwhelm them in the late 1960s. Crossman, always with a nose for opportunistic lurches, concluded that 'immigration could be the biggest vote loser for the Labour Party'.[20] This kind of thinking sparked an increasingly desperate lurch to the right by Labour, to accommodate to the growing racist populism rather than to challenge it. Callaghan denied entry to Kenyan Asians trying to flee to Britain in 1968, even though they had British passports. Cabinet member George Thomas argued that 'to pass such legislation would be wrong in principle, clearly discrimination on the grounds of colour, and contrary to everything we stand for', but he was in a tiny minority. Resistance to anti-immigrant racism did not come from Labour, or even primarily the Labour left, but from new campaigning charities like the Joint Council for the Welfare of Immigrants.[21]

Strife in Place of Unity

After offering limited resistance in Parliament, the left reacted more strongly to the industrial strategy developed by Barbara Castle in the White Paper *In Place of Strife*, designed to deal with shop-floor militancy. With over 2 million days lost every year through strike action since 1964, Wilson had to prove he could tame wild trade unionists, in particular their unofficial wildcat strikes. Over 50 per cent of the strikes took place in just a handful of industries – car factories, shipyards, the mines and docks[22] – and most of these were organised through shop-floor militancy. Many years of full employment and the closed shop gave workers an industrial strength they had rarely possessed before, allowing shop stewards to act independently of any official sanction from their union. While the union chiefs fought to try and keep the wage limits intact, the grassroots of the union had other ideas.

The solution developed by Wilson and Castle was a corporatist one, to further integrate the unions into the affairs of state, and giving them power as bureaucratic institutions rather than workers' movements. Castle believed this was a socialist response to the constant wage claims, but as one contemporary noted 'the trouble with Barbara is that she thinks anything she does is socialism'.[23] The proposals involved requiring official ballots and a 'cooling-off' period for strikes. The hope was that the cooling-off period would give union officials time to step in and placate the workforce or for a deal to be worked out without the need for a strike. In this way, *In Place of Strife* acted as the blueprint for all future anti-strike legislation as it undermined militancy by making the union bureaucracies more responsible for workers' actions, thus allowing them to act as brakes on rank-and-file activity.

At this time, however, the trade union leaders were willing to take action against such legislation. The intensification of the class struggle across industry had produced a leftward shift in the unions. A new vanguard formed around the TGWU and AEU (led by left-wingers Jack Jones and Hugh Scanlon) were furious at the intervention of Wilson and his Cabinet into the movement in such a way. At Labour conference level, this meant millions of affiliated member's votes were now in alliance with the left – the stranglehold of the right over conference was finally ended. Jones and Scanlon were not consistently on the left, reflecting their trade union interests and positions in the bureaucracy, but they were certainly an awkward ally for the Labour Party and hostile to swathes of integrationist policies.

Foot led the opposition in Parliament, attacking Wilson and Castle for having 'been persuaded that the way to establish themselves as big, brave men and women capable of government; the way to prove they have hair on their chest; the way to show they don't give a damn for anybody, except of course the New Mirror or the Daily Statesman [*sic*] and, last but by no means least, the public opinion polls, is to declare war on the trade unions'.[24] The *Tribune* group in Parliament proposed an amendment to safeguard the 'fundamental rights of a free trade union movement'. Favouring a more active approach than the negotiation strategy of the TUC, the CPGB-led Liaison Committee for the Defence of Trade Unions organised a series of work stoppages and a strike on May Day 1968 involving 250,000 workers. As negotiations with the TUC stalled, Castle and the Cabinet looked for a way out. Scanlon and Jones offered them one: abandon *In Place of Strife* in exchange for a 'binding and solemn' pledge that the unions would self-police and prevent wildcat strikes through their own internal mechanisms. But for many workers the damage was done: Labour had proposed introducing regulations into the trade union movement that even the Tories hadn't attempted since the war. For a lot of shop stewards on the factory floors that was unforgivable, but it meant a fragile alliance had been forged with the Labour left who had clearly sided with the workers' movement. This alliance was essential to the subsequent developments of the 1970s.

The political turmoil hit Labour hard. The flagging end of the first Wilson government revealed a revisionist party, wholly reliant on Keynesian demand-management, trapped in an economic straitjacket that provoked working-class resistance while undermining its own ability to implement more progressive social-economic policies. Around 200,000 members left the party during this period. Ken Livingstone described the experience of joining in 1968 as being like 'a rat who was boarding a sinking ship'. Wilson still hoped to win in 1970 – in some polls he was even 7 points ahead on the eve of the election – but he was defeated by Ted Heath who won the election with a 30-seat majority. As Crossman commented in his diary about the collapse in support from the Labour electorate: 'We have given them three years of hell and high taxes. They've seen the failure of devaluation and felt the soaring cost of living.'[25] Labour had alienated its own voting base.

The Realignment of Forces

The experience of the Labour government of 1964–70 had a profound effect on Ralph Miliband. He saw that too many of the left MPs had been bought off with opaque phrases or vague promises of socialism and peace. They confused the rhetoric with the reality and grasped at each left nod from the party leadership as a new principled turn. By the time the second edition of Miliband's *Parliamentary Socialism* came out in 1972 his conclusion was clear enough: Labour was finished as a vehicle for any kind of socialism. Even its Fabian perspective of gradual, incremental moves towards socialism had been abandoned by the party leaders.[26] Now it was a mere shill, a prop for the ruling class, and the Labour left was a busted flush, made up of isolated 'pathetic figures' able to mount 'episodic revolts' but nothing more. Miliband proposed 'moving on' from Labour, building something new. Nevertheless, the years following the publication of the second edition of *Parliamentary Socialism* heralded a renaissance for the left of the party, which went on to achieve breakthroughs in both politics and constitutional arrangements that changed the future of Labour.

The context for the revival of the Labour left from its late 1960s nadir was the huge industrial struggle that took place during the Heath interregnum. In 1972 there were 22 million days lost to strike action – a symptom of the combative spirit of many rank-and-file working-class militants. Even the shop-workers union USDAW passed a motion at its 1973 conference calling for the elimination of the capitalist system. Newly converted left-winger Tony Benn (having been a Wilsonian minister in the 1960s) took up the demands of some of the most radical parts of the trade union movement, and critiqued his own recent past: 'I was part of the policy which is now presented as being so brand new by the Social Democrats, who are really resuscitating a policy that I worked harder on than anyone else, and I can tell you, from experience [that it] fails, it's undemocratic and widens the gap between rich and poor.'[27] This sense was echoed by conference delegates. CLP delegate Gay Walton summed up this view at the 1970 conference:

When in opposition, the leadership of the Party said, 'When faced with an economic crisis we shall nationalise the banks and the building societies,' but when in power and faced by an economic crisis they adopted orthodox and capitalistic methods to combat the crisis, and once again the ordinary people of this country were called upon to make the sacrifice, while the rich people suffered no hardship.[28]

The repercussions of Labour's ousting from government and the scale and strength of working-class struggles at the time had a profound impact on the development of both the left and the wider Labour Party in three areas:

Industrial militancy: The left was bolstered by the militancy displayed by the almost general strike of 1972, thousands of workers taking unofficial strike action in protest at the imprisoning of striking dock workers under Heath's new anti-union laws. The immense surge of anger and action from the trade union movement forced the government to back down and blew a hole in Heath's industrial relations reforms. How the militancy of the trade unions was to be factored into a largely parliamentary perspective became a key part of the debate among the Labour left for the rest of the decade.

Economic strategy: Related to the battles going on in workplaces up and down the country, the workers' occupation at the Upper Clyde Shipbuilders in 1971 proved a turning point for left strategists – here was a 'work-in' and production under workers' control. The workers' campaign forced the Tories to keep the shipyard open, saving 4,000 of the 6,000 jobs. The UCS occupation inspired 200 similar incidents across the country, usually small enterprises facing bankruptcy that were taken over by the workforce. UCS provided a working model for a new way of putting some of the vague promises of Clause IV into action, and forced Parliament to act as a result of a workforce taking matters into its own hands. Benn visited the occupying workers and advocated their cause in Parliament,[29] a moment that established him as the principled leader of the parliamentary left. This was also the time when the Institute for Workers' Control, headed by Ken Coates, became much more prominent within left discussions in the party, advocating more radical concepts of socialist industrial organisation than Labour had historically entertained. The Labour conference in 1973 agreed by a wide margin to support calls for workers' control through 50 per cent of the boards of nationalised industries being made up of trade unionists, and union reps at every level of management having joint powers alongside the managers.[30]

Local government: The third front was the surcharging and barring from office of Labour councillors in Clay Cross in 1972–3 after they refused to implement the Heath government's Housing Finance Act which took control of rents out of the hands of local authorities and put them in the hands of Westminster. Their cause was celebrated throughout the labour movement, as that of principled comrades willing to stand up to the Tories.

Labour was lifted and shifted left by the mass movement outside Parliament which seeped into it. Clearly the post-war order was fragmenting: now was the time for a bolder, more ambitious left with a transformative strategy that could establish a new consensus for future generations.

The Rise of Militant

One organisation that hoped to provide that strategy was gathering its forces. Understandably, in a period of such seismic class struggle, with a working class that was brash, confident and willing to bring down governments, all revolutionary socialist groups were growing quite significantly. One organisation – Militant – had a particular angle that marked them out from the rest: they were wedded to the strategy of working in and through the Labour Party to achieve socialism.

Their goal was to transform Labour into a Marxist party – or at least to have a majority of Marxist MPs in the PLP – where they would use an Enabling Act to swiftly nationalise the top companies across the country, introducing workers' control and ensuring production for need not profit. Militant's leader was Ted Grant, who, alongside Peter Taaffe, recruited a number of serious and dedicated activists to the organisation. Between 1970 and 1974 Militant grew rapidly from 100 to 400 members, rising to a thousand shortly afterwards.

Militant grew primarily because it stuck with the Labour Party Youth Section after every other Trotskyist group had abandoned it.

They methodically organised LPYS branches, recruited to the Militant Tendency, and integrated the branches into their own organisational work. LPYS gave them funds, influence and positions within the party – each LPYS branch could send two delegates to their CLP meetings, giving Militant a voice on local leaderships. In 1972 the LPYS was also given a seat on the NEC, which Militant seized with both hands.

Militant enjoyed support in a handful of CLPs around the country, but the jewel in the crown was Liverpool. Early success in the city in the 1950s had been achieved in a struggle with the old guard leadership, led by Bessie and Jack Braddock, who ran Liverpool as their own fiefdom. Initial opposition by networks of left activists consolidated into an organisation that went on to become the lodestone of Militant in the 1960s.

Though they were a small current compared to the membership of the wider party, Militant were well organised and punched well above their weight. They scored a victory at the Labour Party conference in 1972, getting a motion passed by delegates that called for an Enabling Act to nationalise the largest monopolies in the country. The motion also included a direct criticism of the old integrationist, Fabian approach, calling for Labour to 'formulate a socialist plan of production based on public ownership, with minimum compensation, of the commanding heights of the economy ... This is an answer to those who argue for a slow, gradual, almost imperceptible progress towards nationalisation.' This embodied the core of the Militant perspective and strategy, which remained largely unchanged throughout their time in the party.

How did Militant escape the purges that had fallen on earlier socialist currents? Their growth occurred at a period of quite serious liberalisation in the party structures; its internal culture and level of tolerance was markedly different to ten years earlier. The proscribed list had fallen into disuse and was abolished in 1973. Militant had learned from the previous witch-hunts against the left. Ostensibly they had been part of an organisation called the Revolutionary Socialist League, but that was left to wither away, replaced by a network of sellers of the Militant newspaper. Whenever accusations emerged of a 'party within a party' the response was usually 'it's just a newspaper', and the idea of persecuting someone for selling a socialist newspaper was simply not very popular among lay members. Additionally, the NEC adopted a much more hands-off approach to the Labour youth organisation than they had between 1960 and 1964. Militant were at least a loyal opposition: they did work getting the vote out in marginal seats and they were very active in promoting the Labour Party.

Interestingly, considering they were to become such a target for the right's hatred, most of Militant's politics were not particularly radical. They were pretty standard – for the time – labour movement policies: a 35 hour week, a better minimum wage, more workers' control over hiring and firing, opposition to arms spending and to Tory anti-union laws. On some issues Militant were quite conservative, reflecting a workerist[31] view of class consciousness; they weren't very enamoured with the women's movement, gay liberation or black self-organisation. Their view was that these weren't working-class issues and were divisive for class unity. On Ireland their position was against the initial occupation, but they were only in favour of the withdrawal of British soldiers if a trade union defence force was created to replace them, arguing that this was essential to stop sectarian violence. Most of the rest of the left opposed the presence of British troops in the country on principle, and were in favour of their immediate withdrawal and a united Ireland.

The Alternative Economic Strategy

In their critical analysis of the failures of Wilsonian politics, the Labour left drew quite radical conclusions in the early 1970s. Michael Barratt Brown was active in the Institute for Workers' Control. He in particular developed a criticism of the corporatist policies that fed into a lot of the Labour left thinking of the following decade.[32] Barratt Brown argued for workers being able to encroach on the control of managers, through challenging their 'right to manage', and eventually demanding a say in investment and wider economic concerns. He also warned of the parliamentary fixation – it was inevitable in a system that favoured capitalists over workers (and Tories over Labour) that integrationist tendencies would lead to a co-option of Labour into attacking workers' living conditions. Furthermore he pointed to the prevalence of transnational companies as the key source of competition: it was the centralisation of capital not the rivalry of nation states *per se* that was the problem. As such, his solution to the national crisis posed by the 1960s was a class alliance between working people and national capital against the predatory machinations of international businesses and against the Common Market in Europe. This was the new paradigm for the emerging left to examine Britain's economic problems.

These kind of ideas circulated more widely after the 1970 election. A new analysis formed, becoming for a time the official economic orthodoxy of the party, expressed in the conference motions and programmes passed between 1972 and 1983. It came to be known as the Alternative Economic Strategy (AES). Stuart Holland's book *The Socialist Challenge* (1975) was considered the bible of the AES. It called for workplace democracy, 'opening the books' on private firms to allow for public scrutiny over their finances, and public control of the 25 most profitable companies in the UK.

These policies marked a sharp change in strategy. A commitment to the mixed economy was no longer enough; there was now outright criticism that 'even the most comprehensive measures of social and fiscal reform can only succeed in masking the unacceptable and unpleasant face of a capitalist economy'.[33] The key part of this strategy for the left was the commitment to the nationalisation of the top 25 manufacturing companies in the UK through the mechanism of a National Enterprise Board (NEB) that would buy controlling shares.[34] Under these proposals the NEB would be responsible for job creation, investment promotion, technological development, growth of exports, spreading industrial democracy and several other areas of Labour left concern. It represented probably the clearest commitment to a reformist socialism since 1945, and the hope of recapturing some of the post-war state control and regulation of larger parts of the economy.[35] In the words of the editor of *Tribune*, Richard Clements, writing in 1973: 'for the first time Labour has a comprehensive answer to the ills of our society ... it provides a real basis for challenging society'.[36] The integrative techno-corporatism of Wilson had failed; now a transformative attack on wealth and power in Britain was replacing it.

The AES formed the philosophical core of Labour strategy, culminating in the 1973 Programme, which stands as a crowning moment of Labourite anti-capitalist thought. Unlike 1945 this was not the politics of consent, it was a declaration of struggle against capitalism. Based on the programme, the 1974 election manifesto outlined the intention to 'bring about a fundamental and irreversible shift in the balance of power and wealth in favour of working people and their families'. It specifically called for more economic powers for working people over wages and production decisions. It was a clear high point for both the radical agenda and the necessary policy consequences of a socialist plan for a Labour government.

Despite the enthusiastic energy of Holland in advocating and propagating the ideas of the AES in the policy forums and among trade union policy and political officers, it earned only lukewarm support in the PLP. Wilson himself was clearly not a fan. Therein lay the inevitable problem: if the MPs did not want to implement the manifesto then party members were largely powerless to act. The left was not ignorant of this political bottleneck in Labour. In order to make the AES a reality they relied on a powerful left movement from below: workers, their unions and the grassroots of the party applying pressure on a Labour government to go further and use state power as a weapon against the capitalists. As Holland explained:

In practice, a Labour government is only likely to introduce such a major transformation of British capitalism if it is pressured both by the current economic crisis and by its own supporters in the unions and the party. But, to realise such pressure, workers ... must ensure that they can secure more than a British variant on either state capitalism or state socialism. They must be directly involved in the process of transformation, or the transformation itself is unlikely to occur.[37]

Holland's answer to the Marxist criticism of the state as a defender of capitalism was that the post-war state increasingly went through 'Bonapartist' phases[38] – meaning that the class struggle rose to such a level that the state ended up balancing between the class forces and could at times be prised free of the grip of the capitalists and turned against them. His hope then was that the class struggle would force such a change.

Holland's strategy was, however, flawed in a number of ways. At root the crisis of capitalism had to be resolved either in favour of the working class through socialism or through restoring profitability. Holland recognised that the crisis affecting British capitalism – inflation and lack of growth – were not home-grown: it was a result of the stagnant world economy, greater concentration of capital (monopolisation), and the intensification of competition internationally.[39] But the AES posited that Britain's lack of competitiveness could be fixed by more vibrant state intervention. The poor competitiveness was caused by a lack of investment which was itself a result of low profitability – capitalists won't invest where there is no money to be made. The AES called for planning agreements, but just as with the National Plan these were indicative, drawn up by businesses themselves and then 'scrutinised' by the government.

Holland and his allies focused on the institutional make-up of corporate ownership as a solution. True, public ownership would help the situation by avoiding excessive profits and curtailing speculation, but changing the corporate structures through nationalisation or having more workers on the board of directors doesn't alter the fundamental problem that in a capitalist market economy the primary way to compete is through increasing the exploitation of the workforce, inevitably reducing working conditions and pay. The left advocated protecting British business interests through state ownership and not – in reality – genuine workers' control, only workers' participation in management decisions. This ran the risk of making trade unionists complicit in managing wage cuts and speed ups to keep capitalism profitable.

This pointed to an existential problem for the left's strategy – it relied on promoting private sector growth (through the NEB, investment, etc.) to create jobs, with nationalisation as a way of prompting the rest of the private sector to do better. Yet the left also promoted workers' rights and greater social equality – the very factors that disincentivise private sector investment.[40] No wonder capitalists were more interested in exporting capital abroad, where there were fewer labour laws and weaker trade unions. Additionally, the reliance on import controls would only have the effect of exporting unemployment and poverty abroad, and – ludicrously – the Labour left argued that they did not think Britain putting up import controls would encourage other countries to do so.

There were also social questions raised over Holland's reliance on the massed ranks of a militant workers' movement to deliver a half-way-house socialist transformation of British society. Why would a powerful, well-organised working-class movement, presumably seizing control of their own industries and guided by their own class interests against the bosses, limit themselves to the nationalisation of the top 20 companies and some import controls?

These criticisms were brought into sharp relief by events in South America. The rise of the AES coincided with the crushing of the left-wing Salvador Allende government in Chile, when CIA-backed sections of the military launched a coup that killed thousands and installed a dictatorship. Allende's popular left-wing policies (national-isation of the copper mines, land reform, etc.) were cited as the reason for the right-wing coup,[41] but it was the rising workers' movement that was the most worrying threat.[42] A transformative left government can be destabilised through the usual mechanisms (international economic sabotage, undermining the currency), but the transforma-tive movement from below was what terrified the ruling elites and the US state department. The workers and peasants themselves took over factories and businesses if they suspected the owners of engaging in sabotage. They organised and took over planning and rationing committees. A first aborted coup earlier in 1973 had been met with a massive occupation of factories and a huge march of over one million people. In this context there was an urgent need to think about how extra-parliamentary movements could resist the inevitable violent reaction that would erupt in the event of a strong socialist challenge through parliamentary institutions. A left government backed up by a mass movement had still been defeated by a military takeover, so where did that leave the AES? Despite the events in Chile, Holland still assumed a relatively neutral state with a loyal police force and an army that would not overthrow a radical left government and could be used to enforce any legislative inroads into capitalist power. This was a very big assumption, considering the subsequent testimony of many during the mid 1970s that they were concerned about a possible coup against the Wilson government.[43]

Wilson Redux, Labourism Comes Apart

However, any threat of a British coup there may have been receded rapidly into the background when it became clear that Wilson was intent on ignoring his own party democracy when he took power in 1974. Led by an ailing man still shaken and demoralised from his last time in Downing Street, Labour was not particularly looking to form a government. But when the powerful National Union of Mineworkers (NUM) went to war against Heath, resulting in a three-day working week as coal supplies ran low, Heath called – and lost – an early election and Labour was thrust back into power. After the initial February election, Labour was the largest party but lacked a majority, so they ruled in a voting agreement with the Ulster Unionists. Wilson called a second election in October and scraped in with a margin of only three MPs. Labour was back in government, but not necessarily back in power.

Upon election, Wilson refused to implement the more radical parts of the manifesto. The truth of the matter was that – as David Marquand explained years later – the programme was more of a document in an internal faction fight than a programme for government.[44] The left had no way to force Wilson to implement the election pledges. For his part, Wilson adopted a policy of containment and marginalisation of the left. The routine of putting leading lights of the left in the Cabinet was once again deployed: Foot was made Minister for Employment, which was seen as a concession to the unions; Benn was given the Ministry of Industry with Eric Heffer as his under-secretary.

Although the left commanded the Ministry for Industry they were a minority in the Cabinet. Benn was told in no uncertain terms that he had to make do with a tight budget. Additionally the left found themselves constantly frustrated by the civil service, some of whom threw up any obstacle they could to hinder the more radical ministers. Benn's first meeting with Sir Anthony Part, the senior civil servant charged with industry, saw the urbane Part coolly enquire: 'I presume, Secretary of State, that you do not intend to implement the industrial strategy in Labour's programme?' When the Industry Act finally wound its way through Parliament it was a shadow of the ambitious plan developed in opposition: the NEB was introduced but it had a budget of only £1bn and was initially chaired by Sir Don Ryder, a distinctly non-socialist figure. He was followed by a merchant banker, a clear sign that the new institution would not be used as a weapon in the interests of workers. Despite the original lofty ambitions, the NEB was only ever allowed to prop up failing businesses. Just as the National Plan in 1965 had been voluntary, the NEB also couldn't produce planning agreements, only voluntary codes that businesses were free to ignore at their whim – which they did.

The only significant deal the NEB made was with Chrysler, after workers occupied their factory in Scotland demanding nationalisation. Chrysler was given £40 million to stop its UK business collapsing, then two years later the factory was sold to Peugeot-Citroen without government being consulted. Although the 1974 manifesto had promised that Labour 'shall not confine the extension of the public sector to the loss-making and subsidised industries', any nationalisations were mostly a repeat of the historic practice of only bailing out industries facing imminent bankruptcy: docks, ship building and aerospace were nationalised, as well as British Leyland, which was in dire straits.

Compare the Chrysler fiasco to the Lucas Aerospace shop stewards' proposals in 1976: faced with a cut of 5,000 jobs, after meeting with Benn the union activists put forward an alternative corporate plan, based on workers' democracy and an environmental agenda. The Lucas Plan would be for need, not profit, and phase out weapons production to replace it with 'socially useful' goods, like medical equipment and hybrid batteries.[45] The Lucas Plan became a cornerstone in the thinking of the left desperate to escape corporatism and develop new economic models.

The labour movement establishment still sought a reinvigorated corporatist model. Proving the old maxim that committees are where ideas go to die, the calls for workers' participation in production was put to a committee of inquiry, headed by Oxford academic Alan Bullock. Staffed by union leaders like Jack Jones and representatives of big business, the committee proposed a system of Works Councils – similar to the West German model – with workers representatives co-managing decisions in the company. But this recommendation was torpedoed in part by the trade union leaders themselves, and the discussion was moved to a Cabinet Committee which didn't report until 1978. As Jones noted sadly: 'what was left of the Bullock report sank in the disaster of the winter of discontent'.[46] The corporatist notion of a tripartite system of Labour government, unions and management working together rested on the notion that the unions and Labour were cooperating – an unsustainable proposition by the late 1970s.

Unable to influence the Confederation of British Industry or tackle the conservative mandarins in the Treasury, Labour focused its energies where it had the most power, attempting to win the trade unions over to a Social Contract that would limit wage increases. In this regard they were totally successful. Year on year wages deals with the unions saw pay increasing well below inflation. And despite the popular image of the 1970s, the number of official strikes dropped dramatically. Benn worried about this in his diaries, especially as the newly elected Tory leader Margaret Thatcher was gleefully exposing Labour's role in managing working-class resistance in the interest of business:

> we talked about how to deal with Thatcher's argument, which is that the Labour Government are doing to the trade union movement what the Tories could never do; that in doing it the Labour Government are getting profits up and holding prices down and therefore restoring vitality to the capitalist mechanism; and that by doing so they will

disillusion their own supporters and make it possible for the Tories to return.

Benn worried that the outcome of the Labour Party in power in the 1970s would leave the movement 'broken and divided and demoralised'.[47] His fears were prescient, as was Thatcher's argument, though his diary does not broach the issue of how the future might have been rewritten.

Despite their initial focus on industrial policy and questions of economic democracy, the turning point for the left was the referendum on membership of the European Economic Community in 1975. Callaghan had gone to Dublin to negotiate the terms of Britain's continued involvement in the EEC. But when he returned the deal he had struck was far removed from the party policy that the left had secured at conferences and the NEC. The PLP forced a vote on it but Callaghan secured his position with the help of the Conservatives; a referendum was called on terms deeply unpopular with the left and against party policy. Adamant that a reforming left government was still possible, the left was deeply concerned that the EEC would act to block socialist measures. Tony Benn and his allies rejected the pro-EEC arguments, convinced it was a regime only intended for capital accumulation and ensuring profit. They led the charge to get the UK out of the EEC. But the focus on national sovereignty and economic rights failed to convince the electorate, who saw in Europe a chance for more trade and better jobs. The campaign was a failure; only 32 per cent voted to leave the EEC. This defeat left Benn isolated – portrayed as a zealot for a lost cause – and Wilson took the opportunity to demote him to the much less influential Department of Energy.[48]

Rebellions From Behind and Below

The disappointment inevitably provoked a response from a party that still had a mass base and was still largely committed to socialism. Labour was rocked by a large number of backbench revolts in Parliament and a determined campaign from below in the CLPs. This was helped largely by the evolving make-up of the party. One historian identifies the new middle class, professional, left-leaning trade unionist and women members as 'a more assertive rank and file ... less deferential to parliamentarians (Right and Left!), more determined and persistent in its desire to achieve radical change'.[49] One result of this was the willingness of CLPs to deselect MPs and introduce mandatory reselection for every MP – something that left intellectuals like Richard Crossman had dismissed in the 1950s as 'insanely dangerous'.[50]

From 1973 there was a considerable thawing of the proscriptive, anti-radical politics that had characterised the witch-hunts of the 1960s. Now much more under the influence of the left thanks to the trade unions' leftward drift since 1967, the 1973 NEC saw a more liberal regime introduced in the party. The proscribed list was abolished and the threats of purges of left-wing activists came to an end.[51] These decisions proved to be quite momentous in relation to the grassroots struggles that gripped the party during the turbulent times of the 1970s and '80s. They meant that left-wing groups like Militant could operate without persecution, despite some on the NEC arguing that they were behaving unconstitutionally. Orientated to the youth organisations of the party, Militant was making significant ground in recruiting the more radical and politically ambitious younger generation who were critical of Wilson's prevarications.

At the same time the left's influence in government came under sustained attack. Wilson abruptly resigned in 1976. Both Foot and Benn ran for the leadership and Foot came second with 137 votes, losing to Callaghan. Wilson left Downing Street saying to Callaghan 'sorry about the mess': a forewarning of the problems that lay ahead. Callaghan had once been a trade unionist, a man of the left who signed the Keep Left statement in 1947, but now he was Prime Minister the responsibility of isolating irksome left voices became paramount. The détente with the left MPs was over. Castle was out and Benn was demoted. This did not strengthen his government; the road Labour had embarked upon was a doomed one. In the face of the growing crisis of British capitalism the government was weak, struggling to tackle the economic forces ravaging the country.

Despite the set-backs, the left was often in open rebellion from above and below. The 1974–9 government suffered more parliamentary defeats than any before – many from the bullish and well-organised *Tribune* group. *Tribune* became the bane of the Labour leadership. In 1974 there were 80 MPs associated with the magazine, a strong showing in Parliament for an organisation that appeared determined to carry through the more radical aspects of the manifesto. But the actual strength of *Tribune* was limited. They were noisy and pressed their points often, but only on six occasions could they defeat government legislation. The most important victory was against the Expenditure White Paper in March 1976, which necessitated a vote of confidence in the government the following day. The left hailed the blow as a sign that the government was susceptible to sustained attack and was increasingly reliant on the Tories to maintain itself in power, something that would not be tolerated by the rank-and-file activists from below. What was lacking, however, was the capacity to channel that grassroots anger into a responsive mechanism that allowed them to hold their MPs to account or pressure them. Essentially the left could make no further progress in the current constitutional set up. The guerrilla war in some CLPs to deselect unpopular MPs was the consequence.

A Right to Rule?

The campaign to democratise the party was fought on a number of fronts: removing the leaders' veto over the manifesto (which had seen key left policies exorcised in 1973); empowering the NEC to decide on the manifesto; the mandatory reselection of MPs; and an Electoral College system to decide the leader. Central was the question of accountability of MPs to their local CLPs. The organisation that took this on most effectively was the Campaign for Labour Party Democracy. The CLPD was formed in 1973 with one simple aim: to ensure that the Labour manifesto was actually implemented by a Labour government. Its leading lights were Vladimir and Vera Derer and later Jon Lansman. Vladimir Derer's view was that the left didn't take the reality of the hegemony of parliamentary democracy seriously, constantly counter-posing it to much-hoped-for 'spontaneous' working-class movements while neglecting the living fact that Parliament is where power resides.[52] Fresh from the battles over the first Wilson government and keen to see the more radical demands of the 1974 programme implemented, they proposed the reasonable demand that politicians should act on their manifesto commitments. But such a position was considered scandalous because it cut right though the highly cherished autonomy of the PLP, who believed politicians should act on their own 'good judgement'. This Burkeian[53] reflex was entirely at odds with the principles of democratic accountability in the labour movement – you take a vote and you act on the result. Labour MPs repeated the same philosophy as their Tory counterparts, claiming they were accountable only to the electorate who got them to the Commons at election time. The ultimate test of credibility was the general election. As such, what right did a handful of party activists have to put demands on men and women who had won tens of thousands of votes from 'ordinary people'? Compounding this view was the more prosaic point that becoming an MP in a safe Labour seat was effectively a well-paid job for life. MPs did not want to be threatened with losing their jobs just because of how they voted in Parliament.

This translated into the struggle for the mandatory reselection for MPs. In order to ensure it was fair, and that deselection would not be used as a weapon by the right or the left, the process had to be applied universally. Every MP, right or left, would have to win the nomination of their own CLP at each election before they would be put before the electorate. The idea was popular with lay party activists, frustrated with the privileged elite that made up the right-wing of the PLP. Mandatory reselection first appeared on the conference agenda in 1974, and although it was defeated (by 3.5 to 2 million votes) it returned every year, backed by more and more CLPs, at first only 12 but by 1977 it had the backing of 79 local parties. The CLPD was supported in these endeavours by three left-wing unions, NUPE, the TGWU and Association of Scientific, Technical and Managerial Staffs (ASTMS), who all backed the most radical demands, giving the left an influence beyond the CLPs.[54]

Unsurprisingly, the Labour establishment reacted furiously to attempts to remove MPs who had lost the confidence of their CLPs but were seen as loyal to the PLP hierarchy. Battles in the mid 1970s to deselect Eddie Griffiths in Sheffield Brightside and Reg Prentis in Newham North East were long and bitter, with the media publicising them to show a divided party. Prentis' de-selection made headlines as he had been a Cabinet Member under Wilson. This motivated 179 MPs to publish a public letter supporting him and condemning the local members trying to unseat him. The press joined in the fight to save the right-wing Labour MP, blasting local Labour activists as 'hard left', 'members of the Trotskyist Militant Tendency' (they were not), 'extremists' and, most damningly, 'bed-sit revolutionaries'.[55] Embarrassingly, Prentis proved his critics right when he quit and joined the Tories, fulminating against his CLP. But in 1978 resolutions to conference on mandatory reselection were lost because Hugh Scanlon abstained, against the wishes of his own union delegation.[56] He warned Labour to focus on industrial policies and dismissed the moves to improve party democracy as 'chicken shit'.

What Rough Beast?

In 1975 Labour negotiated with Jack Jones a new Social Contract which would cap wage increases. Such negotiated compromises were largely based on the goodwill of the unions to prop up the Labour government, but there had to be a *quid pro quo*. As a reward for wage limitations, the Social Contract promised to create space for investment in the 'social wage' – for example rent controls and pensions.[57] But the deal was ultimately one-sided. There was no sugar to go with the bitter pill of making the workers' pay for the wider malaise of the economy. As such the Contract was living on borrowed time.[58] The agreement to secure an International Monetary Fund (IMF) loan was the battering ram the capitalists needed to smash through Labour's social programme. Britain was hit by multiple crises at once: stagflation, a run on the pound and capital flight. Investors were selling sterling hand over fist, despite constant protestations from Healey that the pound was undervalued.[59]

One journalist described the concerted efforts of the Treasury and the Bank of England to let the pound slide as a way of forcing policy changes as an attempted 'civilian coup against the government'.[60] Capital controls that would have stemmed the losses were rejected. Afraid to confront the power of the City of London and given advice by the Treasury that he had no choice, Healey went cap in hand to the IMF for a loan to the tune of £2.3 billion. The conditions of the loan required eye-watering cuts to public expenditure. Regular visits by teams of IMF inspectors followed in 1977 to ensure the austerity measures were proceeding according to plan. But to implement the economic restructuring demanded by the IMF meant abandoning Labour's life-long pledge to full employment, and allowing the private sector to be free of restrictions. Once again the law grinds the poor but rich men grind the law.

In contrast the left argued against accepting the IMF loan, calling instead for investment in the NEB, nationalisation of the banks, (controversial) import controls and planning agreements imposed on multinational corporations. Benn argued at Cabinet that 'it would be inexplicable to our movement that we had never even tried our alternative strategy with the IMF and yet more inexplicable that in order to get the loan we have promised not to undertake that alternative strategy'.[61]

But the left's arguments were ignored. There was a final showdown at the conference in 1976 when the left attempted to set out a clear alternative to the proto-monetarist agenda of the Cabinet. Conference re-endorsed a form of the AES and rejected outright any deal with the IMF. Healey spoke passionately against the left's 'siege economy' proposal, arguing that only through bowing to the dictates of the IMF could Britain survive. Tony Benn later mocked this argument: 'their policy was a siege economy, only they had the bankers inside the castle with all our supporters left outside'.[62] Conference rejected Healey's argument and voted overwhelmingly to nationalise four of the largest banks and the majority of the insurance industry. Callaghan contemptuously dismissed the vote, making it clear that it would have no effect on the government. Six weeks later the deal was signed and the AES – at least at national level – was history.

...Towards Bethlehem to be Born

Labour has always faced problems handling economic downturns. Promising prosperity when the economy is booming is not a problem, but promising full employment in periods of severe economic crisis requires serious anti-capitalist measures that restructure the economy away from profit and towards planning for need. This is the rock upon which Labour has been dashed more than once. As the post-war order unravelled, forces in both Labour and the Conservatives developed new ideological responses; in Labour it was the AES, from the Tories Thatcherism. The crucial difference was that Thatcherism became hegemonic in her own party whereas the AES – popular among members and many unions – remained a minority view in the PLP. As outlined above, the AES was not a perfect solution to the problems facing Britain, but at least it was an attempt to resolve the contradictions of British capitalism more favourably to workers and the poor. In rejecting this, Labour in Parliament relied on forcing down wages to buy them more time for the economy to recover of its own volition. The voluntary wage policies agreed in 1976 unravelled in 1978. Like a bucking horse throwing its rider, trade unionists – led by the firefighters (FBU) demanding a 30 per cent pay increase – began to reject the incomes policy. It had been intended to prevent inflation, but as inflation skyrocketed it just led to wages being reduced. Contrary to the enduring myth that it was the 'reckless' trade unions in the Winter of Discontent who brought down Labour by having the audacity to defend their members pay and conditions in the face of inflation, it was actually the austerity demands of the IMF that were the turning point. Just as MacDonald chose to surrender to the Bank of England in 1931, so too did Callaghan and Healey capitulate to the demands of international finance. The deliberate abandoning of the promise of full employment was a retreat from even the revisionists' promises in the 1950s.[63] It set the Labour right on a course to accepting the subsequent Thatcherite orthodoxy. Public sector unions striking for higher wages in 1978–9 were the consequence of both Labour's inability to transform the economy in the interests of the majority and the collapse of its historic programme.

But the IMF loan was also a deliberate weapon used against social democracy and against the trade unions. Healey later confided that he believed the advice he had been given by Treasury officials had been totally inaccurate, that figures were inflated to provide evidence that the IMF loan was inescapable. The actual figure for government borrowing in the crucial year 1976–7 was £2 billion less than the projected total, which was the same amount as the cuts that Labour made.[64] It was a decisive victory for the right in forcing the Labour Party to abandon both its left-wing programme *and* the revisionism of the 1950s, to make it bend the knee before the power of capital and accept the 'new realism'. It was the attempt to manage British capitalism in a time of crisis that eventually consolidated the right-wing of the Labour Party around the new realities of economic orthodoxy. In the words of one historian:

> In 1974, Tony Benn had said the crisis should not be used to prop up an ailing capitalist system but should be the basis for a forward march into socialism. 'We should all be socialists now', he said. But after the 1974–9 Labour government, the Party could not again come into power for another 18 years, when it succeeded in convincing the electorate, under Tony Blair, that none of us are socialists now. That, I would argue, is the fundamental significance of the IMF crisis in 1976.[65]

After being ousted from government in 1979, Labour embarked on the by now familiar approach of moving left to attempt to recapture the base and reinvigorate the party activists. The problem was that although many understood the vicious cycle, there was no way to break it. Labour had moved left when in opposition before only for the Cabinet to rapidly abandon their promises when in power. It was this, as much as any particular ideological strength of Thatcherism, that in 1979 repelled so many voters who had previously looked to Labour as their party.

Despite the strength of the Labour left, when repeated conference decisions were ignored and Callaghan and the Cabinet pursued their own course towards oblivion, there were no mechanisms whatsoever to reverse course. The left did not have a fall-back plan after the AES was publicly crucified by the IMF in 1976. All that could be done was to criticise the leadership and force the issue at conferences, but to no avail. Labour had given in to the power of big capital and international finance once again, unwilling to mobilise the social forces required to defend their programme in power, and was led by politicians who saw appeasing the City of London as more important than guaranteeing workers' wages. It was clear that the party had to be made more accountable if there was to be any hope of avoiding this tragic fate again.

6

The Broad Church Collapses

'The Labour Party is a very broad party, reflecting a wide variety of opinions from Left to Right. This diversity of view is a great source of strength and we must vigorously resist any attempt that is made to drive the Left or the Right out of the party.'

Tony Benn, speaking in Birmingham at the May Day rally, 1979

In opposition the left once again found its voice. They better understood the unravelling of the post-war consensus and raged at the inadequacies of the centre-ground politics of the party leaders. Benn was clear who was responsible: the defeat 'followed thirty years of anti-socialist revisionism preached from the top of the Labour Party'.[1] The intensity of inner-party struggle during this period would produce the most profound constitutional changes seen since 1918. But the fallout from those years would see the Labour left put on the back foot for a generation – until 2015 and Jeremy Corbyn's victory. The first pitched battle against the party machinery was on the question of inner-party democracy. After all, a radical transformative strategy required a radically transformed Labour Party.

Battle for Reselection

Following the election defeat, the party establishment was shaky but the left felt vindicated. Now was the moment to push for the constitutional reforms that would break up the PLP domination of the party. At the 1979 conference a major breakthrough occurred when the NEC changed its position and backed reselection for MPs. At the same time several major unions (TGWU, NUPE and the AUEW) had just passed motions in favour of reselection at their conferences. It was one of those rare moments where the rank and file, the leadership and the unions all seemed to align together. The conference carried the CLPD-inspired motion, though – as with many victories – it was based on a compromise.

Under the new rules each MP could face a trigger ballot if a certain percentage of the local membership backed it, and if that ballot was passed then a full reselection process would begin. Buoyed by the victory but wary of the power of the machine to block change, the left was spurred into action. The CLPD, the Labour Coordinating Committee, Socialist Organiser and others launched the Rank and File Mobilising Committee (RFMC) to keep up the pressure around three central democratic reforms: extending the franchise for leadership elections to unions and members; giving the NEC control over the manifesto; and mandatory reselection. In terms of left unity and its grassroots approach, the RFMC was unique and was instrumental in driving through the structural reforms that opened up space for the left to win ground inside the party.[2]

The specific question of electing the party leader was put to a special conference held in Wembley in 1981. The CLPD made a tactical decision to accept a compromise solution for leadership elections, agreeing to an Electoral College of 40–30–30 (trade unions, PLP and membership). The old way of doing things was eroding and the idea that the constitution could be changed, even in faltering, compromise-laden steps, was a significant victory. Interestingly, the right-wing MP David Owen, soon to split with the right to form the Social Democratic Party (SDP), proposed a One Member One Vote system of elections with the PLP choosing the candidates. This would eventually be adopted under Ed Miliband 30 years later; it was the system that led to Corbyn's election.

But for the left the price of victory was high. The RFMC unravelled under major differences in approach. The CLPD favoured behind-closed-doors deals with the union leaders and bigwigs. Others rejected this as unaccountable and bureaucratic, favouring a more activist grassroots-led approach. This divergence of opinion meant that once the constitutional reforms were achieved the RFMC broke down. Some activists went on to organise Benn's Deputy Leader campaign a year later, others focused on the unions. The Labour left would not be so united for another generation.

The Left Bogeymen

The election of Michael Foot as Labour leader in 1980 and the defection of the right the following year to form the SDP were heralded by many on the left as a turning point in their favour. In fact it precipitated the beginning of a serious counter-attack from the right. Claims of 'infiltration' had been growing since 1976 when Healey had attempted to take the heat out of the IMF debacle by focusing attention on 'Trotskyites' and troublemakers in the ranks. Once again newspaper editors were only too happy to oblige in the witch-hunt, with regular articles condemning and ridiculing the left, a softening-up exercise before the actual purges began.[3] By the time of the 1981 SDP split the centre-right and the soft left around Foot felt they had to prove to the public that Labour was not overrun by the left.[4]

It is a testimony to the rapid hegemony of Thatcherism that the narrative around Labour was so easily dictated by its enemies. The howling attacks on what would soon be known as the 'loony left' came to dominate discussions over strategy and electoral performance. This framing favoured the right against the left and pre-emptively rendered left responses illegitimate. It was during this phase that several 'loony left' media hate-figures emerged: Ken Livingstone at the Greater London Council (GLC); councils like Hackney, Liverpool and Lambeth; Militant Tendency; Peter Tatchell (and LGBT rights more generally); Black Sections; Women's Sections and several others. The loony left label became an insipidly lazy but very effective way of undermining the Labour left, a slur so ubiquitous in the right-wing media it even found its way into internal Labour Party communications. There was a media focus on the idiosyncratic personalities of left public figures – Livingstone's newt collection came in for regular ridicule in the press – but also a potent attack on left policies, especially around gay and black rights. A nervous fear set in that the party was increasingly dominated by an obsession with so-called 'minority issues'. Eric Hammond from the right-wing EETPU union summed up the view of the right: London Labour was full of 'terrorists, lesbians and other queer people'.[5]

The Bermondsey by-election in 1983, where gay rights activist Peter Tatchell stood for Labour, was the scene of disgusting homophobic smears and outrageous bigotry. Despite Tatchell's being picked to stand by the CLP in 1981, the NEC took over a year to approve the nomination. Foot later admitted that he blocked it as he was under tremendous pressure from the soon to be SDP wing of the party, not over Tatchell's 'vote losing' sexuality but because he had advocated a campaign of non-violent civil disobedience against the Tory government.[6] During the by-election itself he received very little support from the national party, and only a few organisers came to help from elsewhere. This lack of support only emboldened the bigots. In an interview about the election, Tatchell recalled: 'I was deluged with hate mail, death threats, attacks on my flat and more than 100 physical bashings.'[7] As he concluded: 'Some Labour right-wingers wanted me to lose in order to strengthen their bid to ditch left-wing policies that had been approved by the grassroots members at party conference.'

Another divisive issue was Ireland. The Official IRA bombed the Aldershot barracks in 1972, followed by a mainland bombing campaign by the Provisional IRA shortly afterwards. The left was put in a difficult situation; many backed the cause of Irish self-determination and a united Ireland but civilian deaths were undermining the cause and making it deeply unpopular with the British electorate.[8] Nevertheless, for some on the left it was a mark of honour to actively promote the activities of Sinn Féin politicians as a snub to the Tories (public) position that there would be no negotiation. In a move that sent *The Sun* into a tail spin, Livingstone invited Sinn Féin leader Gerry Adams to the GLC and Lambeth councillors parleyed with Sinn Féin council-lors.[9] Where the Labour left saw alignment with Sinn Féin was in their shared advocacy of bypassing a reactionary state legislature by focusing on local government and 'community empowerment'.[10] It was also in the context of the fight to promote Irish rights – in particular the cam-paigning for the release of the Birmingham Six and the Guildford Four, men wrongly imprisoned for pub bombings – that a new MP named Jeremy Corbyn came to prominence.

But one man stood out in particular as the firebrand of the left – Tony Benn. The media perpetuated the image of Benn as the dangerous radical, considered public enemy number one in Whitehall. He was certainly moving to the left at a time when many of his contemporaries were surrendering to the integrationists. He had loyally served in Callaghan's Cabinet throughout the 1970s, even after Wilson had crucified him following the Europe referendum. He stood in the tradition of Bevan and Foot, accepting the discipline of Cabinet responsibility in return for greater influence internally. During the heady days of class struggle in the late '70s, however, his Cabinet post was an albatross around his neck, silencing one of the left's key voices. The acid test was to see how effective he had been in his position when it came to influencing government policy; the conclusion would have to be that it did not add up to much.

In the early 1980s Benn was a household name, cast in the role of messiah or pariah by friends or enemies. By then free from Cabinet responsibility, Benn could speak his mind. He was less enamoured with Clause IV and the corporatist paternalism of the traditional labour left, instead looking to the new social movements to overcome the limitations of parliamentary socialism.[11] He articulated a vision of a new Labour Party as a constituency of different social struggles, drawing on the energy of the women's and black movements. This perspective was championed by figures such as Hilary Wainwright and implemented by Ken Livingstone during his leadership of the Greater London Council.

Benn's commitment to socialism was a uniquely esoteric British vision. His version of a socialist society was really one of greater democracy, greater worker involvement in industry, and a more accountable political system. All fine things – though they added up to a curious mix of radical liberal values and workers' control. Benn's rhetoric recalled an older radical tradition dating back to the Levellers in the English Civil War – popular democracy. In a speech to the PLP in 1980, Benn outlined his chief concern over the 'blockages to Parliamentary democracy', citing four major obstacles – the European Community, the IMF, the House of Lords and American military bases stationed in the UK.[12] There was a class argument in there somewhere, but it always presented itself as a demand for genuine national sovereignty, leaving out the question of the capitalist class more generally. Instead Benn's preferred target was the Political Class, meaning the politicians who were standing in the way of genuine democracy.

But as with most things in the Labour Party, it is what Benn *represented* that mattered most. He may have been a constitutionalist political reformer but he was a threat to the interests of the establishment because when he spoke, many people listened. Benn joined the ranks of the Labour left MPs (alongside Corbyn, Heffer and others) who were also embedded in campaigns and struggles, from anti-apartheid campaigns, to CND, to strikes. He was a proponent of *extra*-parliamentary action, as long as it was not *anti*-parliamentary action, because although he believed the House of Commons was still the best vehicle for securing a plural and democratic society, he was aware of the limitations of representative democracy. He called this the mosaic of the socialist movement. The GLC used the term 'rainbow coalition'. They meant the same thing: reaching out to the new left and social forces outside of the electoralist obsessions of Labour.

In this context, although the post was usually considered worthless, his bid for the deputy leadership position led to an almighty clash between different wings of the party. Competing against Healey, it was a hard-fought campaign between left and right, made especially vicious because the right had lost to Foot in the recent leadership contest and were desperate not to lose more ground. Benn did not shy away from accusations of being divisive but embraced them; he wanted to polarise opinion and speak for the many activists disappointed by Labour's lack of socialist vision, arguing: 'you can't go on forever calling yourself a socialist party when you are not...'[13]

Initial PLP support for Benn's candidacy was limited. Foot and Benn fundamentally disagreed on the reform process in Labour. After years of refusing to do so, Benn joined the *Tribune* group of MPs to try and secure some parliamentary backing, only to see them throw their support behind the soft left candidate John Silkin. The Bennite MPs launched their own left organisation called the Socialist Campaign Group shortly after the election. Benn was also attacked by the union leaders for dragging out the 'inner party democracy struggle' even longer. He drew far more support from the rank and file in both the party and the unions. His campaign attempted to overcome the lack of political engagement with the millions of affiliated supporters in the unions. Benn took the Labour Party's internal debates into the hearts of working communities, over the heads of the hostile union leaders, and won considerable support. His campaign focused on large public rallies, left caucus meetings in the trade unions, and fringe meetings at union conferences. His speaking tour took him to small pit villages where 300 miners would come out to hear him speak. Like the best parts of Bevanism, this breaking down of the traditional barrier between party and unions was a crucial component of the strategy of the new left, to forge a working alliance from below to push more radical demands.[14] This made Benn public enemy number one for many union chiefs.

After an exemplary campaign, Benn came within a whisker of winning, achieving 49.6 per cent to Healey's 50.4 per cent. Benn had won 80 per cent of the CLP votes and 40 per cent of the union votes. The narrow loss was made even more bitter when right-wing MPs who had backed Healey decamped to form the SDP only a few months later. The narrative at this time was that Labour was in another prolonged civil war and that the left led by Benn were intent on destroying the party with their 'kindergarten politics'.[15] This had the effect of making genuine attempts to democratise Labour appear to the electorate as utterly self-indulgent, a way of further isolating and invalidating the politics of the transformative wing.

The pressure on the left grew immense as Labour's support collapsed in the polls from 50 per cent in 1980 to 34 per cent and then 24 per cent by the time of Benn's deputy leadership challenge.[16] The right and the unions used this as a stick to beat the left with. The growing movement around Bennism came to a juddering halt in 1982 at a specially convened gathering at Bishops Stortford. It was a meeting of the great and the not so good – the NEC, the PLP, Trade Unionists for a Labour Victory, all together at the ASTMS country club. The SDP was used as a cudgel with which to beat the left – they were blamed for driving them out with the left's incessant demands and disruptions. When the Labour right threatened an all-out war against the left that might destroy the party, Benn bowed to pressure and began to demobilise his followers. The agreement outlined a truce premised on 'the election manifesto being based on the 1981 conference decisions, an acceptance of the current leadership of Foot and Healey and a moratorium on constitutional changes. In return there would be a cessation of witch hunts against the left.'[17] Chris Mullins proposed the truce, backed by Lansman, who argued that 'the left was at a low ebb. A truce was not a defeat.' But Aubrey Wise disagreed, wanting to keep the fight up: 'we had to activate the rank and file to defend their rights.'[18] The truce perspective won out and the left stood down, waiting for the 1983 election to resolve the contradiction – a move that would prove fatal.

The Return of Municipal Socialism

With Labour out of power in Westminster, a number of party activists reoriented to local government. They were initially very successful, with elections in 1978 and 1982 seeing a number of councils fall under left Labour control. These successes heralded a potential return of municipal socialism. The idea was to utilise the institutions of local power to support social causes and workers' struggles. This would widen democratic public participation in decision-making and open up the resources of local government to progressive and community causes. The new municipalists looked back to the decentralising traditions of 1920s and '30s, like those associated with the Poplar resistance and even Herbert Morrison. On the London County Council in the 1930s Morrison had used the rates to redistribute wealth from richer areas to poorer. Livingstone and the GLC saw the opportunity to apply similar principles in relation to transport policy.[19]

The left were keen to develop a new relationship between the party and its base, and between local governments and the residents and workers they represented. As David Blunkett explained in 1982, Labour councils were good at public spending, 'but they tend to be authoritarian: doing the right thing for people, rather than with them.'[20] The municipal socialist strategy required resistance to Thatcherite laws, but the Labour machinery was inveterately hostile to such an approach. For them, respect for parliamentary law was sacrosanct, even when the laws were regressive and unjust.

The turn to local government achieved initial successes in London, South Yorkshire and the West Midlands County Council. Away from Westminster, it allowed the left to implement parts of the AES in the microcosm of local government. Municipal socialism concentrated on job creation through providing local services. In Lambeth for instance, the council opened Consumer Advice Centres for local residents. The GLC launched the Greater London Enterprise Board, a revival of the NEB in the capital. The economic strategy involved 'outright public ownership of companies, equity stakes, part ownership with workers' trusts, the creation of producer cooperatives and "enterprise planning agreements"...'[21] Moreover, Livingstone and his deputy – John McDonnell – opened up the GLC to social movements. They provided meeting spaces for liberation campaigns and involved community activists in committees to ensure a range of voices were heard and to break up political elites and local bureaucracies. This strategy was referred to as 'in and against the state.'[22]

Radical newspapers like *Socialist Organiser* and *London Labour Briefing* were launched, seeking to coordinate and build a base among left councillors in the capital. But tactical differences emerged under the pressure of local administration. There was a fierce debate between *Briefing* and *Socialist Organiser* over whether it was acceptable for a Labour council to raise local rates to offset cuts – *Organiser* opposed the measure as an attack on working people. Nevertheless, *Briefing* achieved significant success with the election of Ken Livingstone to the GLC leadership in 1981 and winning left councillors across the capital. It subsequently played an important role in coordinating the initial resistance to defend local government from Thatcher's attacks. But for the municipal socialist strategy to work it would take an iron-clad united front of councillors and councils across the country to beat

Thatcher. When it came to the fight, as we shall see, the troops proved to be unreliable.

1983: The 'Longest Suicide' Myth

In her first administration, Thatcher was not performing well in the polls, despite her tough talk against the unions and the introduction of the right to buy council homes.[23] Labour looked like it could do well if it united behind its manifesto and pushed for a radical opposition. But political events and Labourite opportunism conspired to deliver the party a historic defeat in the general election of 1983.

After every election defeat there is a process to establish the causes of it. Usually this is more an ideological battle than an objective analysis of voting intentions. The right of the party were absolutely clear on the reason for the 1983 defeat: Britain under Thatcher was moving to the right and the hard left of the party had sunk Labour's electoral chances with 'the longest suicide note in history' – an epitaph provided by Gerald Kaufman MP. This became the standard mantra; in Wainwright's words, the left now had the 'mark of the devil'. The culture of the party changed as the right decided that the time for fooling around with 'utopian' demands was over. The 1983 defeat became incorporated into Labour Party myth, a scary story to tell the children at bedtime, a quick explanation to undermine any left arguments before they had even been made. 'You want to take us back to 1983?' was enough to shut down any criticism of the continuing right-wing drift.

Many blamed the Falklands War for Thatcher's win. When Argentina seized the Falkland Islands, the mainstream press went into a frenzy to agitate for a military response. As Thatcher debated whether to send a taskforce, Foot made the fatal error of goading her in Parliament to send troops. In the initial debate Foot's speech was essentially enthusiastic sabre-rattling. If the hope was that by appearing to be loyal military-loving nationalists, the party would be rewarded by the electorate, the reality was a cruel blow. Thatcher came across as a statesmanlike leader, Foot as an opportunist. The man associated with the Labour left since Bevan's day, a founder member of CND, fell into line behind

Conservative thinking. Thatcher had the satisfaction of seeing a left leader of the opposition submit and argue her own point of view. The subsequent rout at the 1983 election was in part the punishment for Foot's failure to oppose the war.

The actual cause of the defeat was a combination of factors. The first was the SDP, who split the Labour vote. Michael Meacher MP argued that it was not policies but internal politics that were responsible for the defeat. Commenting on Benn's campaign for Labour Deputy Leader in 1981, he said: 'It showed how bitterly the right will fight ... There was never less than half a page of vitriol in the press per day and the source was the right-wing of the Labour Party. They were feeding stuff into the press even though it did cataclysmic damage to the Labour Party. It was something like a bombing raid flattening everything in sight. It was more a cause of the defeat in 1983 than the Falklands.'[24] Before the 1983 election, the *Militant* editorial board concurred, arguing that John Golding, a key right-wing witch-hunter, was 'bleeding the party's election prospects to death' through his continued public attacks on the left.[25]

Meacher was right to point to the conflict between the left and the right of the party. The problem was that the leadership and principal spokespeople didn't really agree with the manifesto. The right had succeeded in securing a majority on the NEC just before the election, removing key left-wingers, which didn't help create a stable party united behind the election campaign. The campaign committee charged with building the campaign was dominated by the right and the centre, and included only a handful of left-wing figures.[26] Those charged with selling the manifesto to the electorate did not believe in it, while right-wing Labour MPs on the ground rubbished it, instead focusing on their individual roles as constituency MPs and distancing themselves from the party leadership. Paradoxically, the right-wing breakaway had pushed the party further to the right, as many Labour MPs tried to win back SDP voters by accommodating their views.

But the 1983 defeat also raises questions about the left's strategy. Subsequent analysis found that, when it came to policies alone, the Labour manifesto was actually *more* popular than that of the Tories.

From employment to inflation and government spending, even on scrapping Trident, the Labour manifesto scored more favourably than the Conservative one.[27] But people won't simply vote for left policies just by being presented with them, even if it is in their class interests. A radically different approach is needed, both patiently explaining the policies and creating the kind of social movement mobilisation that can generate the confidence to realise such goals. Benn's election campaign successfully mobilised the grassroots of the unions, and this could have formed the basis for a movement inside and outside Labour, not just transforming the party but also coordinating workers to take action against Thatcher. Benn may have backed extra-parliamentary struggle but the Bennites lacked the determination to bring it about.

In order to contain the 'wild' left, the right pushed forward a centre-left candidate to replace Foot – Neil Kinnock. He was much younger than Foot and from a solid working-class background, the son of a miner like Bevan. Previously he had associated with the left but now presented himself as a pragmatic candidate who could appeal to all sides of the Labour alliance, a reliable pair of hands. He promised the party that he could win elections – perhaps a foolish boast, but one that many were desperate to hear. Kinnock was a moderniser who argued that his party had to change to be electable. In the post-1983 context, modernisation meant defeating the left.[28]

The Two Fronts: Unions and Local Government

Although on the back foot, the left was still a considerable force within the party, especially at CLP, conference and NEC level, but they had marginal support in the PLP. The non-parliamentary left was very active in CND, supporting the 1984–5 miners' strike, and around various international initiatives. Crucially, it had strongholds that attracted national attention. Both Thatcher and Kinnock – for different reasons – knew that these strongholds had to be overcome and defeated, and be seen to be defeated. Emboldened by her election victory, Thatcher turned her attention to two bastions of socialism that now needed to be removed – the trade unions and the 'municipal socialism' of local government.

The second Thatcher administration proved a turning point. By passing a series of draconian anti-union laws in her first term, Thatcher clearly intended to go to war against workers. The unions were seen as a barrier to the principles of free-market monetarism, as obsolete institutions that frustrated wealth creation. As part of the reorganisation of British society, the unions had to be tamed – and the main enemy was the mighty National Union of Mineworkers, with their leader Arthur Scargill. The NUM occupied the nightmares of Tories after bringing down the Heath government in 1974.

To break the union, US-style policing methods were introduced, involving extreme violence unseen in generations against pickets and protestors. The Tories also prepared for the showdown with the miners by stockpiling coal and buying off other sections of workers in the run up to the fight. The threat of job cuts in the mining industry was seen by the NUM as a provocation which triggered a national strike that lasted almost a year. This was a strategic battle of historic importance – Thatcher versus the Guards Regiment of the British working class. The Tories hated the miners after the humiliation of Heath in 1974; in language that was rooted in the patriotic nationalism of the Cold War, they were the 'enemy within'. The grassroots of the Labour left along with other socialists threw themselves into solidarity work, raising money and food for the strikers and their families in addition to organising speaking tours around Europe and beyond. They also drew together women's, youth and LGBT struggles in support – Labour women contributing with a successful campaign against the page-three girl in the miners' newspaper. While conference delegates were supportive of the struggle, this did not translate into much support from MPs. Only the 'usual suspects', people like Corbyn, Benn, Skinner and McDonnell, threw themselves into the fight, visiting picket lines and using their public influence to back the strikers. But they were the minority – in January 1985, only 12 Labour MPs took part in a direct action protest where they refused to sit down in the Commons in order to force a debate on the strike. Campaign Group MPs took the lead, visiting picket lines and donating money to the miners' relief centres, but it took ten months for the PLP leadership to eventually come out in reluctant support of the strike, broadcasting clear reticence and slowing down efforts by many members to publicise greater support. Kinnock first visited a picket line in January 1985.[29]

Alongside the miners there was the second front: the left in local government. After its initial success in the 1978 and 1982 elections, the 'municipal socialism' strategy collapsed when the local alliance between the hard and soft left fell apart over the campaign against rate capping. The Tories introduced rate caps for several councils, limiting the amount that could be raised through local taxation and forcing cutbacks in services. The resistance strategy involved each local authority that was fighting the rate cap to refuse to set a budget until more money was provided, hopefully forcing a political crisis and a government U-turn. This was intended to occur at the same time as the miners' strike, as a 'second front'. Conference even adopted a motion in support of the councillors who wanted to defy the law, the first time the Labour Party had voted on a motion to endorse law-breaking.[30] But the rate-capping struggle started the week after the miners' strike collapsed, and early on in the campaign Livingstone broke ranks, organising the soft left councillors at the GLC to vote with the Tories to set a rate. His Deputy and Chair of Finance, John McDonnell, was furious that Livingstone had taken the GLC out of the fight so early on. As the threat of legal action mounted, many of the councillors in Town Halls across the country began to peel away from the fight. Within four months, only two councils remained, Liverpool and Lambeth. Their councillors were eventually surcharged and forced from office – but not before the image of left-wing figures like Liverpool's Derek Hatton and Lambeth's Ted Knight had been burned into the public consciousness. Their tenacity of resistance was largely helped by their local implantation – both Militant Tendency in Liverpool (who were influential on the council) and the radical left in Lambeth had built community solidarity campaigns, mobilising them alongside local trade unions to back the fight. Ultimately, without a national intervention by the Labour Party or a firm unity between the councils, it was impossible for a couple of local authorities to resist Thatcher's attack. The rate cap was introduced, eventually forcing Labour councils to pass on massive cuts to services during the late 1980s. Hoping to save their political careers, many on the soft left rounded on the councillors who had fought the cap, accusing them of gesture politics.

One effect of the rate-capping defeat was the rise of Socialist Action. Isolated at the GLC, with few friends on the left, Livingstone surrounded himself with members of the Socialist Action organisation – a split from the International Marxist Group who wanted a long-term orientation to Labour. Socialist Action developed a notoriety for being a somewhat clandestine organisation. Fearing they would fall victims to a purge of the left, they officially ceased to exist, instead maintaining themselves as a network of socialists allied to well-known left figures in the party. Their entire strategy was to adapt and ingratiate themselves with the Labour left, in order to influence it from within. They became passionate advocates of self-organisation for women and black Labour members, as well as supporters of third world anti-imperialist struggles.

But both struggles – the miners in the pit villages and the 'new urban left' in town halls across England – were defeated by the Tory government. The miners' return to work after a decisive defeat was a generational turning point, one that shaped the coming decades. It gave the Tories and the capitalist class confidence to continue to 'modernise' and redirect the economy towards low-paid, service sector jobs, and it convinced the Labour leadership that the old days of class war were finally over. Sensing the opportunity provided by the defeat of the miners, Kinnock singled out Militant for particular vitriol, using his 1985 conference party speech to crucify the Liverpool councillors – an event that has come to symbolise the Kinnock crusade against the hard left.[31] As Kinnock ranted, Eric Heffer, the long-time left MP for Liverpool Walton, got up from his seat on the NEC table and walked out in protest. David Blunkett was reportedly in tears afterwards – the hope of an alliance between the hard and soft left was slipping away.

Modernisation Begins

Kinnock reorganised the party in 1985, establishing the powerful Campaigns and Communications Directorate, headed by Peter

Mandelson and answerable to Kinnock directly, thereby circumventing the NEC. Mandelson wanted a new direction: media savvy, working with focus groups, and recruiting people from advertising. The public relations guru Philip Gould was brought in with the aim of making the party more appealing to the middle classes. The more Labour worried about the Tory spaniels in the press, the more panic at Labour's HQ on Walworth Road grew and voices clamoured for the need to silence the socialists in the party.

One central aspect of Kinnock's leadership was the co-option of parts of the soft left into the agenda of the right. The alliance between soft and hard left broke down as the former accepted Kinnock's integration-ist strategy and turned on their ex-comrades. The *Tribune* magazine and parliamentary group became ardent supporters of Kinnock, after Tony Blair and Gordon Brown played a prominent role in ensuring that the group in Parliament was loyal to the integrationist wing. *Tribune* attacked Benn's call for a general strike to support the miners, siding with Kinnock over Labour's (non-)strategy towards the strike.[32] They sought respectability and responsibility because they were the most shaken by the 1983 election defeat, making them susceptible to the demands for 'party unity' by way of disciplining the left to accept the perspectives and policies of the centre-right. They saw themselves as the moderate wing of the left who were best placed to tackle 'extremism' and undermine polarisation.

Similarly, the Labour Coordinating Committee, which had started off on the left of the party, went from advocating extra-parliamentary activity to being leading proponents of the 'legalistic' Kinnock regime. They removed left leaders, ousting George Galloway who had been central to their operation in Scotland. It was time to build a 'broad democratic left' and to expunge the ultra-left's leaders who had undermined the party's electoral chances with their 'gesture politics, sectarianism and opposition to new thinking'.[33] Kinnock skilfully peeled off the soft left leaders, Michael Meacher, David Blunkett and Tom Sawyer, by convincing them that the 'hard' left were too abrasive in their style, too narrow-minded, too dogmatic and would drive away Labour voters. The Labour leadership looked to break up the Socialist

Campaign Group of MPs by promising its members instant promotion in the PLP, so long as they broke publicly and issued denunciatory statements in labour movement journals like *Tribune*.[34] Some of the soft left backed Kinnock because they believed that it was better to influence him from within his camp than outside of it.[35] The belief that Kinnock was a 'prisoner of the right' turned out to be misconceived – Kinnock had gone over to the right and shared many of their views.[36]

Despite hopes of a turnaround in electoral fortune, 1987 delivered another stinging defeat for the party. The policy review post mortem concluded two years later that removing left policies from the manifesto would help modernise the party and win the centre ground. The assumption in Labour leadership circles was that the right-wing shift in the popular mood was unstoppable – all that could be done was to find ways of accommodating it. As such, 'modernisation' became the new slogan with which to fight an old war. The 1989 conference, under pressure from the modernisers, agreed to remove the commitment to renationalisation of privatised industries, to not restore trade union rights and to scrap unilateral nuclear disarmament, something Kinnock himself had until recently publicly championed.[37] The shadow of Nye Bevan was behind him in the conference hall.

The party was being out-manoeuvred by the Tories, they were compromising excessively and conceding too much ground. Thatcher and the mainstream media taunted the Labour leaders for their socialism, goading them that the handful of cases where socialists in the Labour Party had managed to organise a fight back against the Conservative juggernaut were evidence of the extremism of Labour more generally. They persuaded the Labour right that they had to defeat the left to have any hope of winning. Thatcher had not just won the argument in the country, she had won the argument in the Labour Party too.

Back in 1984 Denis Healey had campaigned for Tony Benn in the Chesterfield by-election to get Benn back into Parliament. He famously compared the unity of the party with figure skaters: 'Healey and Benn are like Torvill and Dean – I can't get the bugger off my back'. Back then the sense of being a united party with different wings who at least had to tolerate each other still had resonance, even with the right, but by the late 1980s this broad church was being demolished.

A united front was established to defend the left in 1986. Labour Left Liaison was made up of the campaigning left organisations in the party, including the Labour Women's Action Committee, the Labour Committee on Ireland, the LGBT and Black Sections, Socialist Organiser and Socialist Action. It published a semi-regular bulletin called *Witch-Hunt News*, detailing all of the expulsions and disciplinary procedures that were mounting against comrades. But the incredibly low vote that Benn and Heffer achieved in 1988 when they challenged Kinnock and Roy Hattersley for the Leader and Deputy Leader positions showed that even Benn's star was waning. Despite his high profile and notorious reputation as a still potent left firebrand, he secured only 11 per cent of the vote. Kinnock saw this as confirmation of his own course and doubled down on his efforts to transform the party.

The Fight for Self-organisation

One point of conflict with the modernisation agenda was over the struggle for self-organisation within Labour during the 1980s. At a time when the NEC was driving to control and streamline the image and governance of the party, self-organisation was viewed as a dangerously destabilising interruption. Women's groups had been active in Labour for years, though they were primarily limited to infrequent, uncontroversial social gatherings. That began to change in the late 1970s when feminist campaigners made contact with party members. Concerns over women's representation in the party structures began to grow. By the mid-decade a more radical organisation, the Labour Women Action Committee, was launched. LWAC formed alliances with parts of the left in Labour, intent on promoting left policies alongside more women representatives on committees and in Parliament. LWAC had emerged from the CLPD, a case of women on the left realising that self-organisation was necessary even to get their own comrades to recognise their political equality. They campaigned for the Annual Women's Conference to have some sovereign decision-making power and to be recognised as such by the party. Some gains were made. For instance, after 1984 every CLP had to have a women's officer. But still the problem of bureaucracy within Labour and the intransigence of those with the power to concede positions to 'uppity' women dogged the women's fight for much of the 1980s.

One crucial aspect to the struggle was that, in contrast to CLPD's line of giving trade unions more influence in Labour – bureaucracy and all – LWAC wanted to challenge the union leadership as well.[38] Their challenge to the power structures in the party was also a challenge to the men in charge of the movement. The right-wing officials of the unions were contemptuous of these moves; 'the problem is feminists and Militant' was the view of one at the time.[39] But they were actually two separate problems – Militant itself was opposed to separate sections or self-organisation in the 1980s, seeing them as distracting from class issues.

Even more controversial was the Black Sections campaign. Black voters had overwhelmingly voted Labour, loyal to the party that had facilitated the post-war Windrush generation's emigration to Britain. In addition the anti-colonial and anti-racist campaigning of some left MPs had made a lasting impression. Most of the migrants were working class and therefore saw Labour as their natural party, even if the actual number of black faces in Labour was often very small. Black members in London branches – prominent among them councillors Sharon Atkin, Linda Bellos, Narendra Makanji, Martha Osamor, Diane Abbott and Bernie Grant – started to organise black caucuses and wanted to network them more formally together to deepen Labour's presence in Black and Minority Ethnic (BME) communities. For the activist Marc Wadsworth, then a figure in Lambeth Labour politics, the urban uprisings in the early 1980s – in Brixton, Liverpool, Birmingham and Leeds – which involved large numbers from the black community, were 'a wake-up call to a society that was either indifferent or hostile to the demands of disenfranchised and disadvantaged black people'.[40] Just as women were doing, black members wanted more representation and – crucially – more policies aimed at supporting their communities. There were no black MPs, few black councillors and no black members on Labour's ruling National Executive. In the face of police violence, stop and search, and systematic discrimination in schools and in employment, Labour should no longer be allowed to rely on black votes without also dealing with black concerns.

By the late 1980s there were 35 Black Sections, mostly in London and the Midlands, but the workerist Militant Tendency in Liverpool were fiercely opposed, accusing sections of dividing the working class along colour lines. More significantly, Black Sections quickly ran into a huge fight with Kinnock's right-wing party-modernisation agenda. An NEC 'Positive Discrimination' sub-group, chaired by Jo Richardson MP, produced a report that supported Black Sections, but it was squashed on the grounds that such a move would create 'apartheid' in the Party. Undeterred, Black Sections lobbied for Black and Minority Ethnic parliamentary and council candidates in places where there were large numbers of African, Caribbean and Asian voters. This was a clear and present threat to Kinnock's plan to ensure that people loyal to him became MPs. Because the Black Sections worked closely with socialists, they were viewed with suspicion by the Kinnockites.

By 1987, being associated with Black Sections could result in a party member being disciplined. Three members of Roy Hattersley's Birmingham Sparkbrook CLP were expelled for setting up a Black Section. The first national explosion was over the removal of Sharon Atkin, a left Labour councillor in Lambeth, who was selected to stand in a parliamentary by-election in Nottingham East. She was the Black Sections chair. The NEC and local MPs responded vehemently – opposing any statements or organisation by the Black Sections and calling for a Birmingham public meeting (addressed by Atkin and Bellos) to be cancelled. When Atkin made comments that were critical of Labour's record on combating racism in response to an anti-Labour heckler at the meeting, they were used by the NEC to justify removing her as Labour's candidate.

Kinnock had Atkin removed and a leadership-friendly candidate imposed who subsequently lost the seat for Labour. After the NEC meeting Benn furiously condemned Kinnock's actions as 'judge, jury and executioner ... I've heard of one member one vote but I did not know that meant that the leader was the one member and his was the only vote.'[41]

There was success in the 1987 election with the election of Bernie Grant, Paul Boateng, Keith Vaz and Diane Abbott, the first black woman MP, after a hard fought campaign in Hackney North. But the left-wing black Haringey councillor Martha Osamor was removed as a candidate in the 1989 Vauxhall by-election because of her association with Black Sections and the hard left, and Kate Hoey manoeuvred into place as a way of neutralising the left in Lambeth. Although there were some victories in the form of the historic new cohort of four black MPs, the Labour Party nullified the more radical demands of the campaign, including its 'Black Agenda' document, diverting it into a case of mere representation and ignoring many of the more radical political points that black members were raising. Marc Wadsworth concluded that 'though the Black Sections managed to get "black faces in high places", the movement itself was destroyed from within by the machinations of an unforgiving Labour Party and some short-sighted opportunists.'[42] Respected Black intellectual Darcus Howe was more critical, arguing that the Black Sections were essentially a 'quest of the black, professional middle class for power-sharing with its white counterparts.'[43] The Black Sections were also inevitably pulled into the machinations of internal Labour politics instead of turning outwards into the urban communities being blighted by Thatcherism.

The Coup de Grace Against Militant

Militant Tendency was singled out for destruction during the late 1980s by Kinnock and the NEC. The growth of Militant in the mid-1970s had been of concern to the party apparatus. The clashes between left and right in the National Organisation of Labour Students became a regular feature of NUS conferences. The right-wing regularly picked fights with Militant, staging walkouts and protests. Exposing the depth of anti-Trotskyist feeling, the right opposition named themselves *Operation Icepick* – a reference to Trotsky's assassination by a Stalinist agent. At the 1981 Labour conference a number of Militant delegates had their credentials revoked and weren't allowed a vote. Outside the student movement, Militant expanded its operation, establishing strong bases in some unions. They offered simple and popular arguments on nationalisation and trade union militancy, to be achieved through a Marxist-led Labour Party.

With Militant influence spreading, Reg Underhill returned to his role as witch-finder general in the fight against entryism, compiling a collection of documents he claimed proved Militant's semi-clandestine activity. The left on the NEC – Heffer, Benn, Jo Richardson and others – were opposed to publishing Underhill's report and used their majority on the organisational subcommittee to block it on the grounds it would provide fuel for a witch-hunt. Right-wing stalwarts like John Golding led the charge, supporting publication of the report and arguing for a return of the proscribed list at almost every NEC, despite being knocked back repeatedly. Eventually Golding's tenacity paid off. His opposition in the party and pressure from the media to control the left pushed the leader and the soft left to agree to an inquiry into Militant. Foot meekly added the proviso that there should be no witch-hunt.[44] The NEC voted 16 to 10 to begin the rehabilitation of the proscribed list, this time revamped as a 'register of approved organisations' which was agreed at the 1982 conference. The unions had no appetite for a witch-hunt and stood firm against immediate expulsions, but at the same time they agreed to the register, which would later be used as the basis for the purge of the left.[45] The register had been a compromise proposal from the soft left, but it served the right's interests, beginning the process of rooting out organised oppositional tendencies.

Militant's editorial board was instructed to provide details of 'its aims, officers, employees, membership and accounts'. This would supply the evidence of a 'party within a party' as well as a hit list for expulsions. Despite Militant's reputation on the left as a sectarian organisation that was hard to work with, a number of left organisations, including the CLPD and the LCC, initially refused to register in defiance of the witch-hunt. This solidarity did not last long however. The purge became possible in the mid-1980s because many of the alliances that the soft left had built around Benn were fracturing. By then a number of *Tribune*

MPs, in alliance with council leaders like David Blunkett and the LCC, were working together in pursuit of a more moderate left strategy in the party. The LCC had defended Militant in 1982, but by 1985 they were handing over 'dossiers' of evidence to the NEC to help expel Militant activists from the party. The NEC expelled Ted Grant and four other Militant editors in 1983 on the eve of the Bermondsey by-election. In response, Militant's conference in Wembley was attended by over 3,000 people, including 1,600 Labour delegates.

The party investigation into Militant activities in Liverpool in 1986 was damning, effectively concluding that it was a Mafia-esque operation that was bringing the party into disrepute. Militant were vulnerable to the attack as their local support base had been eroded. During the rate-capping struggle, they had unintentionally broken their crucial alliance with the local trade unions when Liverpool Council terminated the contracts of many in the council workforce under legal advice. This action was intended as an escalation by the council, meant to expose the full extent of the implications of Thatcher's attack on the city. But the unions and workforce were furious. When the councillors were surcharged the planned 'general strike' of workers in Liverpool failed to materialise.

Eventually key members of the Liverpool District Labour Party were hauled up for questioning. They were confronted with various charges, including intimidation and violence and mismanagement of council funds. The more serious charges of violence were largely ignored; most were expelled merely for being associated with Militant. Larry Whitty drew up charges against 12 members of the Liverpool District Labour Party; Militant responded by lodging an injunction in the High Court against the proceedings on the grounds that they did not conform to natural justice. As the Labour Party is a members' institution, however, they can organise their own internal affairs, including riding roughshod over democratic rights. The NEC ignored the ruling by the judge that natural justice was *advisable* in such a situation, promoting a walkout by the left NEC members. The war of attrition ground on for months, until eventually the political forces of the right managed to marshal the strength and determination to expel several members – some key leaders like Hatton alongside other rank-and-file activists who had merely published articles in *The Militant*.

Nobody witnessing the hearings could have concluded they were imbued with impartiality or natural justice. Eric Heffer described the scene:

> I went along with Derek Hatton as a witness to his interrogation by the inquiry team and I must say that from the behaviour of one person [inquiry chair Charles Turnock] in particular, it wouldn't have been out of place for him to have been wearing jackboots. As a former chair of the Organisation Sub-Committee, I have conducted a number of such inquiries in various areas, but I have never seen anything like this person's behaviour. It was disgusting, nothing but a McCarthyite inquisition.[46]

More expulsions followed and entire CLPs were targeted for suspension and reorganisation in a repeat of the 1950s. By 1991, 215 people had been expelled, but their wider political influence was also neutered. The key turning point was the attack on the LPYS, Militant's main base of support. The NEC cancelled the youth conference in 1987 and then reduced the age limit to cut off the Militant leadership of LPYS. Militant kept a brave face as their entire project of transforming Labour into a socialist party began to collapse under the hammer blows of the right. They hoped that any serious witch-hunt would only strengthen them, as party members would side with them against the bureaucracy. This did not materialise. Abandoned by many on the soft left, Militant's operational capacity to remain in the party was severely limited. They split in the early 1990s, Peter Taaffe leading most of the members out to form the Socialist Party, while Ted Grant remained with a rump of those committed to carrying on.

Thatcher herself was brought down by a combination of internal Tory divisions over Europe and her catastrophic Poll Tax – a supreme piece of legislative hubris from a government that thought it couldn't be beaten. Spearheaded by Militant, socialists both inside and outside Labour helped launch a mass non-payment campaign which saw around 16 million people take part. Pressure was brought to bear on the remaining left-run councils to refuse to collect it, or to find ways of sabotaging collection. Although only 15 Labour MPs backed the Anti-Poll Tax Federation, it was clear that serious numbers of rank-and-file members and – most importantly – the wider public supported a very dynamic campaign. Tommy Sheridan, a Militant member from Scotland, was made the chair of the Federation, triggering his expulsion from the party. But again the class divisions in Labour were exposed. Kinnock was inevitably hostile to any protests and serious mobilisations against the tax, instead proposing an unwieldy alternative local tax system. The Labour Party instructed its councillors to collect the tax in the face of mass opposition, and disciplined or even expelled councillors who refused. Outside of Parliament the tactics of the socialist left succeeded, and after a huge protest in London in 1990 where the police lost control, the Poll Tax was shelved. Socialists had scored a huge victory against one of the most reactionary pieces of legislation dreamt up in the modern age, and the protest movement they helped organise did more to stop Thatcher's policies than all the meek arguments in Parliament from Kinnock. Her flagship policy crushed and with little internal support left, Thatcher tearfully tendered her resignation to the Queen.[47]

Victory For the Right, But at What Cost?

It was a testament to how far the party had come under Kinnock after 1983 that the 1992 manifesto didn't mention the word socialism once. In 1974 the party had declared it had 'Socialist aims and ... [was] proud of the word' – under Kinnock it was ashamed. The red flag was hauled down and replaced by the less radical looking red rose as party logo. These changes didn't do much good. John Major's Tories won the 1992 election, with a much reduced majority but nonetheless big enough to form a government. The resignation of Kinnock after the unexpected election defeat should have gone down as a mark of the failure of his strategy – instead the party chiefs redoubled their efforts to move the party to the right. Voter research from Kinnock's media department found that Labour lost because it 'was still the party of the winter of discontent; union influence; strikes and inflation; disarmament, Benn and Scargill'.[48] Kinnock's legacy for the left was a deeply damaging one, even more so for the fact that as a young man he had been one of them. Now, like Michael Foot before him, he was another monument to the tragic fate of left-wing MPs who became party leaders. When Kinnock visited Eric Heffer on his death bed in 1991, the veteran Liverpudlian MP – bitter and angry at the man who had trampled on his life's work – told him, 'It's you who should be dying, not me.'

The general political and organisational retreat of the left under the hammer blows of the right had given Kinnock a free hand to dispense with remaining troublemakers. The NEC became adept at witch-hunting and smashing the left wherever they were influential. Left candidates for elections were removed by the NEC, to ensure the party had 'the right message' for the electorate. Lol Duffy in Wallasey was rejected by the NEC panel in favour of Angela Eagle, despite being the clear favourite of the local party. Socialist Organiser and the Black Sections were banned, and Lambeth Council had its Labour leaders removed by the NEC in 1991. All fell under the sword of internal investigations, deselection, expulsions or suspensions. The party centralised like never before, policing its ranks and purging dissent as the right secured their position in the apparatus and wielded power mercilessly against socialists.

Despite the fatalistic claims that the drift to the right in the 1980s was inevitable and nothing could be done but find new ways to surrender, there were alternatives. The miners did nearly win – on at least two occasions when workers linked to the coal supply chain threatened strike action Thatcher thought she might lose. There were other opportunities, for instance the strikes by dockers in 1986 or of the print workers in 1987. Labour did little to support these actions both because they reflected the passivity of the TUC and were convinced trade unionism was unpopular. Faced with the most powerful regiments of the working-class movement being picked off one by one, the official leadership of the movement did precious little to save its forces. Kinnock and Labour offered no alternative. But the left at least grasped at something in those days – that there was resistance, and that if it was generalised and given a clear national leadership then a different course of history might be arrived upon. But as with the 1926 general strike, Labour was stuck fast by electoral gravity to its parliamentary orientation, and the Labour left, occasionally heroic and self-sacrificing, were unable to escape the stranglehold of the right of their party.

The isolation of the left through the purging of policies and people was driven primarily by the desire of the integrationist right to accommodate to the demands of British capitalism for a new consensus, championed by the Tory Party and relayed in the editorials of the right-wing newspapers. This whip of accommodation led to some unsavoury decisions concerning inner-party democracy and representation. By the time Kinnock quit as party leader, the conference was a hollowed-out affair, lacking in real debate, setting the scene for the stage managed events of later years. Manifestos were in the hands of the Policy Forum and carefully selected review committees that guaranteed the policies the leadership wanted.

But for the new right, these changes did not go far enough. They wanted a new strategy, one that not only appealed to the populist right-wing agenda of Thatcherism, but that properly subsumed Labour into an emerging neoliberal consensus in a way that the older social democratic generation couldn't do. The problem for the Young Turks on the right was that Kinnock did not go far enough, he was not bold enough in fundamentally altering the nature of Labour's relationship to the unions and capital. Kinnock couldn't offer them anything new. It was this realisation by a group of Labour MPs around Blair and Brown that spurred them on to radicalise the 'modernisation' process and try to change the very nature of the Labour Party itself.

7

The Single Idea

'It is us, the new radicals, the Labour Party modernised, that must undertake this historic mission. To liberate Britain from the old class divisions, old structures, old prejudices, old ways of working and of doing things, that will not do in this world of change.'

Tony Blair, 1999

The 1992 leadership election produced no surprises. John Smith was elected leader, promising a moderate social democracy which would continue the reforming practices of the Kinnock years, keeping the left marginalised and moving the party further to the centre. Under pressure from the media over Labour's links with the unions, Smith successfully won the abolition of the trade union block vote at the party conference in 1993, the same year that Tony Benn was voted off the NEC.

After John Smith died suddenly in 1994, three leadership contenders threw their hats into the ring: John Prescott, Margaret Beckett and Tony Blair. It is revealing at this point that the left in the party was unwilling to field a candidate – centre-left MP Robin Cook refused to stand due to his fear that he would be unpopular with the electorate and might cost Labour the 1997 election. This represented a significant victory for the right: they had indoctrinated the left in the fear of their own unelectability.

Tony Blair emerged as the 'obvious choice' candidate and won. Young, professional and ambitious, he presented himself as the leader to get Labour back into power. The new leadership based itself on the managerial machine that Kinnock had built in his war against the left. Ensconced in Millbank Tower, the inner leadership formed a party within a party, autonomous and highly centralised. Unlike Kinnock,

Blair had never been a socialist or even a social democrat. His father was a conservative-minded self-made man and Tony was largely apolitical until his wife Cherie recruited him to Labour. He wasn't 'betraying' his roots as he had no roots to betray. Nevertheless, Blair saw himself as destined to fulfil the revisionist project: 'With Neil Kinnock's election as leader we began a long march of renewal. That project was taken forward by John Smith. We owe it to them both ... to finish the journey from protest to power.'[1] This Kinnockite mantra, that the left was only good for protesting and only ruthless right-wing pragmatism could achieve power, was by now an article of faith among the moderates. Being 'a party of protest' was both reckless and useless – only parliamentary success mattered. The Millbank Tendency replaced the Militant Tendency as the insurgent faction. In 1996, funded by rich backers like Lord Sainsbury, the Blairites launched a pressure group called Progress to further their aims in the party.

Blair and his allies were clearer than their predecessors about what needed to be changed. New Labour architect Peter Mandelson cited the Labour left in Lambeth by way of explaining his scorn for socialists: 'I remember being warned by a local Labour activist as we canvassed in a local estate one Sunday morning that the party must at all costs avoid "compromising with the electorate".'[2] Mandelson believed that compromise was essential – compromise with the right-wing media, with big business and with rich entrepreneurs. New Labour was founded on an appeal to class forces traditionally outside of Labour's voting base – not to win them to a specifically social democratic politics, but to accommodate their prejudices and the assumptions of post-Thatcherite Britain. Mandelson frankly admitted that New Labour was comfortable with people 'getting filthy rich'.

For What Shall It Profit a Man, If He Gain the Whole World, and Suffer the Loss of His Soul?

The landslide 1997 electoral victory produced a huge sigh of relief from millions across the country exhausted after 18 years of Tory rule. Labour won 418 seats in the Commons. After the election, the MPs crowded into Parliament to hear a speech from a triumphant Blair during which he warned against backbench rebellions which brought down Labour governments in the past: 'They were all swept away, rebels and loyalists alike. Of course, speak your minds. But realise why you are here: you are here because of the Labour Party under which you fought.'[3] The Blairite dream promised electoral victory, but only if the party was willing to forfeit its soul, to abandon its traditions and assumptions and embark on a new path.

Many of the party membership, worn down after years in opposition, were willing to follow Blair to his promised land. Despite the Blairite trumpeting of the 'new mood', New Labour was born out of defeats, not victories. Even some of the old guard could see what was happening. Kinnock initially railed in private against the new leader, despairingly concluding: 'he's sold out before he's even got there ... Tax, health, education, unions, full employment, race, immigration ... It won't matter if we win, the bankers and stockbrokers have got us already, by the fucking balls, laughing their heads off.'[4] Gordon Brown was an ally of Blair throughout this period, though always with more concern to appease the old Labour crowd. Roy Hattersley was inveterately hostile to Blairism, describing it as 'a Cuckoo in the nest', building a new party from within Labour.[5] A similar view was expressed by John Golding, who had relished his role in breaking the 'loony left' in the 1980s but was circumspect about what followed. After the Labour Party conference in 1998, travelling back on a train with his nemesis Dennis Skinner, he bitterly summed up the rise of Blairism: 'we both lost; your socialism and my Labour.'[6]

The right have always built their politics around the economic orthodoxies of the time: in the 1950s it was the mixed economy, in the 1990s it was the free market and globalisation. Socialism seemed dead and buried by the '90s; Thatcherism and the fall of the Berlin Wall had seen to that. Now the party leadership spoke with one voice, making an unequivocal claim to represent the 'pensée unique'[7] of individuals and overwhelming market forces – neoliberalism. Like all reformers, Blair adopted a new ideology to remake the party in the image that he thought would best accord with the new era – the Third Way. Blair described the Third Way as 'draw[ing] vitality from the uniting of the two great streams of left-of-centre thought – social democracy and liberalism – whose divorce did so much to weaken the progressive policies across the west'.[8] Social democracy was now to be replaced with social liberalism – a qualitative ideological shift. This represented a hybrid, taking the apparent vitality of the market driven economy and integrating it into the public sector. The tone was set early on, with the proposal in 1995 to replace the social democratic Clause IV with a more liberal version – closer to the spirit of Jean-Jacques Rousseau than to Hardie – scrapping the commitment to the socialisation of industry and replacing it with a vaguer commitment to 'a common endeavour'.

The fight for the defence of Clause IV mounted by Arthur Scargill and others was intense. The debate happened across the party, with Blair personally touring CLPs and working-men's clubs. In order to bypass the 'cranks and extremists', CLPs were instructed to ballot every member, not just local party delegates. Blairite union leader Alan Johnson convinced his members in the UCW to back the new Clause IV. The leadership frantically worked the media to pitch Blair as the modernising reformer against the tired old backward-looking left. The new wording wasn't released until a month before the vote, and the tight deadlines meant the Defend Clause IV campaign had an almost impossible task to mobilise the constituents.[9] A specially convened conference voted overwhelmingly to change the constitution. Blair had pushed this 'symbolic change through a demoralised party, desperate for electoral success, and willing to pay almost any price for it'.[10] This was followed in the 1997 manifesto by a promise that unions 'would get fairness but no favours from a Labour government'. Taken together, Blairism was a package of measures designed to erode and eventually cut the link with the working-class base of the party, the better to serve the needs of the global elites. Most of the newer members fervently believed in the new ideology; many older Labour members went along with it as the price they had to pay to get back into government.

For Blair and Mandelson, their own politics and that of the New Labour project more broadly descended not from a specific Labourism or the principle of working-class autonomy or representation, but from a more nebulous 'progressive' movement. The term 'progressive' encapsulated the liberal tradition of Gladstone and Lloyd George as much as – if not more than – Keir Hardie.[11] The Progress philosophy was set out in Blair's 1999 Labour Party conference speech: 'The 21st century will not be about the battle between capitalism and socialism but between the forces of progress and the forces of conservatism. They are what hold our nation back. Not just in the Conservative Party but within us, within our nation.'[12]

But the Blairites weren't only a new ideological current. They were the product of the realignment of British society under Thatcher, the destruction of old industries and unions, of old communities and ways of living, to be replaced by the emergence of the new media economy, and the growing influence of public relations and lobbyists. They were people who lived in a world of corporate shindigs, Non-Governmental Organisations and political consultancies, part of a revolving door of connections between money, capital and politics. For them, neoliberal politics was the new common sense; they lived that world, just as Hardie and Nye Bevan had lived the world of the blue-collar working class years earlier.[13]

The left were faced with the enormous challenge of carving out a space in the New Labour project. The Blair years were characterised by retreat, both organisationally and politically. New Labour was not merely a rebranding exercise, it was a different kind of party, one in which the left were to be completely isolated and, preferably, driven to extinction. Members left in droves over policies they could no longer stomach, resulting in a rightward spiral where – with a handful of exceptions – only Blairites became MPs and many CLPs were seized by the right. The Socialist Campaign Group, the radical left-wing of the PLP, made up only 7 per cent of the MPs after the 1997 Labour landslide.

New Labour was a party built for globalisation, an aggressive advocate of neoliberalism and the benefits of incorporating profit-making enterprises into the public sphere. Nationalisation and collectivism were considered dead and buried, to be replaced by public-private partnerships and Private Finance Initiatives, mediated through the market.

Attacks on asylum seekers, hounding people on welfare, pandering to the reactionary newspapers and increasing the prison population were no longer the preserve of the Tories. The pernicious targeting of some groups was deeply worrying; Alan Simpson MP felt that 'In the same way that the Mafia asks you to destroy something precious to demonstrate loyalty, [New] Labour MPs were asked to give a kicking to some of the most vulnerable in society.'[14] Even policies heralded as progressive, such as funding increases for the NHS and schools, came with a sinister logic according to which the private sector had to be integrated into, and profit from, the public sector. Even the national minimum wage was brought in at very low level to reassure business interests.

The Vice Grip

New Labour was an exercise in management. Blairites would *manage* conferences, *manage* dissent, *manage* risk, *manage* the media, all with a focus on procedural conformity and centralism. Convinced that the media decided elections, they became obsessed with the tabloids to the point of paranoia.[15] Although party managers wanted to move away from the 'dogmatic, activist driven culture' they associated with old Labour generally and the left more specifically,[16] the Blairites themselves acted with the passion and discipline of Bolsheviks, believing fundamentally in the historic and essential role of a disciplined party in the furthering of their politics.[17] Management became the new form of integrationist logic, involving the application of ruthless measures to ensure electoral success. This required preventing the crystallisation of a transformative left by blocking any avenue for possible left influence.

Labour conferences became thoroughly stage-managed affairs, more of a corporate networking opportunity than a policy-making body. The rules were changed in 1998 to stop CLPs submitting motions directly to conference; instead they had to go to the National Policy Forum, a tightly controlled 'consensus' body run by the Blairites. Central to this consensus was weakening the union link. Social liberalism had no love for trade unions. The goal was to render them mere subordinates in a partnership that prioritised business interests. At the national conference in 1995 the union votes were reduced to 50 per cent of the conference total – a sign of the new commitment to distance the party from its trade union past. In *The Road to the Manifesto*, Blair explained that the New Labour approach was 'based on stake holding, not an old-fashioned war between bosses and workers'.[18] As we have seen, Labour's leaders had never really believed in the 'old-fashioned war'. But Blairism rejected old fashioned solutions; it was deeply antagonistic to corporatism and collectivist socio-economics. New Labour constantly reassured the public that there would be 'no return to flying pickets, secondary action, strikes with no ballots or the trade union law of the 1970s' – in other words, to the time when trade unionism was an effective movement. A telling indication of the direction that Blair wished to travel was his praise for Amicus leader Ken Jackson, who called for the TUC to scrap its annual conferences and merge with the CBI, to end the 'us and them mentality'.[19]

After the successful alliances forged in the 1970s between the trade unions and the left, the acquiescence of the unions was a particular blow to the socialists in Labour during this time. For instance, during the debates at the joint Shadow Cabinet/NEC meetings to agree the 1997 election manifesto, Dennis Skinner argued for greater workers' rights and more comprehensive unemployment benefits, but none of the trade union delegates would second his proposals, despite them being union policy.[20] These retreats by the unions were largely due to the collapse of trade unionism as a direct action movement in Britain. By 1999 the number of days lost to strikes was only 242,000 – a number that steadily declined throughout the following years. Just as New Labour had absorbed the Thatcherite consensus into its bones, so too the unions had absorbed Thatcher's anti-union rhetoric; they also believed that strikes and working-class militancy were things of the past. The union leaders ruthlessly policed their own members using the anti-union laws. Without sustained left pressure from their grassroots, union bureaucrats could freely side with the New Labour bureaucrats without fear of repercussions from their own members.

The key factor sustaining the control exercised by the Millbank Tendency was the sheer relief felt by the unions that Labour was electable again. They may have grumbled in public but within the Labour Party their half-hearted opposition was easily defeated by the might of the Blairite machine. Millbank operators kept the unions in line by threatening a return of a Tory government if they didn't back the vision and course of action of Blair. This vice grip was too much for some – the RMT and FBU unions quit Labour during this period. The FBU disaffiliated after the 2002 firefighter's strike, which was savaged by the Labour government and led to defeat. The RMT – a founding union of the party – was the first in its history to be expelled, after it backed socialists standing against Labour in Scottish elections.

A Last Stand?

The marked difference from Wilson's day was the lack of even rhetorical concessions to the left when Labour won in 1997. It was depicted as a victory for New Labour, for the values of the new Progress wing of the party; everything else was irrelevant. The left's concerns – for a restoration of trade union rights, for reinstatement of the recently sacked Liverpool dockers, for renationalisation – were all ignored. Even the jewel in the crown of the NHS came under attack from the social liberal agenda as private sector interests ate away at the core of the health service.

Although Blairism was hegemonic it was not unchallenged. As New Labour raced giddily on, opposition grew from within and without the party. There was still a mood among many in the rank and file of the party that was critical of the move to the right. Well-known leftists such as Skinner, Livingstone and Diane Abbott all got sizeable votes at the NEC elections, as did Jeremy Corbyn, 'internationalist and indefatigable campaigner for everything the leadership disdains',[21] who got 25,000 votes. Even centre-ground candidates like David Blunkett and Robin Cook had to trade on some left rhetoric to ensure a larger share of the vote. To stop this the rules were changed in 1998 to prevent left MPs from being elected through the constituency seats. To get rank-and-file members elected, the Centre Left Grassroots Alliance (CLGA) was launched by activists around the CLPD, and succeeded in getting four left-wingers elected to the NEC in 1998 amid fierce media criticism. Their victory was seen as a huge blow to Millbank who had spent a fortune promoting their slate. But on the NEC the CLGA members proved hopelessly outnumbered, in most votes they were the only four to oppose the leadership.[22]

Outside of the NEC, the left pushed for more constituency-based organisation. In 2004, along with CLP activists, a number of unions both inside and outside Labour (RMT, FBU, CWU and BFAWU) set up the Labour Representation Committee, chaired by John McDonnell, to push for left policies. As Owen Jones described it in 2011: 'Like LRC 1.0, it has the same underlying argument: working-class people currently lack effective political representation, and something should be done about it.'[23] The LRC was an explicitly socialist organisation in the belly of the New Labour machine. In the unions, left leaders like Mark Serwotka in the PCS and Billy Hayes in the CWU became more common, forming a block dubbed 'The Awkward Squad' in the media. The level of industrial militancy was far below what it had been in the 1970s, but they stood out for their opposition to the Blairite party managers.

Others were also uncomfortable with Labour's lurch to the right, and in 2003 the centre-left Compass group was launched. Its manifesto *The Good Society* argued that New Labour had gone too far towards 'unaccountable and unacceptable concentrations of wealth and power' that 'not only remained untouched, but have been encouraged'. The soft left, led in Parliament by John Cruddas, saw their role as being to challenge the outright free-market orientation, but they also distanced themselves from the actions of the 1980s 'hard left'. Cruddas himself had been in the core Blairite team until 2001, but he and the others who went on to found Compass became disillusioned with the extreme neo-liberalism of the New Labour message. Instead of direct 'campaigning' as the left understood it, Compass favoured an orientation to NGOs and pressure groups to lobby for policy changes on issues like an energy windfall tax. Attempting to carve out a space for a more plural party culture, Compass was a prolific publisher of pamphlets and organiser of conferences but found itself perpetually frustrated by the 'command and control' nature of the New Labour administration.[24]

Opposition occasionally found its way onto the conference floor, though the balance of forces meant that only one set-piece battle could be launched each year. These fights ranged from pensions to civil liberties to foreign policy. While the left or the unions occasionally managed to win a vote at conference, the right either forced it to be taken again until they won, or Blair and Gordon Brown declared in advance they would ignore the vote – as Labour leaders had done previously.

One notable victory against the regime was when Ken Livingstone defied the Blairite machine and won the election for London Mayor in 2000. Livingstone was the firm favourite to stand as the Labour candidate, 60 per cent of party members backed him and 72 per cent of the union affiliates, but he was ousted by Blairite manoeuvring and replaced by Frank Dobson. Ignoring Millbank, Livingstone submitted his papers to stand and was immediately expelled from Labour. He won the election by over 200,000 votes (beating Dobson into third place), clearly supported and buoyed up by many London Labour Party members who were willing to campaign even for a non-Labour candidate, in anger against Blair's reforms.[25] Labour allowed Livingstone back in during his first term, realising that his support among members was substantial.

Livingstone's time as London Mayor was seen as a continuation of his time at the GLC – he even started his victory speech with the knowing 'Now, where was I?', before using the (far more limited) resources of the Greater London Assembly to pursue many of the same community projects he had been involved with in the 1980s. Once again he surrounded himself with Socialist Action associates, including John Ross as director of economics and business, and Simon Fletcher as his chief of staff. The secretive network had spent much of the 1990s ingratiating themselves into various organisations like Labour CND, and saw themselves as promoting 'broad left' politics, i.e. backing soft left politics as a way of promoting progressive politics more generally. They later pushed a form of Stalinism, calling for alliances with 'progressive capitalists' which fitted a wider softening of their previous socialist

politics.[26] But their icon Livingstone appalled many of his comrades
on the left when in June 2004 as mayor he urged tube workers to cross
RMT picket lines – clearly seeing it as his job to 'keep London moving'
at the expense of workers' demands.

It was foreign policy that gave the Labour left a chance to escape
the party straitjacket and reconnect with the wider public. The scale
of the opposition to the Iraq war in 2003 was phenomenal, producing
a social movement unrivalled in modern British history, larger even
than the Poll Tax protests. The democratic deficit between the British
public, including many Labour members, and the leaders of the PLP
was obvious. Many felt the attack on Iraq was based on spurious
claims, motivated by an imperial agenda coming from Washington,
and that Blair was supporting an illegal war. The struggle outside
found its way into the Commons as Blair was rocked by two huge
backbench rebellions, one in February 2003 and the next a month later.
He allowed a debate in Parliament in March on the eve of the attack,
giving his reasons for supporting the US-led invasion, citing the threat
of 'Weapons of Mass Destruction' and the continued instability in the
region created by Saddam Hussein. Corbyn, McDonnell and the others
on the left opposed the war on principle. They rejected the arguments
around the WMDs and argued for Iraq's national sovereignty in the face
of unwarranted international aggression. Robin Cook resigned from
the Cabinet in protest, followed by Clare Short. In all, 121 Labour MPs
voted against the war in February, rising to 139 in March, in one of the
largest backbench rebellions in parliamentary history. Alan Simpson
MP, from the Socialist Campaign Group, launched Labour Against the
War with the backing of Benn and Corbyn, which provided a much
needed profile for the beleaguered left in the party. Internal challenges
to the leadership over Iraq saw manoeuvres at the conference in 2003,
where the entire Labour foreign policy was bundled together, forcing
delegates to vote down everything if they wanted to oppose the Iraq
invasion.[27]

Very few of the protestors joined Labour – why would you join the
war party? – but it established a relationship of trust and camaraderie
between many thousands of people alienated from mainstream politics

alongside left Labour activists. Jeremy Corbyn in particular was a prominent figure in the Stop The War Coalition. This alliance would be renewed again during the anti-austerity struggles after 2010, with McDonnell and Corbyn also playing key roles in the various campaigns that were launched. That at least some Labour MPs were on 'the right side of history' was clear to many thousands of people desperate for change.

The Cost of Blairism

New Labour tried to create a new ideology for the modern age. But the idols of free-market social liberalism turned out to be false. It was a reactionary creed, an economic and social philosophy that, termite-like, ate away at the social base. In its policies, Blairism succeeded in building an alliance with the liberal and conservative middle classes, an electoral calculation that was sustainable for a while, but at the expense of Labour's working-class vote. The neoliberal policies did little to rebuild communities shattered by Thatcherism where precarious ser-vice-sector jobs continued to replace the industries that used to give communities a sense of pride and purpose. The rise of the BNP and then UKIP attested to the alienation of huge swathes of deindustrialised England and Wales; racist demagogues provided easy answers to the generational social crisis facing many working people.

By triangulating into the centre, social liberalism blurred the lines between New Labour and Conservatism. Bill Morris, head of the T&G in 2002, summed up the problems of New Labour in an article for his union's magazine: 'My fear is that by pursuing policies like foundation hospitals, university top-up fees and describing decent trade unionists as wreckers and dinosaurs, Labour is creating a dangerous divide between the party and its natural supporters.' This was a very real problem between 1997 and 2007. Studies showed that members' views on traditional issues such as state intervention in the market, strong trade unions and redistributionary policies remained positive.[28] Alienated from New Labour, voters looked for alternatives. The Scottish National Party grew by stealing Labour's social democratic clothes, and by promising to free Scotland from the unrepresentative rule of Westminster. Even the Liberal Democrats – at the time led by the SDP wing – were winning votes from Labour in 2005 by posturing to Labour's left. George Galloway's election as a Respect MP off the back of fighting Islamophobia and opposing the Iraq War also stung Labour.

If we cut through the spin of the Labour right about how successful Blairism was, it is worth noting that five million voters were lost between 1997 and 2010, marking the beginning of a dramatic decline of support in working-class heartlands in the north and Scotland. The grip of Blairism on the party eroded both the membership and the voter turnout. Membership fell from 405,000 in 1997 to only 176,891 in 2007.[29] This had an obvious effect on the activist base. By May 2006, one MP could complain that 'the Party has disappeared. There are no local parties. There's nothing to campaign with. It's all top down and instructed from Party headquarters; all the regional organisers have gone.'[30] Of course, this was not a concern for the Blairites, who anyway preferred a smaller 'professional' party with the elected politicians doing all the campaign work. They could be easily managed. But it fostered resentment and frustration in the remains of the ranks that the party was being treated only as an auxiliary to the politicians.

It was this combination of factors that precipitated the explosive return of the Labour left – the voters lost, the decline of trade unionism, the crisis of working-class representation and the sense that politics was too elitist, too stage-managed: in essence too *Blairite*. However, within the party, all that remained were the few huddled survivors of the transformative aspirations of the Labour left. Groups including the LRC kept the egg warm waiting for better days. The key factors in the historic revival of the Labour left included contingent internal changes in the Labour Party rules (more on which in the following chapter) but also their life-line links to mass forces in campaigns and struggles outside the party. The space for the socialist left was perhaps only an inch, but as the saying goes, it is in that inch that we live or die.[31]

8

The Corbyn Supremacy

'We didn't lose – we threw it away! Four years after gifting power to Margaret Thatcher, that's how I summed up the 1983 general election for Labour. What we in the Labour Party have to ensure is that we never throw it away again. And to do that we have to make certain that the Party never again comes under control of the left.'

John Golding, MP for Newcastle-under-Lyme.

When Blair's resignation eventually came in 2007, the left fought to get the nominations to put up a candidate. John McDonnell had been campaigning for almost a year to stand, earning support from the broad left of the affiliated Labour unions. After a brief period in which Michael Meacher attempted to launch a rival left candidacy, McDonnell was the only left MP seriously trying to get onto the ballot.

McDonnell's approach represented a clear break from Blairism: investment in public services not predicated on private sector finance – a new form of public ownership which would 'involve the workers who deliver those services, the people who receive them and elected representatives of the local community'. These would not be state-owned industries in the classic corporatist sense. McDonnell explained his strategic vision: 'some people will remember the pre-GLC discussions about being in and against the state. That's what government should be about in terms of socialist practice – you go into the state to transform the state.'[1] The union leaders and soft-left groupings like Compass backed Brown instead of McDonnell, depriving the membership of a contest. By the deadline McDonnell was 16 nominations short, and Gordon Brown, as the only other candidate, was crowned leader despite the Blairite wing having mixed feelings about his loyalty to the New

Labour project. The deputy leadership contest went ahead with six candidates. The unions and the left backed Jon Cruddas from Compass, but despite the £140,000 spent on his campaign – money mostly from the unions – he came third, losing out to right-winger Alan Johnson and the eventual winner Harriet Harman.

The attempt to get a left candidate onto the ballot had the effect of boosting LRC membership with people critical of the state of the party. The 2007 LRC conference declared that 'we do not have a Party of Labour, the task is to build one'. They still saw Labour as the main vehicle to achieve socialism but were increasingly pessimistic about their chances of 'reclaiming Labour'. Since so many socialists and left-wing activists were now outside Labour – disillusioned with the stranglehold of Blairism – the LRC amended its constitution to allow non-Labour members to join, as long as they weren't in organisations that stood against Labour in elections. PCS General Secretary Mark Serwotka addressed the LRC conference in no uncertain terms: 'I haven't come here to tell you to leave the Labour Party – we need the Labour left to fight. But if you think that calling for people to join or re-join the party to reclaim it is a strategy then I'm afraid we have a disagreement.'[2] Though reclaiming Labour seemed like a distant prospect, efforts to build a credible party of the left outside Labour also floundered. Attempts to launch new workers' parties with the RMT produced only electoral coalitions, not democratic parties. Both George Galloway's Respect Party and the Scottish Socialist Party had suffered catastrophic splits by 2007. Labour was a cold place for socialists but it looked colder still outside. In 2011 Compass followed suit, becoming a broader coalition which included Scottish Nationalists and Greens – stepping back from involvement in internal Labour elections.

Brown's rule was an unhappy one. The man who claimed to have ended boom and bust was hit with the 2007–8 economic crisis, one many feared would be as severe as Ramsay MacDonald's in 1929. Brown's attempt to forge a new centre ground politics was fatally undermined by the global financial meltdown. Faced with the possible collapse of the western banking system, he resorted to nationalising the debts of the major banks, while leaving their profit-making activities in the private sector. Mainstream commentators and politicians approved and similar policies were adopted across the world. The Tories supported bailing out the banks at enormous public expense and then in the 2010 general election blamed the resultant levels of debt on Labour's profligate spending.

For the Labour left the crisis exposed the fundamental problems of neoliberalism. Compass proposed social democratic reforms, banking regulation and rebalancing the economy away from the free market. The LRC went further, calling for the nationalisation of the banking sector both as a response to the crisis and as part of a wider anti-capitalist strategy. However, McDonnell, the leading light of the LRC, articulated a different approach. In a *Guardian* column in 2008 he suggested that the part-nationalised banks be forced to adopt a 'new lending strategy [which] must prioritise tackling the worst effects of the recession. We need to promote employment through investment in major public works schemes to meet the UK's needs.'[3] This proposal later became a central plank of 'Corbynomics'. So hegemonic was neoliberalism that even McDonnell's mild social democratic alternatives were considered transformative threats to the integration of Labour into the neoliberal world order.

By 2009, David Cameron's resurgent Tories were eating away at Labour's vote, winning the argument in the minds of the electorate that the global banking crisis was caused by Labour's over-spending. It was a testament to the lack of economic conviction from Labour that they were unable to defeat this pernicious myth. Labour was defeated at the 2010 general election – and a hard-faced austerity programme became the order of the day. But the Tories didn't have a majority, so they looked to the Liberal Democrats for support. Their Liberal allies abandoned their previous left orientation and facilitated a right-wing Tory-led coalition government. The coalition cut away at the welfare state and public spending, slashing, burning and selling off everything they could get away with as they ferociously tore down the remains of post-war social democracy.

To return to power, Labour's key task was to both explain the crisis and offer an alternative to austerity while mounting opposition to the cuts alongside the wider movement. While New Labour was ideologically incapable of performing this task, the left was organisationally incapable. The Socialist Campaign Group of MPs had been reduced in number to just 13. Both John McDonnell and Diane Abbott (the chair and the secretary of the SCG) put themselves forward to stand for leader in 2010 after Brown stepped down. With such small forces, splitting the left vote undermined both candidates. Some Campaign Group members even backed Ed Miliband and Ed Balls. There was little momentum or unity in the parliamentary left and in the wider membership the LRC was shrinking. The union weight was behind Ed Miliband, Ralph Miliband's son, who they saw as the only candidate with a chance of ending Blairite rule, especially as his Progress backed brother David Miliband seemed most likely to win.

Ed's Not Red

Ed Miliband's leadership election victory represented a shift to the centre for the party. But to what end was not clear. Putting centre-left intellectuals like Cruddas in the core policy team seemed an explicit attempt to forge a social democratic renewal. But although 'Red Ed' had narrowly won the leadership (thanks to the trade union votes) he was still a prisoner of the party right. They controlled the party apparatus and had the political capital of three electoral wins behind them. Unwilling to build a movement among the membership and desperate to avoid the perception of being in an alliance with the unions, Miliband walked a tightrope between left and right.[4] The result was 'One Nation Labour', a stillborn project that failed to inspire the public imagination. It was billed as 'radical and conservative'[5] by Tristram Hunt MP, but neither radicals nor conservatives were convinced.

Initially, Labour opposed the austerity agenda of the coalition government and expressed some sympathy with the protesting students in 2010 and the trade union demonstrations against austerity. The integrationist wing retained control, however; they used polling data showing that Labour wasn't trusted on the economy to force Miliband away from any socialistic policies. In the tradition of previous

Labour leaders, Miliband emphatically came out against strike action by public sector trade unionists fighting to save local services. Not that there was much strike action to speak of. The unions opposed austerity but industrial action against public sector cuts was pitifully low. Local authority budgets were slashed to the bone, but Labour councils across the country agreed to impose the cuts – albeit with heavy hearts. The history of local government resistance to cuts seen in the 1980s was either forgotten or actively denounced by sitting Labour councillors.

In January 2012 Miliband and Shadow Chancellor Ed Balls declared a dramatic policy U-turn and announced that Labour supported austerity economics. It led to howls of protest from left figures like Owen Jones, who rightly pointed out that there was not much political space for an austerity-lite Labour Party and even if there was, was it right to adopt austerity measures which impacted on the poorest the hardest?[6] Prominent Keynesian economists argued that austerity economics were primarily ideologically driven, but the Labour leaders were so desperate to prove themselves 'serious' on economic issues they fell in line behind Tory arguments. Disaffection spread among the membership as the familiar triangulation took place, destroying any hope of Labour carving out a specific space for itself on the electoral map. Instead, the Green Party seized the opportunity to present themselves as the 'anti-austerity party' and enjoyed a 'Green Surge' in membership.

In 2013 a public row with Unite – the biggest financial contributor to Labour – caused a significant rift with the unions. A Unite member who had been elected chair of Falkirk CLP began recruiting local union members with a view to getting a Unite member as the parliamentary candidate. The outgoing MP accused Unite of 'flooding' the party by signing members up *en bloc* and paying their subs – an accusation that caused outrage among the unions. Labour was after all the party they had established and if Blairites could 'flood' it with middle-class professionals then why couldn't the unions bring in their own people? The Labour right urged Miliband to 'deal' with the union link once and for all.[7] With unintended irony Mandelson warned Miliband at the 2013 Progress conference that the unions were trying to take over the Labour Party. Labour passed a dossier of evidence to the police to carry out an investigation into Unite. Although the union was exonerated, the Falkirk episode propelled Labour's biggest funder onto a collision trajectory with the Labour right.

As a result of the Falkirk affair, Labour initiated a review by Lord Collins into the unions, party funding and elections. In future there would be clearer rules around union involvement in internal elections and union money entering the party. Collins proposed abolishing the Electoral College entirely in favour of one member one vote for the Labour leadership. It was this change that opened the door to the unexpected events of 2015 – a textbook example of the law of unintended consequences.

Despite these internal schisms, the Labour Party looked set to do well at the general election in 2015, perhaps well enough to force a hung parliament. But the election ended in disaster. The Tories gained seats while the Liberal Democrats were reduced to only nine MPs – a punishment for their compromises to gain power – meanwhile the SNP dominated in Scotland. Labour won back a million votes from 2010 but lost MPs. While the defeat was the product of a number of factors, it is clear that Labour's muddled message and lack of strategic thinking led to the loss of votes across Britain (including from a large number of people on the receiving end of austerity politics).[8] The right immediately tried to establish the narrative that the party lost because it was not 'aspirational' enough for the demands of the neoliberalised middle classes. The left pointed to the lack of clear economic alternatives and the adoption of Tory-lite policies. The stage was set for a battle for the future of the party.

Demand the Impossible

No one predicted Corbyn's leadership victory in 2015, least of all the left themselves. At a diminished meeting of the parliamentary Labour left a week after the election it was clear they were short of candidates. Eventually Corbyn offered to stand to give the left a voice, suspecting he would not get the nominations to get on the ballot. His candidature – secured at the last minute by a deal with some on the right in the PLP to nominate him as a token candidate for the left – was greeted with derision. Erstwhile SDP candidate Polly Toynbee labelled him 'a 1983 man, a relic of the election that brought him to Parliament when Labour was destroyed by its out-of-Nato, anti-EU, renationalise-everything suicide note'.[9] Journalist Dan Hodges went further, prophesying that 'Jeremy Corbyn will have no role to play in that contest. He can't win. For all the grandiose rhetoric, he's a political pygmy. He'll be crushed. Marmalised. Utterly humiliated.'[10]

The right was clearly confident. The organised Labour left was small and Corbyn was considered 'hard left' and out of touch with the electorate – he would not even appeal to the unions as Miliband had done. Only a brave few put money on the 100–1 odds for Corbyn to become leader. Winning the leadership in September 2015 was historic, around 250,000 members voted for someone from the left of the party. So why did he win where Abbott and McDonnell had failed previously?

For many young people Corbynism was a cry of rage against the bleak future offered to them. For others Corbyn represented a reflex desire for a return to an older form of Labourism, of social democracy against social liberalism. The movement behind Corbyn represented a decisive rejection of 40 years of neoliberalism and six years of austerity, the continued decline of communities, the lack of decent jobs, low wages, sky-high rents and unaffordable homes, racism, imperialism and the corruption of the political class exposed by a series of parliamentary expenses scandals. The increasingly desperate calls by the old guard to reject Corbyn and his politics, to adhere to the integrative strategy of appeasement and triangulation, fell on deaf ears. The left's success was largely a product of the way in which the right's politics had failed working people. Bending the knee to the status quo earned some Labour MPs fat expenses accounts, lucrative after-dinner speaking tours or seats on the boards of companies, but surrendering the principled opposition to food banks and tax cuts left Labour MPs without an alternative vision and bereft of a clear argument. Many people felt that they had been sacrificed at the expense of the continued privileges of the 1 per cent. Corbyn built an alliance of both contemporary and traditional Labour values: a 'libertarian socialist – critical of the top-down model of nationalisation advocated by old Labour ... sounded fresh to a new generation.'[11] Corbynism represented a mixed economy, some wealth redistribution, undoing the most egregious policies of Thatcher and Blair (the anti-union laws, student fees) and a willingness to explore new economic models away from the obsession with the free market. McDonnell in particular advocated a far greater expansion of cooperatives as an alternative to the private sector. Anti-neoliberal without being anti-capitalist. Corbyn himself described his election manifesto as 'depressingly moderate'. Nevertheless it was considered dangerous radicalism by the establishment.[12]

This also has to be seen in an international context. Corbyn was not the only left politician to surprise the commentariat. Across Europe, austerity was being challenged by new social movements and political parties that were outside the mainstream. Social democratic parties committed to neoliberalism had implemented austerity leading to disastrous electoral results. The crushing of Pasok and the rise of Syriza in Greece was an example of what could happen. Some expected to see Labour's own 'Pasokification'. Instead, because of the first-past-the-post system in Britain, the reinvigoration of the left happened *through* Labour – though in opposition to the Labour establishment. Alternative left parties simply could not get any credible electoral traction. But Syriza was also a warning to left governments of how entrenched power and capital can undermine and destroy your ideals – just as they had done with Syriza's attempt to end austerity in Greece.

Corbyn, the scrappy outsider, had to utilise every tool available to build support. His campaign launched Jeremy for Leader and combined traditional labour movement rallies and ring rounds with a social media operation that eclipsed the other candidates. Corbyn came across as principled, modest and human during the TV debates, in contrast to the focus-group robots with their carefully chosen buzz words. This challenge was possible because Ed beating David Miliband had knocked the wind out of Progress and their allies in the party machine. Although Miliband's era was ultimately a failure, it showed that different avenues were possible after years of neoliberal hegemony. David Miliband's defeat disillusioned many Blairites, who began drifting away from the party, as David was to do himself. This damaged the party management apparatus of the Blairites, and as a result the internal regime was no longer so stifling. The increasingly desperate opposition to Corbyn only served to highlight his break with the old regime. Now themselves outsiders, Blair and Mandelson repeatedly intervened in the media to denounce Corbyn and even called for a unity candidate to stand against him – every time only boosting his popularity.

The Labour establishment had failed to notice the growing discontent with its rightward drift. They had assumed their voters were right-wing, that UKIP was the direction of travel. In fact the mugs emblazoned with 'Control Immigration', leaders pandering to *The Sun*, and the years of serving entrenched wealth and power, especially during a time of devastating austerity, had left many Labour supporters angry. There was a hunger for a more principled leader. What was perhaps the single event that most tipped the balance was itself a product of the integrationists' drive to appear 'sensible' on the economy. When the Welfare Bill came before the Commons – a bill that proposed slashing benefits to vulnerable, poor people – the acting leader Harriet Harman instructed the Labour front bench, which included Yvette Cooper and Andy Burnham, to abstain. The Progress candidate Liz Kendall needed no instruction to attack welfare. This left them to be pilloried among the rank and file and by anti-austerity activists. Corbyn naturally voted against, establishing himself as the only principled candidate who would stick to his guns to fight Tory policies. Harman probably did more for Corbyn's victory than any other Labour MP.

Corbyn's stand against the Welfare Bill and the rising tide of support for him in the rank and file of the labour movement meant that it was increasingly difficult for the union leaders not to back him. This was the other decisive shift in the left realignment – in 2015 Corbyn was backed by serious union muscle – Unite, UNISON, TSSA, BAFWU and the CWU all endorsed him, the latter doing so explicitly to 'oust the Blairites'. This shift in the union's allegiance from the right or the centre ground had a profound impact – for the first time a candidate from the left of the party was backed by the unions. After years of the unions being treated as unwelcome friends (often labelled as dinosaurs or wreckers during the Blair era) and fleeced for money in return for nothing, there was a mood for a pro-trade-union leader. Moreover, the union leaders themselves were in a weak position as they had delivered little for their members since 2010. Failure and collapse on every campaign from public sector wages to pensions meant that the union bureaucracies were not in a strong position to sell to their own members support for someone like Burnham who was willing to abstain on issues like welfare reform. While the unions were arguably moving left in their rhetoric,[13] when it came to successful industrial campaigns they had little to show. Just as after the defeat of the 1926 general strike, the failure of industrial action led to a renewed interest in politics. But the support of the unions was not automatic – struggles had to be fought for their endorsement. Key figures in UNISON preferred Yvette Cooper, and Unite's leadership originally favoured Andy Burnham. It took left networks in the unions and Labour-link forums to pressure them to back Corbyn.

Finally, reminiscent of Benn's deputy leadership campaign, it was a change in the constitution which allowed the left to take advantage after the Collins Review. Ironically it was the introduction of one member one vote, originally a proposal from David Owen and the right of the party in the early 1980s, which opened the door to a new transformative era. Many on the left had opposed the Collins Review reforms, seeking to defend the constitutional trade union link on principle, even though historically it had been an essential component in the power of the right. The inclusion of supporter status was seen by the right as a chance to undermine the members. What most on the left did not see at the time was that this was an opportunity for the thousands of disaffected, alienated members (the 'cranks and extremists'), frustrated at the undemocratic nature of the party, to regain their voice. When people outside of Labour saw a chance to crack apart the neoliberal pro-austerity consensus, they joined with Labour members and the unions to use the right's democratic reforms against them.

Corbyn was their revenge.

Under Fire From Day One

Corbyn won the leadership election with nearly 60 per cent of the vote. The Progress candidate Liz Kendall came last with less than 5 per cent. The left's victory was historic and decisive. But Corbyn's Labour was an unstable entity – a transformative leadership wrestling with the powerful integrative tendencies of the PLP and the wider political establishment. While Corbyn was inevitably mocked, derided and attacked in the press, the worst blows came from his own side. Corbyn did not quake in the face of the Tories but he was constantly under fire from his own backbenchers.[14] Many of the hardened Blairites refused to serve in his Shadow Cabinet, but Corbyn was able to stitch together a compromise Cabinet between the left and the right (though he did place his key ally McDonnell in the Shadow Chancellor role). Despite this attempt at a broad church Shadow Cabinet, the constant talk of his lack of 'electability' by the Labour right was designed to make it a fact on the ground – the wish was father to the thought. The media mocked the left while lavishing praise on their opponents who conformed to the kind of Labour the rich proprietors of the newspapers wanted to see: business friendly, pliant and loyal to the diktats of the powerful. When Corbyn won the election, some staffers in HQ wore funeral attire.[15]

The campaigners who came together to secure his election went on to launch Momentum, a tool to organise support for Corbyn's policies. Launched by Clive Lewis MP and headed up by Jon Lansman (CLPD), it aimed to be both a platform inside Labour and an organisation for building social movements outside. Writing in the *New Statesman*, Lewis outlined the ambitions of the newly revived left: 'a social movement to work for a more democratic, equal and decent society inside and outside the Labour Party ... It will work with Labour members to transform our Party into a democratic institution ... [and] strive to bring together progressives campaigning for social, economic and environmental justice across the country.'[16]

Corbynism

The PLP were in no mood to give Corbyn time to establish himself, because they feared that he and the forces behind him were uncontrollable. Through public division, the right hoped to make a left-led Labour unelectable. They were willing for the party to take the hit of another five years in opposition to prove that Corbynism was a doomed experiment never to be repeated – to revive the myth of 1983. Such an outcome would largely be the responsibility of the right of course, as it was in 1983, but they believed they could seize control of the narrative just as they had done before.

Their line was, in the words of Dan Hodges: 'He may be a nice man. He may be a principled man. But he is not a leader, and he never will be.'[17] Of course, the best way to show up Corbyn's lack of credentials was to be ungovernable as a PLP. In order to destroy his credibility, the right sought key set-piece battles to deliver blows against him. Initially they focused on Trident renewal, and then most notably on military intervention into Syria, where Hilary Benn gave a well-received pro-war speech and was subsequently touted in the media as a potential alternative leader in the PLP. They were, however, faced with the problem that Corbyn had more than doubled the party's membership to over 500,000 and clearly retained a lot of support among the rank and file. Thus the battle lines were drawn: most of the MPs versus most of the membership.

The febrile atmosphere caused by the strained balance of power was finally broken by the EU referendum. Despite the opportunities arising from the Tories being in chaos after David Cameron resigned, the narrow vote to leave the EU was immediately seized upon by the Labour right to accuse Corbyn of weak leadership. The near invisibility of the Labour remain campaign, headed up by Alan Johnson, was skated over. All the underhand tactics of the Blair years were dusted off and deployed for action. The whispering campaign in the press against Corbyn became a guttural shout as Hilary Benn and others organised a planned mass resignation of as many ministers as they could.[18] Front bench Labour MPs resigned throughout the day, spaced out equally on the hour to ensure constant rolling news coverage and create maximum pressure on the leadership. Even Cameron yelled it at him across the Commons as the calls for Corbyn to resign became cacophonous. But their plan hit a disastrous obstacle: Corbyn simply refused to resign. He argued that he had a clear mandate from the membership and that that was the basis for his continued position. The coup ran aground as the opposition tried to force a leadership election only to struggle to find a serious candidate. Although Angela Eagle initially put herself forward, she was ditched in favour of Owen Smith. The Labour rebels hoped Smith would be their champion against the man they considered 'a critical threat to the future of the Labour Party'.[19] Smith's campaign revealed the peculiar twist of the Labour right – imitation as the most insincere form of flattery. His left policies were designed to echo many of Corbyn's (though he differed on key issues like Trident and tuition fees), but he was pitched as 'electable'. It was a clear attempt to win over the soft left and split them from the Corbynista wing.

Corbyn now faced a second election in the space of a year, the first Labour leader to suffer that ignominy. His supporters considered it a profoundly undemocratic coup attempt by the PLP in alliance with the party bureaucracy.[20] The sight of establishment figures ganging up on Corbyn only riled party members even more. This was exacerbated when it became clear that this leadership campaign was not to be fought on fair grounds – certainly there were apparently arbitrary changes made from the 2015 election that looked biased against the incumbent's support base. First the NEC, under the control of the right, agreed to set the date for eligible voting membership as June 2016, disenfranchising thousands of members who had joined after the leadership election was announced. They also increased the fee for supporter status from £3 to £25 to dissuade people from registering to vote. In addition there was a new round of purges by the compliance unit: thousands of members were expelled or suspended on spurious grounds (sharing a tweet, allegedly posting negative comments on Facebook, etc). In addition, Wallasey CLP was suspended on charges of homophobia – strenuously denied by the local officers and later found to be false.

The left decried these actions as blatant gerrymandering. In that context the CLGA slate swept the board on the NEC for the CLP sections; all six candidates were elected. There were growing calls for party secretary Ian McNichol to resign. Despite the machinations of the right, Corbyn was re-elected with an increased majority; 61.8 per cent backed him (313,000 votes). The rebels fell silent again. The plotters retreated, licking their wounds, but planning future attempts to seize back power once again. The left had delivered another victory and Corbyn was secure for another year at least.

While Corbyn looked like he couldn't be beaten electorally by the right, this didn't stop contradictions opening up within his own support base. Concerns over anti-immigration policies and Brexit left some supporters feeling uneasy. Prominent left-wingers like Paul Mason and Owen Jones urged compromises around issues like NATO. Momentum itself ran into problems as a deep division opened up between those who aimed to restrict it to being a tool for mobilising the vote and others who saw it as a lobbying body to put left pressure on the party more generally. Refusing initially to endorse substantial democratic reforms, Momentum preferred to promote the CLGA slate on the NEC, even though centre-left NEC members voted to suspend entire CLPs (for instance in Brighton) that had been won by the left. Instead Momentum's leadership around Lansman launched a red scare against the Alliance for Workers' Liberty (the descendants of Socialist Organiser) and imposed a constitution on the organisation that con- solidated the control of a small office faction. Amid the wrangling, the organisation saw widespread disaffection with the process. Interven- tions in the media from left celebrities calling on prominent left-wing activists 'from a Trotskyist background' to be expelled from Labour also started a process of splitting the soft left from the hard left – a repetition of the same divide and rule strategy from the 1980s. Momentum's leadership was clearly terrified of being associated with 'wild' elements and wanted the protection of respectability. It cancelled a conference planned for early 2017 and shut down Momentum's regional organisa- tion. The unity of the left in the early '80s in the face of a party machine intent on expulsions no longer existed.

The need for compromise with the right of the party also saw the demobilisation of important initiatives. One of the first retreats was over local government. Left activists were calling for Labour councils to refuse to pass on government cuts, as this had been a huge battleground between 2010 and 2015. But within two months of taking leadership, Corbyn, McDonnell and Jon Trickett put out a letter to Labour councillors confirming that there was no pressure on them to do 'illegal budgets'.[21] This was a clear compromise with party councillors who were overwhelmingly hostile to Corbyn and acted as a political base for the right-wing opposition. There was also little appetite for Momentum nationally to support trade unionists in struggle against Labour councils as they fought to save public services, despite mobilisations by local groups.

Amid these controversies, very little direction was coming from Corbyn's office – the apparent energy of the leadership campaigns had dissipated, replaced by a grim political paralysis. And behind the scenes the right were still chipping away. In February 2017 Mandelson felt confident enough to reveal that 'however small it may be – an email, a phone call or a meeting I convene – every day I try to do something to save the Labour party from [Corbyn's] leadership'.[22] By March 2017 the contradictions at the heart of the party were beginning to take their toll.

Oh Jeremy Corbyn!

Despite arguing for a year that she would not do so, in April 2017 David Cameron's replacement Theresa May called a snap general election. Her *volte face* decision was motivated by both hubris and opportunism. With Labour 24 points behind the Tories in the polls and Corbyn's personal approval rating at historic lows, the Tories hoped to deliver a swift and decisive victory, increase their own majority by a hundred, and crush the Labour Party and its left in one fell swoop. May also faced opposition from her own backbenchers over plans for Brexit and needed to command a stronger majority to ensure her hard Brexit plan could be implemented.

Still dominated by the right and sure that the election would be an annihilation, the Labour machine fought an entirely defensive strategy around MPs in marginal seats. All sitting MPs were automatically re-selected and the NEC and regional committees imposed candidates in the other seats. A number of prospective left candidates were blocked in favour of people more amenable to the right. Some MPs standing for re-election began by issuing public statements damning Corbyn's electoral liability. Ex-Progress Chair John Woodcock even declared he would 'not countenance ever voting for Corbyn as Prime Minister'. Other MPs ran campaigns entirely on their local record, acting almost as independents, distancing themselves from Corbyn and issuing instructions to canvassers not to mention the party leader on the doorsteps. In addition, news leaked out in late April that the staffers at HQ would 'strike' if Corbyn refused to step down following a heavy election defeat. They felt vindicated when Labour suffered bad results at local government elections just before the general election, losing 382 councillors.

For their part, the left was energised and highly determined, driven partly out of desperation that this might be their one shot at going to the electorate with a left Labour leader. Relying on new, younger voters to turn out, voter registration drives were organised in the initial stages of the election. Left activists, partly coordinated by Momentum, partly motivated by their own enthusiasm, started pouring into Tory marginals, fighting to win despite the terrible polling. Corbyn himself visited the key Tory marginal of Croydon Central to deliver his first speech of the campaign, a clear sign that the leadership and membership were ambitious to make gains.

The tricky issue of the manifesto remained. Although very few people read election manifestos, they can set the tone of the media reporting of the campaign and decent policies are often pushed on the doorstep. A week before its formal adoption a draft was leaked to the press in a move that proved to be a master stroke. The popularity of the draft among the party membership closed down space for the right to undermine the more transformative proposals. When *For the Many Not the Few* was officially launched, it was a fully costed, tax-and-spend manifesto depicting a return to a mixed economy and a more equitable form of capitalism – in short, Keynesianism. In many ways it picked up some of the tone of Miliband's One Nation era, arguing for a fairer society and regulating the markets to deliver social justice. However, unlike 2015, the manifesto also contained enough popular issues that mobilised real energy: a living wage, nationalisation of the railways, free university education, progressive taxation, opposition to austerity, 100,000 council homes to be built, and the promise of government intervention in the economy via a National Infrastructure Bank. It was the most radical manifesto in decades that Britain had seen from a party that could potentially form a government.

Despite that, the manifesto was a clear compromise between the left and right of the party. It was agreed unanimously between the Shadow Cabinet and the NEC, a sign that enough was in there to placate the right as well as give the left a platform to campaign on. Ideologically it was a pretty thin document – limiting itself to a criticism of inequality and with no mention of socialism, it was reminiscent of Wilsonian era Labour, advocating a technocratic vision of improving technology to develop the economy. The concessions were clear though – it accepted that there would be no free movement after Brexit, even stating that immigrants would not be able to access public funds while living in Britain. Previous talk of massive expansions of workers' cooperatives was abandoned. In line with conference policy, it committed Labour to keeping Trident, instead pledging that a Labour Prime Minister would only be 'extremely cautious' in deploying nuclear bombs. This put Corbyn in some tricky positions in debates as his stance against nuclear weapons was widely known. Nevertheless it was Teflon proof for any 'suicide note' labels that the right might wish to attach.

While some on the right remained perplexed about Corbynism's popularity they couldn't grasp the essential nature of what was at stake. Despite its mild social democratic objectives, the general line of the Labour campaign captured a public mood. It chimed with people exhausted by a socio-economic order based on debt, insecurity, cuts and the absence of a public service ethos. It captured the long-repressed *desire* for a transformative agenda. Corbynism was seen as a rebellion against a socio-economic system that was actually lowering standards of living for so many people. As the campaign gathered pace, the polls continued to shift further and further towards Labour. Nevertheless, the Labour right was absolutely set on the view that the election would be a crushing defeat for the party, no doubt hoping it would allow them to finally end the nightmare of Corbyn. His position would look untenable if Labour lost too many MPs. Rumours circulated that several MPs planned to launch leadership challenges within days of a derisory election result.

Labour's campaign was helped by Theresa May's spectacularly bad performance. Appearing cold and inhuman, she failed to connect with voters. The Tory manifesto offered nothing positive, only more austerity, while disastrously targeting the Conservative voting elderly with cuts to pensions and forcing people with dementia to sell their homes to pay for social care. The Tory campaign was in disarray within weeks, reduced to negative attack ads on Corbyn and Diane Abbott. Rod Liddle thundered in *The Spectator* that 'this is the worst Tory election campaign ever'. In contrast, Corbyn was in his element, campaigning across the country, speaking to huge crowds and performing well even in hostile interviews. His past support for the Irish liberation struggle was spun as his being a supporter of the IRA, and was a regular question topic from interviewers, as were concerns that he was not brave enough to 'push the button' in the event of a nuclear attack. In the face of regular criticisms about his ethics and his past associations he won consider-able support from voters by appearing principled and honest. Another crucial factor was the mobilisation of younger voters. Corbyn – a man in his late sixties – effortlessly appealed to their existential fear that the country, perhaps even the world, was going from bad to worse in the face of Brexit and Trump. Perhaps it was time to take a leap of faith. He was publicly and vocally backed by grime artists like Stormzy which helped cement a massive youth following. Middle-aged voters also swung behind Labour – only the elderly largely remained stubbornly pro-Tory. As Labour members spent day after day getting out the vote and convincing wavering electors, the polls began to move even more dramatically, closing the gap with the Tories.

The election result defied expectations. Labour gained 30 seats while the Tories lost their majority. It was so close in several marginal seats that Labour was only 2,227 votes away from forming a government. The result cemented Corbyn's position as Labour leader while throwing the Conservatives into chaos. Labour regained seats in Scotland and even won in 'true blue' seats like Kensington and Canterbury. The election results were greeted in cities across the country with young revellers pouring out from bars and pubs, chanting the name of the Labour leader. A man who had been considered an electoral liability had inspired a further 3.5 million people to vote Labour, the fifth largest vote Labour had ever achieved and the biggest vote share since 1966. It felt like Labour had won the election even though they lost it.

The result provoked something of a crisis in the professional commentariat. The paid professionals in the media had all predicted a Labour wipe-out but now had to rush into the TV studios or into print to explain why that had not happened. The pundits overnight started to praise Corbyn's 'radical campaign', his 'youth movement' and the manifesto, anything they could find to explain why Labour had gained seats in the face of such intense hostility and a supposedly incompetent leadership. Labour MPs on the right, many of whom had feared they might lose their seats, publicly admitted that the leader had delivered a good campaign and they had misjudged him. Progress member Woodcock, who had started his campaign calling for Corbyn's head, issued an apology days after the election, saying that Corbyn had 'a right to lead' and that 'the pitched battles and bad blood that have marred the last two years are over'.[23] He also revealed what was in the minds of many other Progress members that night when he admitted 'I don't know what's going on in British politics!'[24] Other leading lights of the PLP right, such as Chuka Umunna and Wes Streeting, either grudgingly applauded the left-led campaign or at least publicly announced that no leadership challenge would ensue as a result of the election. Only Chris Leslie and Yvette Cooper remained committed to the fight: Cooper was tepid in her praise of Labour's campaign and Leslie toured TV studios attacking the result as not good enough in the context of such a weak Tory campaign.

While there was no appetite for a leadership challenge to Corbyn, it was clear that the fundamental contradictions in Labour had not gone away. Some critics were quietened by the possibility of winning power under a left leadership as the 'unelectable' label was peeled off. But backbench rebellions over Brexit were followed in the media by reports of moves by the right to consolidate their hold on the NEC. Unable to remove Corbyn, the fight was still on to isolate him internally. This constant factionalism has a purpose – to some the prospect of a left government is in itself a disastrous outcome – they wanted Corbyn unelectable because they were worried he might win and undo the social-liberalist project they were committed to. As Tony Blair bluntly stated at the Progress Conference in 2015: 'I wouldn't want to win on an old-fashioned leftist platform. Even if I thought it was the route to victory, I wouldn't take it.'[25] Better dead than red.

Outside of the machinations of Whitehall, a few weeks after the election Corbyn spoke to a mass audience at Glastonbury festival. Facing the largest crowd ever at the festival, Corbyn was greeted with cheers, the kind of reaction a rock star might get, not a politician. He delivered a familiar speech, challenging inequality, calling for a fairer economy, preaching unity against division. He concluded with lines from Percy Shelley's revolutionary poem 'The Masque of Anarchy':

> Rise, like lions after slumber
> In unvanquishable number!
> Shake your chains to earth like dew
> Which in sleep had fallen on you:
> Ye are many – they are few!

The old struggle to transform the Labour Party – to transform the world – had started a new chapter.

9

'From Ancient Grudge Break to New Mutiny...'

In November 2021, on Radio 4's *Today Programme*, the Labour leader Keir Starmer refused five times to say whether he thought Corbyn would have made a better Prime Minister than Boris Johnson. For the Labour leadership, the Corbyn era had been a terrible mistake. It was not just that Labour had been defeated in two general elections while led by the left; for the Labour establishment a left-led Labour government would at best have been a historical error, at worst an abomination to be destroyed.

How things had changed. The relative success of Labour in the 2017 general election shocked the right of the party. Demoralisation seeped into the ranks of the anti-Corbyn wing, staffers resigned, MPs announced they would stand down, those that remained began to conspire to split the PLP. The assumed – even hoped for – humiliation of the left when facing the electorate hadn't occurred. This also caused a degree of political confusion. Corbyn's opponents had believed their own propaganda that a left-led Labour Party would be an utter catastrophe. If this one-sided view of politics had proved false and then what else might be false?

Nevertheless, the prevailing view from the Labour right was that the Labour left was illegitimate as a political force and that Corbyn must never become Prime Minister. Dusting themselves off after the set-back of 2017, they had to continue to erode public confidence in the Labour leadership and delegitimise it on political, economic and personal levels. In this they were in lock step with the British establishment of the media, the security services and the Conservative and Liberal Democrat parties. Whatever the political strength of the Labour left, it was clear that the British ruling class was in no mood to compromise; there would be no repeat of 1945. They viewed even a return to left social democracy as politically illegitimate, an insurgent force, a dangerous political tendency.

The downfall of the left after the 2019 general election was a textbook example of the structural and political problems that the Labour left will always have in trying to 'reclaim' the party. After the 2019 election defeat, the new leadership moved rapidly to erase the memory of Corbynism, which was now relegated from inspiring tale of hope to scare story, a warning of the path never to be travelled again. The legacy of the movement built around Corbyn was traduced and trampled, his policies abandoned with ease, key figures from the period marginalised, suspended or even expelled.[1] The revenge of the moderates, as they reasserted what they saw as their natural-born right to rule Labour, was vicious and merciless. After all, the Labour Party is less a weapon of class war than a battlefield in which that war is fought out, one in which socialists are always considered an unwelcome element.

The Insurmountable Contradictions

Internally within the left there were also disagreements that proved to be dynamite built into the foundations. The two primary political issues that could not be resolved were antisemitism and Brexit. Differences were also apparent over the scale and radicalism of the project to transform Labour. Corbynism fell to specific political crises that could not be overcome within the confines of Labourism, and as such point to the culmination of the historic problems of the Labour left in their battle for control of the party. It is not just a story of missed opportunities but also a tragic account of left politics – a tragedy in the dramatic sense that the ultimate downfall was caused by what we could consider character flaws within the movement itself.

There is not enough space here for a blow-by-blow account of the various arguments, but it is necessary to examine the way the crises intersected with the Labour left's project and strategy.

Brexit proved to be an impossible hurdle for Labour. The left itself was split between those actively endorsing a Brexit of some kind as a blow to EU imperialism, and those advocating a second referendum or a fight to stay in the EU, concerned about the growth of nationalist rhetoric and the underlying anti-immigrant argument behind Brexit. A Lexit tendency emerged, drawing on the Bennite arguments from the 1970s and highlighting the dangers of an EU superstate and the erosion of democracy. From this perspective, a radical programme of national-isation would be impossible within the legal structures set by the EU. The debate that tore through the left was partly about an assessment of the balance of forces. The left-remain argument saw Brexit as a nationalist populist reactionary force from which nothing good would come. As Corbyn himself had predicted in 2012: 'It would be a mistake to leave the EU under conditions determined by the Eurosceptic right, who would then be in a strong position to reshape Britain's internal and external relations.'[2] But the Eurosceptic argument had narrowly won the 2016 referendum, posing a democratic issue for anyone proposing to overturn the result. Lexit supporters believed that, despite the reac-tionary nature of many of those backing Brexit, leaving the EU was an inherently good thing, and it was possible to leave in a way that would be favourable to the working class, though it was often unclear what a Left Brexit might mean in the absence of a Labour government. The left-remain argument was popular among Labour members, and a social movement was built around it – something that the Lexit side was unable to do as the pro-Brexit argument was dominated by Nigel Farage and forces even to his right. Because the remain movement was dominated by liberals and the Labour right, association with it was seen as being in alliance against Corbynism. Essentially there was, and could be, no agreement on the way forward.

But it wasn't primarily the divisions within the left that were the problem, it was that Labour's electoral coalition was split along Brexit lines that intersected with divisions between post-industrial and metropolitan regions, between town and city, and according to age or ethnicity. Most of Labour's members still backed remaining in the EU, and many of their younger and immigrant voters felt likewise. But many

Labour MPs in leave-voting seats were feeling the electoral pressure from their constituents. The post-industrial Labour voting areas voted out, but most of the bigger cities and Scotland voted to stay in. Labour's 2017 manifesto squared the circle, temporarily, but the Brexit contradictions only deepened subsequently, as MPs in Parliament fought over what to the public seemed arcane arguments about the different Brexit options.

As an electoralist party, Labour failed to present a persuasive alternative to the Conservatives' Brexit plan and failed to take an argument into any of the crucial communities. It was reduced to fighting a rearguard action to hold together a fragile voting coalition. In a country that was polarised, Labour struggled to accommodate both its remain and leave voters, something that no other political party had to do as they largely represented one side of the debate or the other. All it could do was try to reflect back what different fractured voters wanted, like a cracked mirror.

These battles were in part played out on the conference floor, and the contradiction was not resolved but merely offset by the decision to campaign for a second referendum. As Brexit polarised the nation, the Labour leadership couldn't shift the conversation or convince enough voters that another referendum was a good idea. The weakness of their position was partially obscured by Theresa May's incompetence and the infighting in her own party, but even that potential advantage was soon to be lost.

The Antisemitism Crisis

The row over antisemitism in the Labour Party became one of the defining and most damaging episodes of the Corbyn era. In the wake of Corbyn's victory, a number of antisemitic comments and views expressed by Labour members were unearthed on social media, including Corbyn's 2012 defence of a mural in East London that used antisemitic tropes. The right of the party argued that the left was institutionally antisemitic because of a historic 'socialism of fools' which associated Jews with capitalists and because of their pro-Palestinian views. In response Corbyn's leadership team asked Shami Chakrabarti to produce a report into racism in the party and to propose new methods for dealing with any complaints that emerged. While the actual reported instances of antisemitism from party members remained relatively low, the denial by some on the left that the issue existed at all only added fuel to the fire.[3] The leader's office attempted to deal with the growing crisis by improving reporting and disciplinary procedures and by adopting the IHRC definition of antisemitism, though that sparked a further public argument about whether the examples that came with the definition, such as criticism of Israel or referring to it as a racist endeavour, might constitute racism against Jewish people.

The party was essentially split three ways on the question, between those who believed that antisemitism was not a problem and that the accusations were essentially a conspiracy against Corbyn, those who believed that there was an issue but it was being exaggerated, and those who believed that antisemitism was extensive, pervasive and primarily driven by the Labour left. The leadership around Corbyn made it clear that they would tackle any antisemitism and rejected the claim from some of the left that the entire issue was simply a smear.[4] It later emerged that a lot of the failures around disciplinary action had occurred in the first part of Corbyn's leadership, before the left took the position of General Secretary.[5]

Danger to the Realm

Alongside the constant accusations of antisemitism was the constant drip-feed from the British state and its loyal media lieutenants that Corbyn was a security risk. As early as 2015 there was an unprecedented intervention into politics by General Sir Nicholas Houghton, the Chief of the Defence Staff, criticising Corbyn for being against the nuclear weapons programme. Within a week of Corbyn being elected, the *Sunday Times* published a story quoting someone they described as a senior serving general, warning: 'There would be mass resignations at all levels [if Corbyn became Prime Minister] and you would face the very real prospect of an event which would effectively be a mutiny.'[6] This was only the beginning; throughout Corbyn's time as leader there was a regular drip-feed of stories to the right-wing press intended to highlight his alleged links to the IRA or Hezbollah, and to warn that he 'wouldn't clear the security vetting' at MI6.[7] Incidents of Red Scare security-threat articles peaked around the 2017 and 2019 general elections.[8] In April 2019 footage emerged of young British soldiers using photos of Corbyn for target practice. The army described the soldiers' actions as 'totally unacceptable', but chose only to discipline them rather than sack them.

Alongside the stick there was the carrot. Senior Corbyn officials and Shadow Cabinet members were invited to meetings with MI5 and MI6, where they were reassured that the 'reds under the bed' fear from the 1960s and '70s was long in the past, and that the British state was willing to work with any potential Labour government led by people who they had previously held files on. This was the lure of integration and respectability if the Corbynites played nicely and publicly disassociated themselves from any political movements that were not in Britain's imperialist interests. This time around the Labour Party didn't advocate anything like the 1983 manifesto promise to make the security services 'properly accountable institutions'.

The security-threat storyline was only the most extreme example of the constant undermining and delegitimising of the Labour left in general. From the early days of Corbyn's time as leader, the usual Conservative line of attack over economic questions was ubiquitous – only this time the Labour right joined in. Senior Labour MPs and ex-prime ministers like Brown and Blair weighed in to deride Corbyn's economic policies – the term 'disaster' was the one most commonly associated with what the Labour left were proposing.

In response the Labour left put out two conflicting messages: on the one hand, their economic proposals were indeed the most radical set of ideas that had been proposed in decades; on the other, they were actually nothing that wasn't just common sense in Scandinavian social democracies. Again the struggle between being transformative or integrationist, between challenging capitalism or merely refining its functions, was being fought out at the heart of the left's agenda.

What was not made particularly clear to Labour activists was what would happen if a left Labour government were to face a sustained economic attack (a run on the pound, capital flight, etc.), or even some kind of constitutional coup. The recent experience of Syriza in Greece was barely mentioned, beyond being used as an example of the treacherous reactionary nature of the European leaders. The election in Greece of a left government on a radical anti-austerity agenda with the backing of social movements had seen the dream turn to dust within a month, as Syriza was forced by the combined might of European capital to abandon its entire programme and loyally implement austerity. Would a similar fate befall a Corbyn-led government?

The Labour Left Divided

As well as the arguments over Brexit, the pressure of managing Labour began to take its toll on the left as disputes over strategy and direction deepened. An open and public split emerged within the Corbyn coalition, between the radical wing of the party on the one side, and Unite and other ostensibly left trade unions on the other. The division reopened old wounds from the Bennite era of the early 1980s, in particular the tension between democratising the party for the left, but not eroding what the trade unions saw as their historic and political right to have their interests and internal positions defended. The disagreement blew up in the summer of 2018 over the replacement of Iain McNicol as General Secretary. Unite pushed for Jennie Formby but Lansman threw his hat into the ring as well. Responding to this split, Owen Jones commented in the *Guardian* that 'Momentum is an organisation in a hurry, because its leaders worry that Corbyn's successor may not be rooted in the left, which makes structural changes to the party rather urgent.'[9] But it was precisely this structural change that Unite and the other left unions were weary of. Lansman came under huge pressure to withdraw his candidature, eventually doing so while calling for an end to Labour's 'command and control' culture.[10]

The proposed reforms to the MP selection process being pushed by Momentum included a form of mandatory reselection. But at the 2018 party conference, Unite and other unions conspired with the leader's office and more establishment voices to bring in a trigger ballot instead of outright open selection. Conference CLP delegates were shocked to see only the FBU vote for the mandatory reselection proposals, and Unite (which had a policy on backing mandatory reselection) vote to back the NEC's less radical version. This marked the high point of Corbynite attempts to reform the party in any meaningful way and deal with the historic problem of the power of MPs and the PLP to act autonomously from the membership. Some on the left were scandalised by Len McCluskey and Unite's actions, but in reality they were only pursuing their own bureaucratic interests in defending what they saw as the right of the unions to select the MPs they wanted. McCluskey himself saw it as a loyalty test for backing Corbyn's NEC.[11] At the eleventh hour, Momentum also texted all its delegates on conference floor to back the NEC proposal against open reselection, a move that came at a serious cost to the organisation's credibility. There was a complete lack of any rank-and-file left challenge in Unite, largely because Momentum had spent the last four years fiercely defending the existing union leadership from all criticism because McCluskey was seen as a key ally of Corbyn. The Labour left respects the separate orbits of the unions and the party, even though it is this separation that has fatally undermined radical politics in Labour historically.

For their part, the unions had little interest in accommodating the more radical politics of the newer left initiatives. The Labour for a Green New Deal (LGND) campaign, tacitly endorsed by the party leadership, saw their motions opposed by the GMB and pressure brought to bear to remove the most radical policies around nationalisation and carbon targets. Although Labour conferences supported the LGND motions (as well as the more moderate GMB ones), there was no mechanism to force those policies into any subsequent manifesto. Campaigners who opposed the third runway at Heathrow were ignored as Unite doubled down on a jobs-first policy which betrayed their hopeless sectional interests and limited vision.

Obstruction wasn't just limited to the unions, however. After a morning session of the 2019 Labour Party conference passed a motion in favour of free movement, Diane Abbott confirmed by the after-noon that the motion would in no way alter Labour's existing policy of supporting 'a new system of work visas'.[12] Considering the left were justifiably enraged when Blair ignored conference policy every year, the way in which a left leadership did the same reveals something more fundamental about Labourite politics and the scope for members' democracy.

Within the party itself the psychological toll of four years of grim factional warfare was apparent. There was the war between right and left, where both sides saw the other as intolerable idiots who were destroying the party, but there were also the factional struggles within the left, between those on the soft left (seen as too soft), those who considered themselves Corbynite loyalists, and those who backed Corbyn but critically dissented on key issues like Brexit or believed the economic programme was not radical enough. The factional battles were intense, gruelling and unforgiving. Members on all sides sought to drive their opponents out of politics, undermining their mental health by creating cartoonish villains and encouraging social media outrage designed to isolate and demoralise the enemy. This was particularly intense within the left, where some individuals and groups were singled out for what can only be described as systematic bullying. It left many on the left with a bunker mentality, endlessly rowing on social media instead of building a meaningful movement within the working class.

The Road to Defeat

The European Parliament election of April 2019 sent a warning shot across the bows of the Labour leadership. Nigel Farage's newly formed Brexit Party, only six weeks old, won the election by a wide margin, coming first in nine of the eleven regions. The Liberal Democrats came second followed by Labour and the Greens, but Labour's tally of MEPs dropped from 20 to ten. The real concern was that Labour's vote in the cities had started to desert them. If the pro-remain youth and migrant voters of the major cities were beginning to look elsewhere, then Labour would lose any semblance of being a credible electoral proposition.

By June 2019 Corbyn and his allies, including Ian Lavery and Rebecca Long-Bailey, were publicly supporting a second referendum position, despite private misgivings. But Labour was caught in the Gordian knot of Brexit – it could neither please its leaver voters nor satisfy its remain voters. By July 2019 one poll had Labour at 18 per cent, trailing in fourth place. Labour support had been down to 8 per cent among leave voters in January of that year, and 25 per cent among remain voters – down from 48 per cent. Corbyn's repeated challenge to May to 'go back to the people' with a second referendum on any deal was aimed at pleasing both sides of the divide, but it didn't cut through.

During the summer of 2019 Boris Johnson became leader of the Conservative Party and provided the right mix of ruling-class arrogance and boosterish infantilism needed to improve the Tories' poll ratings. He was the polar opposite of Corbyn. Whereas the Labour leader was urbane, principled, considered and thoughtful, Johnson was the Eton dining-room bully, a rabble-rouser without a shred of political integrity. In a world increasingly moving rightwards under populist politicians like Donald Trump and Jair Bolsonaro, Johnson connected with a layer of the socially conservative electorate who had been recently politicised. He brought with him a new direction, one not grounded in austerity and misery, but in a vision of a new Britain with more money, a rebuilt industry and a role to play in the world. Most importantly, he would 'Get Brexit Done', an appealing prospect in a country exhausted by years of division.

It was clear that the battleground had changed. Labour was no longer fighting a divided and weakened Tory Party with no policies. It now had a more dangerous opponent. When Johnson called an election for December 2019 it was clear that the trap had been set and the chances of a Labour win were slim to none. But Labour had to dutifully vote for the election and commence battle – this time with little of the vigour and hope of 2017. Owen Jones has described the lack of focus, absence of election strategy and collapse in morale at the top of the party during the following autumn. One example was how the party cycled through different slogans throughout the election campaign, unable to settle on one that was clear enough to make an impact.[13] The defiant insurgent energy of the 2017 campaign wasn't there, and the intractable political problems – antisemitism and Brexit – remained unresolved. But there was also no clear political message that cut through. When Labour revealed unredacted documents from trade negotiations that showed how the NHS would be further privatised and sold to US private health-care providers, the Conservatives and media spun it immediately into a story about Russian hackers, insinuating that this was connected to the Labour leader's dubious political allegiances internationally.[14]

The 2019 defeat reversed Labour's gains of 2017 and forced an exhausted Corbyn to resign as leader of the party. While Labour's vote tally remained higher than 2010 or 2015, the vote share was much lower thanks to a Tory vote that surpassed even Thatcher's in 1983. Although Labour under Corbyn did get a very credible vote in both elections, it couldn't beat a historically divided Tory Party led by a weak leader like Theresa May in 2017, and it was soundly defeated when facing a boisterous Bullingdon club thug like Boris Johnson in 2019. There were few new ideas in the Labour 2019 manifesto that cut through; those that were new, like free broadband, were met with depressed resignation from voters that they were simply too utopian. Decades of neoliberalism had eroded the horizons of many voters, leading to scepticism about Labour ambitions; disaster nationalism seemed more credible and immediate than soft social democratic revival.[15] It was Johnson who somehow managed to generate a sense of change, promising an end to austerity and a period of national renewal with more money for infrastructure and a jobs bonanza.

Every election is ultimately defined by the narrative spun out of it, and as far as 2019 was concerned the Labour right had their story loaded and ready to go: Corbyn was an out of touch left-wing extremist who couldn't connect with ordinary working people, and his divided party and confused stance on Brexit had driven millions of voters away. This was the story the Labour left's enemies had wanted to tell in 2017, when they were unexpectedly frustrated by the surge in support for Labour.

A YouGov survey of ex-Labour voters at the election found that they had lost faith in Corbyn as a credible leader (35%) and that they didn't agree with the Brexit policy (19%).[16] Interestingly, the survey also found that only a small minority thought Labour's position had been too pro- or anti- Brexit one way or the other – the majority just thought the party looked weak and divided on the question. Another survey found that 1.9 million remain voters didn't back the party in 2019, compared to 1.8 million leave voters. A million young people who hadn't even voted in the 2016 Brexit referendum also rejected Labour. The crucial shift for the Tories was the mobilisation of two million mostly older former non-voters, who supported leave and, most importantly of all, had 'an overwhelming and intense negativity towards Jeremy Corbyn'.[17] In the most marginal Labour seats lost, it wasn't upset Labour voters abandoning the party due to Brexit that led to the switch to the Tories – the result was mostly driven by non-voters from 2017, people who had stayed at home then, but had been motivated in the following two years to vote to keep Corbyn out no matter what the cost. This was in part a déclassé anti-left vote, from a regressive anti-political, anti-progressive part of the population energised and mobilised by the same kind of reactionary populist message that Cambridge Analytica had pioneered in the Brexit referendum. It was the British equivalent of the electorate that had backed Trump in the USA.

The Ashcroft survey of ex-Labour voters focused on the more backward arguments: 'former Labour voters in our groups lamented what they saw as [Corbyn's] weakness, indecision, lack of patriotism, apparent terrorist sympathies, failure to deal with antisemitism, outdated and excessively left-wing worldview, and obvious unsuitability to lead the country'.[18] The fact that they abandoned Labour in 2019 and 2017 is an indication of the strength of the character assassination campaign against Corbyn and of the sinister drip-feed of misinformation about him.[19] For instance, after fake tweets went viral within hours of the London Bridge attack only days before the 2019 election, one journalist reported being shown them by an enraged London black-cab driver who supposed Corbyn was in sympathy with terrorist actions.[20]

There was also the subjective factor of the energy and vision of the leadership. The general election of 2019 was a world away from the Halcyon days of the autumn of 2015, when it seemed that anything (everything?) was possible and there was genuine momentum behind the Corbyn insurgency. Four years later it was an exhausted and battered Labour left that went to the electorate. When Corbyn announced his resignation after four gruelling years doing a job that he hadn't wanted, it marked the end of the Labour left's hopes for gaining power any time soon. Corbyn had repeatedly said that the struggle wasn't about him, it was about the movement – but as he stood down that movement was already falling apart.

The Labour Right Reasserts Itself

Keir Starmer emerged as the front-runner candidate early on because he best exemplified what the average Labour member wanted to hear – a message of unity, of building on the recent political achievements, from a man with integrity projecting a sense of social democratic middle-of-the-road confidence. In a party that was desperate for victory, the left candidate, Rebecca Long-Bailey, was too associated with the existing leadership, seen as too partisan, too mired in the extreme edges of the project that had failed at the election. Just as Corbyn was a swing to the left after Ed Miliband, now the pendulum had swung back.

Summoning a spectre of untold horrors, the Blairite journalist John Rentoul castigated the left's choice: 'Long-Bailey's big policy announcement is bloodshed, infighting and purification by fire.'[21] Whatever the fears of centrist commentators, Long-Bailey struggled to hold together the broad coalition of Labour members that had overwhelmingly supported Corbyn as leader twice before. It proved an impossible task. Union support fractured rapidly; UNISON's centre-right leadership rammed a policy of support for Starmer through its Labour Link, and sent out an endorsement before the Corbyn-supporting wing had any real idea what was going on. USDAW followed suit. The GMB backed Lisa Nandy. Unite, CWU and the FBU backed Long-Bailey, but the acrimony behind the scenes between Unite and Momentum clearly carried through into her campaign.[22]

While Long-Bailey struggled to get a majority of Labour members to back her, Starmer knew he had to make inroads into the Corbynite wing to guarantee victory. He did this, as Kinnock had done in 1983, by posing as left. Standing on a platform that emphasised his left-wing credentials – invoking the miners' strike, the Wapping dispute, his work on the McLibel trial in the late 1990s, and promising continuity with key left policies from the previous regime – Starmer presented himself as the natural successor to the activist Corbyn. He explicitly praised Corbyn's leadership, saying at a rally in January 2020: 'Jeremy Corbyn made our party the party of anti-austerity and he was right to do so. He made us the party that wanted to invest more heavily in our public services and he was right to do so. And we must retain that, we build on that, we don't trash it as we go forward.' He concluded that 'We should treat the 2017 manifesto as our foundational document, the radicalism and the hope that [it] inspired across the country was real.'[23] This was enough to convince a large section of the Labour membership, and Starmer romped to victory with 56 per cent of the vote, leaving Rebecca Long-Bailey on 27.6 per cent and Lisa Nandy on 16.2 per cent. In the deputy leadership election, Angela Rayner came first, backed by Momentum, while the left MP Richard Burgon came third.

But Starmer's promise of party unity and building on the legacy of Corbynism was an illusion. His wing of the party felt in their bones that they had to destroy every last remnant of the Corbyn era to make the party 'electable' again. Goaded on by establishment forces and the conservative media, Starmer proved ruthless in his crusade to isolate the left of the party.[24] This was a Hegelian repetition of history, but both times as a tragic and inevitable reassertion of the integrationist logic of Labourism over the 'wild' Labour left. The spectre of Philip Snowden haunted the party as it realigned itself with its traditional modus operandi – that of the integrationist strategists, of those closest to capital, closest to the narrow logic of electoralism and enmeshed in the insular parliamentary bubble.[25]

Long-Bailey's defeat was the clearest indicator that the Corbynist wing of the party was in retreat. Starmer's win purportedly represented a victory for the middle ground, but in reality it was a decisive shift to the right. The logic of the internal factional struggle would push him further. Long-Bailey's position in the Shadow Cabinet was ended within months, and Corbyn was suspended from Labour and the PLP, in both cases after allegations of antisemitism. But isolating and removing the old left leadership was not enough – the purge had to go further. Within a year of Starmer's leadership win, hundreds of members had been expelled, many ostensibly for accusations of antisemitism. Socialist Appeal members were dismissed en masse, and a number of others who had been interviewed by or written guest articles in their newspapers were also summarily expelled.

At the 2021 Labour Party conference an amendment was introduced to bring back the Electoral College. The left opposed it, seeing it as an attack on the one-member, one-vote policy brought in under Miliband, and that had won Corbyn his leadership role. On the eve of the conference the amendment was withdrawn – to cheers from the left – only to be replaced by one raising the nomination threshold for potential leadership candidates to 20 per cent of the PLP. This removed one of the major democratic changes brought in under Corbyn, demonstrating how fragile the left's gains were over the previous four years.

The left had to settle for the guerrilla war of holding what ground it could, and go back to the thankless task of winning motions at conferences only for them to be ignored by the party leadership. Inevitably, there was another debate among people on the left about whether to stay in the party or leave. Many took to social media to express their frustration and rage at the rightward shift under Starmer; others urged them to stay, to continue the fight. The bitter cycle of defeat was playing itself out again, even more bitter this time considering the temporary gains of the previous years.

The Inertia of Momentum and the Left

The course that Momentum took is the clearest example of the integration/transformation dynamic at work. It began with a transformative, insurgent energy that had not been seen in Britain since the anti-Iraq-war movement of 2003. The media scare stories that the organisation was a hard-left phalanx of radicals intent on subverting the very institutional basis of the Labour Party was pure reds-under-the-bed propaganda, and it gave Momentum a dynamic edge and notoriety which the left hadn't enjoyed for years. Its social media reach had an important impact on reaching voters, and its ground campaign was hugely important in winning a number of new seats at the 2017 general election.

But well before 2019 Momentum had lost a lot of its activists and was a hollow shell of what it had originally been. Its initial growth and success were largely squandered by its increasing centralisation and lack of independence from the leader's office. It never took its internal democratic structures seriously, and it increasingly relied on paid staff and its extensive social media and mailing lists instead of healthy local organisations. Arguments within its own ranks festered as they were never resolved through any conference or democratic vote. The summary cancellation of the first Momentum national conference in January 2017, and the imposition of a new constitution designed to empower the leadership against the membership, marked a turning point from which the organisation never recovered. This occurred on the same day that Corbyn gave a speech in Peterborough in which he declared that 'Labour is not wedded to freedom of movement for EU citizens as a point of principle' and began to talk about managed migration; this collapsed a key part of the left argument and gave ground to the Conservative Party.[26] Just at the point when the Labour left needed an independent lever to help push the party consistently to the left, Momentum instead became an organisation whose sole purpose was to protect and bolster the existing leadership. It was these integrationist moves – toning down the most radical and important parts of the political argument while limiting the horizon of politics to manoeuvres within the Labour Party – that sucked the life out of the project. This was the inevitable result of Labourism. It would have been even worse if Labour had won an election, as the pressure on the left to silence its criticism and fall in line behind a leadership facing huge coordinated resistance from capital would have been overwhelming.

The opportunism necessary for electoralism is also a factor in eroding the basic principles of the left's politics. One example during Corbyn's leadership was when Labour adopted a policy of adding an extra 10,000 police and 5,000 border guards. Any truly socialist organisation would have a clear position in opposition to expanding a police force under capitalism, but during the Corbyn era the electoral expediency of promoting social democratic politics took precedence. Momentum actively promoted arguments critical of cuts to police numbers as part of the wider cuts to the public sector.[27] After Corbyn had resigned and the Black Lives Matter movement emerged in response to the horrific killing of George Floyd in the USA, as well as several other murders by police, Momentum's social media output became far more critical of the police.

In 2020 Momentum held elections to its National Coordinating Group (NCG). Two main slates emerged: Forward Momentum and Momentum Renewal. These represented a split among the existing organisers, with Momentum Renewal representing a form of Bennism aligned with younger Stalinists who had re-emerged under Corbyn, and Forward Momentum representing a new left tendency promising a more member-led organisation and a break from some of the practices of the past. The Forward Momentum slate won the election easily, but despite the new leadership there was no break with the organisation's NGO style of top-down politics that it had practised since 2017. The new NCG first published a five-year strategy document with no consultation, and then embarked on a torturous 'refounding process' which excluded most standard aspects of rank-and-file democracy.[28]

With the route to party leadership barred possibly for years to come, the real test of Momentum was whether it could mobilise its 25,000 members in an active campaign against the Conservative government's attacks on immigration and the right to protest.[29] But the paper membership of Momentum didn't translate into a real-life campaign response, partly because it had spent years focusing almost exclusively on organising internally within Labour. This is another instance of the historic failure of the left to establish Labour as a campaigning party between elections in a way that makes it credible in working-class communities. To Kinnock's claim that Labour can be a party of either protest or power, the left's best response is to say that when the party is not in power then it has to be a party of protest, it has to be mobilising people beyond its own ranks, engaging in issues that politicise and radicalise people.[30] Socialists know that ideas change in struggle, that if you want a radical workers' movement it has to be one that is confident, energetic, self-mobilising and capable of breaking down divisions within its own ranks. Otherwise you only encounter workers as voters, as just another demographic to canvass, to passively reflect back their own views and prejudices in the hope of securing votes.[31] When Labour went to the electorate in 2017 and 2019, it would have secured a far higher share of the vote had it linked key aspects of its manifesto to actual struggles around housing or the living wage. But the Labour left squandered its power and influence. Even when it won entire regional committees of the Labour Party, like in London, it did nothing with its gains, failing to engage with trade unionists in struggles against austerity, until it was swept out in the next set of internal elections. The inertia of Labourism had thoroughly infected the left of the party.

Conclusion
'Where Civil Blood Makes Civil Hands Unclean...'

The continual rise and fall and rise again of the left of the Labour Party could give its advocates hope that whatever the temporary setbacks their cause lives on. Alternatively, it could be the sign of a movement trapped in the prison of Labourism, constantly wishing but forever failing to achieve its goals. This book took as a starting point Leo Panitch's view of the two wolves inside Labour, the radical transformative wing and the pro-capitalist integrationist wing. The tale of the battle between these two outlooks lies at the basis of Labour history, but, as we have seen, the integrationist tendency is the most powerful one. It exists even on the left and ultimately is the cause of the left's defeat.

One noticeable problem facing the left is the ephemeral nature of any apparent victories gained by any transformative shift. The blood, sweat and tears of the Corbyn years produced policies that were abandoned within months of Starmer becoming leader. Momentum and others fought a rearguard action to encourage members to 'stay and fight', but it wasn't clear how to fight. Leading socialist activists with decades of party membership were expelled with little recourse to natural justice – attempts to discuss their expulsions at CLPs led to chairs and secretaries also being expelled. The open door that allowed Corbyn to get on to the leadership ballot in 2015 was closed at the 2021 conference as the rule book was amended to increase the threshold for nominations. The Socialist Campaign Group was split between hard and soft left MPs. To rub salt in the wound, even Corbyn was excluded from the PLP in 2020, and rank-and-file members had no way of forcing his reinstatement as all discussion of it was blocked at CLP level.[1]

The two wings of Labour are no longer uneasy comrades in an alliance, if they ever were. They are now bitter opponents who exist in a state of war. Surveying the history of the Labour Party, what becomes apparent is not only how deeply divided the party is on a fundamental level but also the sheer hatred the two wings have for each other. The experience of attempting to win elections during the Corbyn era was marked by acts of internal sabotage likely never seen before in a British political party. The right of the party saw the left as a cancer and desired in their marrow for its growth to be cut out. On the surface Labour appears to be a party that can be run by either the left or the right – as a neutral vehicle, much like social democracies view the capitalist state – but in reality the party is wedded by its very structures to maintaining the functioning of capitalism, and therefore it will always treat the left as an insurgent and unwelcome force. This becomes even more the case the more the contradictions of capitalism make reformist agendas harder to implement – the Labour right have consolidated their polities around a form of vicious anti-socialist liberalism that they view as post-Thatcherite common sense.

The rage and fury of the civil war in Labour under Corbyn was more stark than it had been in any previous internal feud. This points to the historic changes in the party over the decades – to the fact that the Labour left is no longer seen as a legitimate component of the Labour family. The sight of someone like Denis Healey going to Chesterfield in 1984 to help get a left stalwart like Tony Benn elected was simply unfathomable by 2017 – by then the Labour right was seeking to sabotage, undermine and outright defy the left's leadership at every turn.

The extent of this was exposed in 2020, when an 850-page internal report into the antisemitism issue in Labour was leaked after Starmer had intervened to prevent its publication. Much to the rage of the new leader and his allies, the report detailed at great length how the party bureaucracy, the people actually running the machinery, fiercely hated everything Corbyn stood for and were actively organising against Labour while he was in charge. They delighted in scouring social media for people to expel, a full-time job they gloatingly called 'trot busting' or 'bashing trots'. One of the staffers proudly called himself 'trot smasher in chief'. Messages calling Diane Abbott 'repulsive' and Karie Murphy a 'bitch face cow' revealed the extent of the hatred directed at the left. They wanted Labour members to die in fires or be used as dartboards.[2]

The report detailed extensive acts of sabotage from day one of Corbyn's election as leader. Appointments for staff were blocked or slowed down, offices were provided without chairs or computers.[3] Subsequent leaks showed how party officials from the right of the party also prevented a proper accounting of the complaints of antisemitism because the 'abnormal intensity of factional opposition ... inhibited the proper functioning' of the complaints procedure.[4] During elections funds were diverted to right-wing Labour MPs, while acts of sabotage included staffers paying for targeted social media adverts that only Corbyn and his inner circle would see.[5] This was intended to give a false impression of the campaign being conducted on Facebook and elsewhere.

This is before we factor in the constant battle with the PLP, and the Labour councillors across the country who acted as a bulwark against the left locally. The lessons of the Corbyn era show that for the Labour left to successfully 'take over' the party they would have to win control of most CLPs; have a majority of the PLP being firmly on the left; have control of the party apparatus, the NEC and the leadership; and have firmly left trade union leaders in position as well. The stars would have to align perfectly at the right time for anything approaching a transformative Labour Party to materialise, and this before it has even taken power to implement a radical programme.

The Labour left will fail to achieve its goals for two reasons, one political and the other structural. During the Blair era a popular T-shirt worn by some socialists bore the slogan 'Labour: I prefer their earlier work'. An understandable sentiment perhaps, but every Labour government has seen its role as that of preserving British capitalism and Britain's place in the world as a 'great power', and as a result has attacked parts of the working class and pursued colonial policies abroad. The constant battle of the Labour left to 'reclaim the party' is based on a total misunderstanding of Labour's history. While the rhetoric of Labour was more avowedly pro-socialist in the past, its actions in government and during significant moments of class struggle have demonstrated the essential nature of the party. When there is a choice between integration into the existing structures of capital and the state or transformation, Labour always takes the path most beneficial to sustaining capitalism.

Labourism conceived as the integration of the working class into managing capitalism points to the reality that Labour is a counter-revolutionary party, formally constituted in 1918 precisely to stop the spread of revolutionary socialism in Britain. Behind its appeals to a common endeavour and its occasional socialistic rhetoric, it is a party based in completely abject loyalty to parliamentary politics, to the state and to British imperial rule. It is the party of MacDonald and Snowden on their knees before King George. It is not a party that has ever sold out because it was *built* to facilitate co-option; its founders supported not the revolutionary overthrow of capitalism but its accommodation and gradual reform. The Labour left has often raised valiant and valid criticisms of aspects of Labour government policy, but it has always been trapped within the logic of a parliamentary party and the compromises that come with it. Even the leading figures of the Labour left like Bevan and Benn served in governments that directly attacked trade unionists, slashed living conditions and pursued militarist policies. Their criticisms and organised fight-backs always happened when Labour was in opposition. Furthermore, whenever the Labour left fights battles within the party to improve policy or democratise the party, this is always spun to voters as 'another Labour civil war', implying structural instability and a party not fit for government. Not until the left is decisively defeated is Labour reported to be back to its winning ways, as for instance when Bevan capitulated in 1959, Benn demobilised his movement in 1982, or Corbyn was beaten in 2019.

The result is that in order for the left to be allowed to run the party they must also make strategic compromises with capital and accept Britain's role as an imperialist country. This means that Labour cannot lead a serious class struggle against British capitalism, and must instead position itself as a loyal opposition that is acting in the national interest. Anything less will be bitterly opposed on every front by the established powers. Even when they do meet this demand – and Corbyn's era was replete with examples of a softening of positions on everything from NATO to fighting the anti-trade union laws – the Labour left will still never be trusted by the British Establishment to run a government. This is why it only nationalises bankrupt or near bankrupt industries. Even the proposal for a four-day working week under Corbyn was articulated as something that was good for British business. This is the position that must be adopted in order to win elections, not to prosecute a struggle for socialism.

These are the exact same problems that the New Left identified in the 1960s, problems that arise when the radical left becomes absorbed into the deathly bureaucratic structures of the Labourite labyrinth – the place where democracy goes to die. As Raymond Williams put it in his *May Day Manifesto 1968*:

> When it [the left] chooses the electoral campaign it becomes of necessity involved in the same kind of machine politics, the same manipulation of committee votes in the names of thousands, the same confusion of the emptying institutions of the movement with the people in whose name they are conducted ... it is directing energy into the very machines and methods which socialists should fight.[6]

Labour left activists end up as committee-people, focusing on internal manoeuvres and political sleights of hand. Momentum originally promised a social movement that would change politics and bridge the gap between the party and wider society. But by the end Momentum and others on the Labour left ended up implementing undemocratic manoeuvres similar to those of Progress decades previously, like parachuting candidates into CLPs over the heads of local activists. The very nature of Labour politics bound them to the logic of integration and realpolitik.

The struggles that needed to be waged – for instance building rank-and-file left movements in the unions – were abandoned by the Labour left in favour of a tenuous alliance with trade union leaders supposedly on the 'left'. The failure to take the initial Corbyn surge into the unions as a strategy to challenge their bureaucracies led directly to the debacle of the 2018 Labour conference, where Unite led the charge to prevent open selection. In reality Momentum and the rest of the Labour left could not have openly challenged the union leaders because of the logic of Labour leftism, according to which alliances with sympathetic vote-wielding General Secretaries will always take priority over an insurrectionary radical movement of workers from below. Forget it, Jake. It's Chinatown.[7]

In 1920 Lenin argued that:

> of course most of the Labour Party's members are working men. However, whether or not a party is really a political party of the workers does not depend solely upon a membership of workers but also upon the men that lead it, and the content of its actions and its political tactics. Only this latter determines whether we really have before us a political party of the proletariat. Regarded from this, the only correct point of view, the Labour Party is a thoroughly bourgeois party because, although made up of workers, it is led by reactionaries, and the worst kind of reactionaries at that, who act quite in the spirit of the bourgeoisie.[8]

This gave rise to the Marxist view that Labour (alongside other social democratic parties) is a bourgeois workers' party, a party whose support rests on working-class votes but which ultimately defends the interests of the capitalist class. The traditional view of Marxists has been that it is possible under certain conditions to become active in the Labour Party in order to foster the existence of a radical left, and then when faced with the inevitable attacks from the right split them away to form a class struggle socialist organisation. That was not possible under Corbynism largely due to the lack of class struggle outside of Labour, but also due to the political incoherence of the left of the party and the undemocratic politics of organisations like Momentum. For those forces it was Corbyn or bust – and in the end it was bust.

This political contradiction at the heart of Labour is why the Labour left itself has struggled to understand the difference between social democracy and socialism – one is a modification of capitalism through a mixed economy and strong labour laws, while the other entails the removal of the capitalist class from power. Some on the Labour left believe that they exist on the same spectrum, that the former is merely a step towards the latter – the gradualist approach. This cuts to the core of the historic debate in the socialist movement between those who favoured parliament and legislation as the method for achieving socialism and those who knew that it would require class struggle and revolution.

Writing in the 1920s on Labourism, the Russian revolutionary Leon Trotsky argued that the Labour left acted like 'a sort of safety valve for the radical mood of the masses'.[9] This was not necessarily a role it consciously undertook, but the essential problem the Labour left will always have is that people join the party to make a difference and then end up being ground down by its internal bureaucratism, constantly in a battle with the right and the full-time apparatus, both of which act to frustrate, diffuse and ultimately nullify any serious radicalism. In this sense the Labour left 'represent the expression of a shift but also its brake'. We can see this in the way that the shift to the struggle internal to the Labour party meant the end of the anti-cuts movement on the streets, and the lack of any serious attempt to organise meaningful large-scale strike action by the Labour-affiliated unions during Corbyn's era.

This doesn't mean that the struggle in Labour is a diversion, as if there is a perfect revolutionary class struggle outside of the party, and people wasted their time in factional struggles in CLP meetings. The class struggle is not only strikes and mass protests; the battle inside Labour – the mass party of the trade unions as the organised section of the working class – is also part of it. Engels remarked that the class struggle happens on the industrial, political and ideological terrains.[10] Labour had half a million members under Corbyn, and as such the ideological battle within the party was an expression of wider social forces and an important fight to have. Socialists have to be fighting alongside the most advanced layers of the working class even when they are blundering into a hopeless fight. This does not mean, of course, that one should withhold criticism of what is happening and why it is doomed to fail. It is also important for socialists never to limit their focus to social movements and the trade unions – there is always a fight for power and political questions need political organisation in response.

Labour is a battlefield for socialists. It is the party that the British labour movement has built, for good or ill. As Bevan warned Jennie Lee in the 1930s: 'it is the Labour Party or nothing ... I know all its faults, all its dangers. But it is the Party that we have taught millions of working people to look to and regard as their own.'[11] The perennial problem for the British (increasingly the English) left is that while it can view Labour as a party built on a rotten compromise with capitalism, it has also never been replaced by anything better.[12] The first-past-the-post system makes building a credible left alternative very hard to achieve, and the trade unions are wedded to Labour through the institutional relationship between the union and party bureaucracies. Labour as a party has never been and never will be a socialist party because it does not have a conception of class struggle as the primary motor of politics. The Labour left might believe in the class war, but they are too enmeshed in the logic of Labourism to realise a strategy around this struggle. For socialists, being in Labour can only ever be a tactic dependent on the political conditions and struggle of the time, not a strategy for socialism.

If there is to be another opportunity for the Labour left along the lines of Corbyn, then the movement would need to be serious about building and supporting workers' struggles in practice, about building a fighting force in the trade unions, about being wary of both party and union bureaucracies, about constructing an independent left that acts to pressure the leadership, not merely defend it against the right. Many involved in Corbynism have drawn these conclusions well after the movement was defeated, but will the lessons be learned for next time? Will there be a next time?

In their account of the Labour New Left, Panitch and Leys conclude that the experience of Corbynism could be read as evidence for Ralph Miliband's conclusion that 'continuing with the attempt to convert the Labour Party into an effective force for democratic socialism is a "crippling illusion"'.[13] Nevertheless, given the failures of alternative electoral projects, it is understandable that young activists will continue to look to Labour as the key site for political struggle with the hope to 'fundamentally change it'.[14] The contradiction is obvious – Labour is incapable of adopting the politics necessary to overthrow capitalism, and yet the workers' movement hasn't built a credible electoral alternative to it. There is no easy solution, but Panitch and Leys do acknowledge that, given the existential nature of the climate crisis, the threat of inter-imperialist war and the inability of capitalism to guarantee any quality of life in even the richer capitalist countries due to cyclical decline, the stakes have never been higher – and time is not on our side. Waiting for the stars to align to rebuild a parliamentary left capable of smoothly winning power is a recipe for paralysis. Ralph Miliband accused Labour of being fetishistic about parliamentary democracy, and it is this fetish that the Labour left needs to move beyond. We need mass social movements to be built now in the face of fierce authoritarian capitalist opposition, and we need a revolutionary socialist alternative capable of using the overlapping crises of capitalism to build a different kind of power, not one fixated on parliament and the rotten institutions of imperialist Britain, but one founded on new forums of mass democracy built out of struggle.

There is an old Irish joke about a city man from Dublin in the rural countryside of the west who asks a farmer how to get to Cork. The farmer scratches his head for a minute and replies: 'I wouldn't start from here.' So it is with the Labour Party.

Notes

Introduction

1. See for instance O. Jones, *This Land: The Story of a Movement* (London: Penguin 2020); G. Pogrund and P. Maguire, *Left Out: The Inside Story of Labour Under Corbyn* (London: Random House, 2020).
2. Leo Panitch's arguments around Labour's integrative nature were developed in 'Ideology and Integration: The Case of the British Labour Party', *Political Studies* 19:2 (1971), and in *Social Democracy and Industrial Militancy* (Cambridge: Cambridge University Press, 1976). Alan Warde, in his *Consensus and Beyond* (Manchester: Manchester University Press 1982), uses these terms, though differently to my interpretation. See also R. Miliband, *Parliamentary Socialism: A Study in the Politics of Labour* (Pontypool: Merlin Press, 2009), p. 19.

Chapter 1

1. H. Pelling, *The Origins of the Labour Party* (Oxford: Clarendon Press, 1965), p. 225. William Gladstone was a Liberal leader and Prime Minister who carried out a popular reforming agenda.
2. Cited in G. Elton and B. Elton, *'England, Arise!': A Study of the Pioneering Days of the Labour Movement* (London: Jonathan Cape, 1931), p. 177.
3. J. Schneer, *Labour's Conscience: The Labour Left, 1945–51* (London: Unwin Hyman, 1988), p. 4.
4. *What Socialism Is*, Fabian Tract No. 13 (London, 1890).
5. Keir Hardie and Richard Bell, the first Labour MPs in Parliament.
6. *Labour Leader*, 8 February 1907.
7. C. Collette, *For Labour and for Women: The Women's Labour League, 1906–1918* (Manchester: Manchester University Press, 1989), p. 19.
8. G.D.H. Cole, *The British Working Class Movement 1787–1947* (London: George Allen and Unwin, 1952), p. 321.
9. G.D.H. Cole, *A Short History of the British Working Class Movement: 1900–1937* (London: Routledge 2002), p. 70.
10. The Great Unrest involved mass strikes by miners, dockworkers, transport workers and workers in many other industries.

11. G.D.H. Cole, *The World of Labour* (London: Taylor & Francis, 2010), p. 38.

12. B. Holman, *Keir Hardie: Labour's Greatest Hero?* (Oxford: Lion Books, 2010) pp. 167–8.

13. Holman, *Keir Hardie*, p. 168.

14. A. Leventhal, *Arthur Henderson* (Lives of the Left) (Manchester: Manchester University Press, 1989), p. 8.

15. Leventhal, *Arthur Henderson*, pp. 8–9.

16. Cited in Leventhal, *Arthur Henderson*, p. 42.

17. R. Groves, *The Strange Case of Victor Grayson* (London: Pluto Press, 1975), pp. 66–9.

18. Grayson mysteriously disappeared in 1920 leaving nothing but rumours about his fate.

19. Quoted in Cole, *Short History of the British Working Class Movement*, p. 117.

20. Cole, *Short History of the British Working Class Movement*, p. 118.

21. Unsurprisingly as Blatchford and Hyndman had combined their socialism with a particularly nationalist viewpoint, both supporting the war against Prussian militarism while ignoring their own country's particularly militaristic position.

22. Cited in R.E. Dowse, *Left in the Centre* (London: Longmans, 1966), p. 20.

23. Dowse, *Left in the Centre*, p. 22.

24. *Daily Chronicle*, 14 September 1914. MacDonald's attitude was not unrepresentative of the mainstream view of the labour movement, which was opposed to conscription but in favour of voluntary patriotic efforts to win the war.

25. E. Shinwell, *Conflict Without Malice* (London: Odhams Press, 1955), p. 115.

26. Henderson went on to win the Nobel Peace Prize in 1934.

27. 209 delegates from Trades Councils and local labour parties and 294 delegates from the ILP, among others.

28. Dowse, *Left in the Centre*, p. 29.

29. 'Distribution and exchange' were added in the late 1920s.

30. T. Nairn, 'The Nature of the Labour Party, Part 1', *New Left Review*, I/27, September–October 1964.

31. P. Seyd, *The Rise and Fall of the Labour Left* (London: Palgrave, 1987), p. 202.

32. R. Crossman, Introduction to Walter Bagehot, *The English Constitution* (London: Fontana, 1963), p. 42.

33. Miliband, *Parliamentary Socialism*, p. 62.

34. V. I. Lenin, *Selected Works in Three Volumes*, Volume 3 (London: Progress Publishers, 1967), p. 346.

35. Cited in M. Shipway, *Anti-Parliamentary Communism: The Movement for Workers' Councils in Britain, 1917–45* (New York: Springer, 2016), p. 70.

36. J. Schneer, *George Lansbury* (Manchester: Manchester University Press, 1990), p. 60.

37. Though as Maxton argued at the 1919 ILP conference: 'Shinwell, so far from being an inciting factor in the whole of the forty-hour movement, was there all the time as a restraining element among the strikers.' ILP Conference Report, 1919, p. 72.

38. Also known as Black Friday, when miners had their wages reduced by the mine owners. Their union's alliance with rail and transport unions should have triggered solidarity action to help the miners get their wages back. But the rail and transport unions did not take action, leaving the miners isolated and defeated. The wage reductions were a huge social blow to the often impoverished mining communities across the country. Black Friday was a profoundly demoralising experience for trade unionists as their organisations rejected a path of solidarity, undermining the entire basis of trade unionism.

39. F. McLynn, *The Road Not Taken: How Britain Narrowly Missed a Revolution* (London: The Bodley Head, 2012), p. 371.

40. Cited in Miliband, *Parliamentary Socialism*, p. 95.

41. F. Brockway, *Inside the Left* (Nottingham: Spokesman, 2010), p. 220.

42. P. Ward, *Red Flag and Union Jack: Englishness, Patriotism, and the British Left, 1881–1924* (Martlesham: Boydell & Brewer, 1998), p. 193.

43. Miliband, *Parliamentary Socialism*, pp. 95–6.

44. J.N. Evans, *Great Figures in the Labour Movement* (London: Pergamon, 1966), p. 109.

45. Cited in Davies, *To Build a New Jerusalem* (London: Abacus, 1996), p. 124.

46. A.J. Davies, *To Build a New Jerusalem*, p. 125.

47. P. Snowden, *An Autobiography* (London: I. Nicholson and Watson, 1988), p. 596.

48. Brockway, *Inside the Left*, p. 148.

49. Cited in J. McNair, *James Maxton: The Beloved Rebel* (London: Allen & Unwin, 1955), p. 187.

50. Brockway, *Inside the Left*, p. 198.

51. R. Arnott, *The Miners: A Year of Struggle* (London: Allen and Unwin, 1953), p. 430.

52. Cited in N. Bevan, *In Place of Fear* (London: William Heinemann, 1952), p. 41.

53. Bevan, *In Place of Fear*, pp. 20–1.

54. A quote from the Prussian Minister Von Puttkamer in the 1870s.
55. K. Laybourn, *The Great Strike of 1926* (Manchester: Manchester University Press 1993), p. 4.
56. Laybourn, *The Great Strike of 1926*, p. 71.
57. J. Paton, *Turn Left!* (London: Secker & Warburg, Ltd., 1936), p. 245.
58. Bevan, *In Place of Fear*, pp. 17 and 25.
59. Bevan, *In Place of Fear*, p. 25.
60. MacDiarmid cited in C. Ferrell and D. MacNeil, *Writing the 1926 General Strike* (New York: Cambridge University Press, 2015), p. 126.
61. Dowse, *Left in the Centre*, pp. 128–9.
62. K. Laybourn, *The Rise of Labour: The British Labour Party 1890–1979* (London: Edward Arnold, 1988), pp. 54–5.
63. A.F. Havinghurst, *Britain in Transition: The Twentieth Century* (Chicago: University of Chicago Press, 1979), p. 201.
64. Cited in Miliband, *Parliamentary Socialism*, p. 153.
65. M. Woodhouse and B. Pearce, *Essays on the History of Communism in Britain* (London: New Park, 1975), p. 180.
66. Woodhouse and Pearce, *Essays on the History of Communism*, p. 188.
67. Bevin is recorded as saying 'I believe that even in our own country there will have to be the shedding of blood to attain the freedom we require.' A. Bullock, *The Life and Times of Ernest Bevin: Trade Union Leader, 1881–1940* (London: Heinemann, 1960), p. 75.
68. K. Marx, 'A Contribution to the Critique of Political Economy', in *Selected Writings* (Indiana: Hackett, 1994), pp. 209–13.
69. The government severely curtailed the rights of trade unions and forced them to alter their funding for the Labour Party – a direct attack on both the workers' industrial struggle and their political representation. A similar scale of interference by a Tory government in the political representation of workers would not occur until the proposed Trade Union Act in 2015–16.
70. W. Knox, *James Maxton* (Lives of the Left) (Manchester: Manchester University Press, 1987), pp. 72–3.
71. W. Kenefick, *Red Scotland! The Rise and Fall of the Radical Left, c. 1872–1932* (Edinburgh: Edinburgh University Press, 2007), p. 200.
72. Knox, *James Maxton*, p. 75.

Chapter Two

1. Knox, *James Maxton*, p. 84.
2. I.S. Wood, *John Wheatley* (Manchester: Manchester University Press, 1990), p. 181.

3. *New Leader*, 14 August 1931.
4. Cited in Wood, *John Wheatley*, p. 187.
5. N. Riddell, *Labour in Crisis: The Second Labour Government 1929–1931* (Manchester: Manchester University Press, 1999), p. 160.
6. A. Morgan, *J. Ramsay MacDonald* (Manchester: Manchester University Press, 1987), p. 187.
7. Morgan, *J. Ramsay MacDonald*, p. 187.
8. R. Pearce, *Attlee* (London: Routledge 2014), p. 47.
9. Cole, *A Short History of the British Working Class Movement: 1900–1937*, p. 73.
10. C. Attlee, *As It Happened: The Autobiography of Clement R. Attlee* (New York: Viking Press, 1954), p. 4.
11. J. Lee, *Great Journey* (London: MacGibbon & Kee, 1967), pp. 108–9.
12. J. H. Brookshire, *Clement Attlee* (Manchester: Manchester University Press, 1995), p. 57.
13. G. Elliott, *Labourism and the English Genius: The Strange Death of Labour England?* (London: Verso, 1993), p. 47.
14. Brockway, *Inside the Left*, p. 238.
15. R.K. Middlemass, *The Clydesiders* (London: Hutchinson, 1965), Chapter 12.
16. J. Lee, *My Life with Nye* (London: Jonathan Cape Ltd, 1980), p. 67.
17. P. Hollis, *Jennie Lee: A Life* (Oxford: Oxford University Press, 1998), pp. 64–5.
18. Party of Marxist Unification, led by Andreas Nin.
19. Several ILP members were killed in the fighting. Bob Smillie, a youth leader in the ILP, died suspiciously in a Republican prison in Spain in 1937. Arthur Chambers died fighting alongside an anarchist unit the same year. In all, 13 of the ILP volunteers were wounded or hospitalised. From 'The ILP and the Spanish Civil War', at www.independentlabour.org.uk.
20. Cited in R. Vickers, *The Labour Party and the World: Evolution of Labour's Foreign Policy, 1900–51*, Volume 1 (Manchester: Manchester University Press, 2004), p. 99.
21. M. Foot, 'Credo of the Labour Left', *New Left Review*, 49, May–June, 1968, p. 20.
22. *Political Quarterly*, July–September, 1932.
23. B. Betts, 'Youth and Peace', *Socialist Leaguer*, No. 5, October–November, 1934.
24. Labour Party Conference Report, 1934, p. 159.
25. Labour Party Conference Report, 1933.
26. G. Bennett, *The Concept of Empire: Burke to Attlee, 1774–1947* (London: Adam and Charles Black, 1953), p. 406.

27. M. Bor, *The Socialist League in the 1930s* (London: Athena Press, 2005), p. 288.
28. Bor, *The Socialist League in the 1930s*, pp. 290–305.
29. M. Worley, *Labour Inside the Gate: A History of the British Labour Party Between the Wars* (London: I.B. Tauris, 2005), p. 158.
30. B. Pimlott, *Labour and the Left in the 1930s* (Cambridge: Cambridge University Press, 1977), pp. 41–2.
31. Leo Panitch gives a slightly unwieldy definition of corporatism as 'a political structure within advanced capitalism which integrates organised socio-economic producer groups through a system of representation and cooperative mutual interaction at the leadership level and mobilization and social control at the mass level'. 'Trade Unions and the Capitalist State', *New Left Review*, I/125, January–February, 1981, pp. 21–44.
32. Scheer, *Lansbury*, pp. 65–6.
33. G. Foote, *The Labour Party's Political Thought* (Basingstoke: Palgrave, 2002), p. 181.
34. D. Coates, *The Labour Party and the Struggle for Socialism* (Cambridge: Cambridge University Press, 1975), p. 36.
35. Coates, *The Labour Party and the Struggle for Socialism*, p. 34.
36. Coates, *The Labour Party and the Struggle for Socialism*, p. 35.
37. P. Corthorn, *In the Shadow of the Dictators: The British Left in the 1930s* (London: I.B. Tauris, 2006), p. 41.
38. L. Davies, *Through the Looking Glass* (London: Verso, 1996), p. 191.
39. Cited in Corthorn, *In the Shadow of the Dictators*, p. 46.
40. K. Martin, *Harold Laski (1893–1958): A Biographical Memoir* (London: Victor Gollancz, 1953), pp. 105–6.
41. T. Buchanan, *The Spanish Civil War and the British Labour Movement* (Cambridge: Cambridge University Press, 1991), p. 204.
42. Cited in B. Pimlott (ed.), *The Political Diary of Hugh Dalton, 1918–40, 1945–60* (London: Jonathan Cape, 1986), p. 229.
43. B. Pimlott, *Hugh Dalton* (London: Jonathan Cape, 1986), p. 181.
44. H. Dalton, *Memoir: The Fateful Years, 1931–1945* (London: Muller, 1957), p. 130.
45. J.T. Murphy, *New Horizons* (London: John Lane, 1941), p. 321.
46. R. Groves, 'The Socialist League', *Revolutionary History*, 1, 1988.
47. Brockway, *Inside the Left*, pp. 269–70.
48. Coates, *The Labour Party and the Struggle for Socialism*, pp. 187–8.
49. A point made by Tawney in 1931, quoted in R. Harrison, 'Labour Government: Then and Now', *Political Quarterly*, 41:11 (1970), p. 78.
50. Pimlott, *Hugh Dalton*, p. 229.
51. Schneer, *George Lansbury*, p. 174.

52. Cited in K. Laybourn, *A Century of Labour: A History of the Labour Party 1900–2000* (Stroud: Sutton Publishing, 2000), p. 67. Bevin was even less kind after his victory: 'Lansbury has been going about dressed up in saint's clothes for years waiting for martyrdom. I set fire to the faggots.'

Chapter Three

1. Cited in N. Thomas-Symonds, *Nye: The Political Life of Aneurin Bevan* (London: I.B. Tauris, 2014), p. 92.
2. Bevan in *Tribune*, 10 March 1939.
3. Schneer, *Labour's Conscience*, p. 159.
4. Hollis, *Jennie Lee: A Life*, pp. 103–7.
5. Hollis, *Jennie Lee: A Life*, p. 108.
6. Hollis, *Jennie Lee: A Life*, p. 113.
7. I. Kramnick and B. Sheerman, *Harold Laski: A Life on the Left* (London: Allen Lane, 1993), p. 441.
8. C. Beckett and F. Beckett, *Bevan* (London: Haus, 2004), p. 41.
9. Hollis, *Jennie Lee: A Life*, pp. 97–8.
10. D. Kynaston, *Austerity Britain, 1945–1951* (London: Bloomsbury, 2007), p. 87.
11. Schneer, *Labour's Conscience*, p. 25.
12. A. Mitchell, *Election '45: Reflections on the Revolution in Britain* (London: Bellew Publishing, 1995), p. 67.
13. S. Brooke, *Labour's War: The Labour Party During the Second World War* (Oxford: Clarendon Press, 1992).
14. After the Tory R.A. Butler and Labour's Hugh Gaitskill.
15. A. Davies, *To Build a New Jerusalem* (London: Abacus, 1996), p. 210.
16. Davies, *To Build a New Jerusalem*, p. 227.
17. A.A. Rogow and P. Shore, *The Labour Government and British Industry, 1945–1951* (Oxford: Blackwell, 1955).
18. Hansard, 17 February 1943: 1818.
19. See Angus Calder's *The People's War: Britain 1939–45* (London: Jonathan Cape, 1969).
20. Davies, *To Build a New Jerusalem*, p. 228.
21. Havinghurst, *Britain in Transition: The Twentieth Century*, p. 410.
22. Davies, *To Build a New Jerusalem*, pp. 225–6.
23. E.E. Barry, *Nationalisation in British Politics: The Historical Background* (Stanford: Stanford University Press, 1965), p. 377.
24. It is worth noting that Attlee had backed an amendment to the 1933 Labour Party conference, moved by Cripps, to abolish the House of Lords, as described in Brookshire, *Clement Attlee*, pp. 57–8.

25. A. Thorpe, *A History of the British Labour Party* (London: Palgrave Macmillan, 2015), p. 122.

26. M. Jenkins, *Bevanism: Labour's High Tide* (Nottingham: Spokesman Books, 2012), p. 83.

27. Cited in Schneer, *Labour's Conscience*, p. 32.

28. Vickers, *The Labour Party and the World*, p. 170.

29. G. DeGroot, *The Bomb: A Life* (London: Pimlico, 2005), p. 219.

30. Schneer, *Labour's Conscience*, p. 44.

31. Vickers, *The Labour Party and the World*, p. 170.

32. *New Statesman*, 16 April 1949.

Chapter Four

1. M. Foot, *Aneurin Bevan: A Biography: Volume 2, 1945–1960* (London: Davis-Poynter, 1973), p. 304.

2. Foot, *Aneurin Bevan*, p. 305.

3. Foot, *Aneurin Bevan*, p. 342.

4. Jenkins, *Bevanism*, p. 291.

5. As Miliband points out, the re-privatisation of steel and road transport was something of a boon for the leadership, because outspoken opposition to it gave something to throw back to the activists (*Parliamentary Socialism*, p. 322).

6. Bevan, *In Place of Fear*, pp. 97–9.

7. Jenkins, *Bevanism*, p. 150.

8. E. Shaw, *Discipline and Discord in the Labour Party* (Manchester: Manchester University Press, 1988), p. 47.

9. Cited in Jenkins, *Bevanism*, p. 158.

10. L. Hunter, *The Road to Brighton Pier* (London: Arthur Baker Publishing, 1959), p. 52.

11. M. Beech and K. Hickson, *The Struggle for Labour's Soul: Understanding Labour's Political Thought Since 1945* (London: Routledge, 2004), p. 15.

12. D. Kynaston, *Family Britain, 1951–1957* (London: Bloomsbury, 2010), p. 429.

13. Thorpe, *A History of the British Labour Party*, p. 144.

14. F. Parkin, *Middle-Class Radicalism: The Social Bases of the British Campaign for Nuclear Disarmament* (Manchester: Manchester University Press, 1968), pp. 38–9.

15. Cited in Foot, *Aneurin Bevan*, p. 576.

16. Cited in Thomas-Symonds, *Nye*, p. 231.

17. Thomas-Symonds, *Nye*, pp. 236–7.

18. Miliband, in D. Coates, *Paving the Third Way* (London: Merlin Press, 2003), p. 60.
19. The book *Must Labour Lose?* (Harmondsworth: Penguin, 1960), by Mark Abrams and Richard Rose, made a similar assertion: that the working class was being stratified by 'embourgeoisement' and that class was a cultural relationship in society, not necessarily an economic one.
20. R. Miliband in Coates, *Paving the Third Way*, p. 57.
21. D. Marquand, *The Progressive Dilemma* (London: Heinemann, 1992), pp. 197–8.
22. W.H. Greenleaf, *The British Political Tradition: The Ideological Heritage*, Volume 2 (London: Routledge, 1983), p. 470.
23. R. Crossman, *Towards a Philosophy of Socialism* (London: Turnstile Press, 1952), p. 27.
24. The rush to the right in Britain was part of an international trend within European social democracy, following similar capitalist dynamics (and integrationist tendencies) in other countries. The German SDP conference at Bad Godesberg also agreed to formerly abandon their socialist programme and commit themselves to working for capitalism with a human face.
25. Labour Party Report of the 58th Annual Conference (London: Labour Party 1959), p. 154.
26. Cited in S. Matgamna, *Seedbed of the Left* (London: W.L. Publications, 1993), p. 7.
27. 'Warning to the Unilateralists', *Guardian*, 6 October 1960. Gaitskell also argued that 'I sometimes think, frankly, that the system we have by which great unions decide their policy before even their conference can consider their executive's recommendation is not really a wise one or a good one.' It seems that when union policy which favours the right is decided by union leaders and not the union members then this democratic deficit goes unremarked. But on the rare occasions when this favours the left, the right became very agitated about this.
28. A party memorandum, circulated a few week before the conference by Morgan Phillips, was clear: 'The Parliamentary Party could not maintain its position in the country if it could be demonstrated that it was at any time or in any way subject to dictation from an outside body which, however representative of the Party, could not be regarded as representative of the country.' Cited by Julian Lewis, 'Labour's Constitutional Crisis, Conservative Political Centre', September 1992, www.julianlewis.net/essays-and-topics/2942: labour-s-constitutional-crisis-13.
29. Membership continued to decline throughout this period – although the official numbers were artificially inflated by CLPs having to affiliate with

at least 800 members (later raised to 1,000). This meant a lot of 'ghost' or paper members as many CLPs affiliated to the party claiming exactly 1,000 members which was usually an over-estimate.

30. Report from Anthony Greenwood, cited in 'The Young Socialists', *International Socialism Journal* 10 (1962), pp. 3–14.

31. J. Scholefield, 'Labour Youth Against the Bureaucracy: 1960–64', *Permanent Revolution* 6 (1987).

32. The Healy group – when it eventually formed the Workers' Revolutionary Party some years later – was characterised by an explosive mixture of sectarianism mixed with opportunism, a revolutionary organisation that in its Labour Party entryism days repeatedly presented itself as only a reformist current.

33. Beech and Hickson, *The Struggle for Labour's Soul*, p. 17.

34. Foot, *Aneurin Bevan*, p. 624.

Chapter Five

1. As the Cabinet papers explain: 'The re-nationalisation of the steel industry by Harold Wilson's Labour government in 1967 did not involve the entire industry but just 14 of the largest firms. Importantly, there was cross-party consensus on nationalisation and, by 1971, it was established that the Conservatives would not de-nationalise the industry.' Cabinet Papers Summary, http://www.nationalarchives.gov.uk/cabinetpapers/themes/after-second-world-war.htm

2. P. Foot, *The Politics of Harold Wilson* (London: Penguin, 1968), p. 172.

3. *Observer*, 24 November 1985.

4. For more details, see Shaw, *Discipline and Discord in the Labour Party*, pp. 129–40.

5. The seamen were on strike to try and force a shorter working week, from 56 hours to 40 hours. Their strike was solid, with many large ports grinding to a halt as ships couldn't be unloaded. When Wilson declared a state of emergency that would allow him to use the Royal Navy to take over the ports and ensure the goods could still be transported he hypocritically tried to cover himself by appealing to national interests: 'The government must protect the vital interests of the nation. This is not action against the National Union of Seamen.' The Labour left came out unequivocally in support of the strikers, and Wilson hesitated on the issue of actually breaking the strike using the armed forces, but clearly he wanted to take action against the NUS because their strike threatened the precarious work being done to balance the deficit and restrict wage rises. In the end the strike was settled with a compromise deal.

6. Beech and Hickson, *The Struggle for Labour's Soul*, p. 17.
7. Foot, 'Credo of the Labour Left', p. 21.
8. R. Opie, 'Economic Planning and Growth', in W. Beckerman (ed.), *The Labour Government's Economic Record 1964–70* (London: Duckworth, 1972), p. 170.
9. R. Miliband and J. Saville, 'Labour Policy and the Labour Left', *The Socialist Register 1964*, pp. 149–56.
10. David Wood, quoted in Shaw, *Discipline and Discord in the Labour Party*, p. 162.
11. First reported in *The Times*, 5 March 1967.
12. Foot, 'Credo of the Labour Left', p. 22.
13. Foot, 'Credo of the Labour Left', p. 23.
14. Cited in P. Foot, 'Harold Wilson and the Labour Left', *International Socialism* (1st series) 33 (1968), pp. 18–26.
15. J. Prescott and C. Hodgins, *Not Wanted on Voyage: The Seamen's Reply*, National Union of Seamen Hull Dispute Committee (1966).
16. J. Saville, 'Labourism and the Labour Government', *The Socialist Register 1967*, p. 67.
17. Livingstone cited in M. Collins, *Ireland After Britain* (London: Pluto Press, 1985), p. 16.
18. S. Howe, *Ireland and Empire: Colonial Legacies in Irish History and Culture* (Oxford: Oxford University Press, 2000), p. 185.
19. Anti-Jewish and anti-Irish jingoism had existed pre-Second World War, but the nature of racism shifted due to the quantity of immigration after Windrush.
20. Cited in Thorpe, *A History of the British Labour Party*, p. 180.
21. C. Knowles, *Race, Discourse and Labourism* (London: Routledge, 2005), p. 90.
22. C.T.B. Smith and R. Clifton et al., *Strikes in Britain: A Research Study of Industrial Stoppages in the United Kingdom* (London: Department of Employment, 1978).
23. Barbara Castle obituary, *Guardian*, 4 May 2002.
24. Cited in A.C. Crines, *Michael Foot and the Labour Leadership* (London: Cambridge Scholars Publishing, 2011), p. 55.
25. R. Crossman, *The Diaries of a Cabinet Minister*, Volume 3 (London: Hamish Hamilton and Jonathan Cape, 1977), p. 925.
26. Miliband, *Parliamentary Socialism*, pp. 372–3.
27. Cited in A. Freeman, *The Benn Heresy* (London: Pluto Press, 1982), p. 52.
28. Cited in P. Bell, *The Labour Party in Opposition, 1970–1974* (London: Routledge, 2016), p. 15.
29. T. Benn, *The Benn Diaries* (London: Hutchinson, 1995), pp. 241–5.

30. K. Coates (ed.), *What Went Wrong* (Nottingham: Spokesman Books, 2008), p. 129.

31. Workerism in Marxism generally refers to an accommodation to the perceived prejudices of what socialists think working-class people believe.

32. Michael Barrett Brown outlines his key arguments in *From Labourism to Socialism* (Nottingham: Spokesman Books, 1972).

33. *Labour's Programme for Britain* (London: Labour Party, 1973), p. 30.

34. Holland looked to the Italian Instituto di Riconstruzione Industriale as a model, focusing not just on saving ailing industries but on directing investment and growth towards prosperous sectors too.

35. N. Thompson, *Political Economy and the Labour Party* (London: Routledge, 2006), p. 217.

36. Cited in M. Wickham-Jones, *Economic Strategy and the Labour Party* (Basingstoke: Macmillan, 1996), p. 53.

37. S. Holland, *The Socialist Challenge* (London: Quartet Books, 1976), p. 155.

38. A reference to the form of state rule in France under Louis Bonaparte after 1851.

39. D. Coates, *Labour in Power? Study of the Labour Government, 1974–79* (New Jersey: Prentice Hall, 1980), p. 248.

40. Coates, *Labour in Power?*, p. 251.

41. As Henry Kissinger argued: 'I don't see why *we* need to stand by and watch a *country go communist* due to the *irresponsibility of its people.*'

42. Heffer describes a visit to Allende months before he was murdered in the coup. Allende said that the Chilean revolution would not be like Russia with its vast bureaucracy, but 'freedom, democracy, music and dance. Then he added: "If they let us."' E. Heffer, *Never a Yes Man* (London: Verso, 1991), p. 143.

43. *The Sunday Times* published an article on 29 March 1981 outlining rumours of a coup plan in 1968. See also A. Morgan, *Harold Wilson* (London: Pluto Press, 1992), p. 331, and J. Medhurst, *That Option No Longer Exists* (London: Zero Books, 2014), p. 93.

44. Marquand, *The Progressive Dilemma*, p. 159.

45. For more see H. Wainwright and L. Elliott, *Lucas Plan: New Trade Unionism in the Making?* (London: Allison and Busby, 1982).

46. J. Jones, *Union Man* (London: Collins, 1986), pp. 315–16; see also K. Hickson (ed.), *New Labour, Old Labour: The Wilson and Callaghan Governments 1974–1979* (London: Routledge, 1994), p. 81.

47. Benn, *The Benn Diaries*, p. 361.

48. He was replaced by Reg Varley, an ex-miner. Years later Ken Coates mocked the lack of principles of these supposedly radical-minded trade

unionists as they wound their way into a Labour Cabinet: 'as a mine-worker [Varley] had been an effective partisan of workers' control ... when he became a member of Parliament he favoured parliamentary control, and once he was a Minister he was immediately converted to ministerial control'. Coates, *What Went Wrong*, pp. 129–30.

49. Seyd, *The Rise and Fall of the Labour Left* p. 53.
50. Seyd, *The Rise and Fall of the Labour Left* p. 87.
51. Shaw, *Discipline and Discord in the Labour Party*, pp. 172–6.
52. D. Panitch and C. Leys, *The End of Parliamentary Socialism: From New Left to New Labour* (London: Verso, 2001), pp. 136–8.
53. Edmund Burke argued that elected representatives in the House of Commons should be free to make their own decisions and vote in accordance with their own views, unimpeded by having to follow the wishes of their electorate. Put simply, elect a politician to act as they see fit, assuming it will be for the general good.
54. J. Callaghan (ed.), *Interpreting the Labour Party: Approaches to Labour Politics and History* (Manchester: Manchester University Press, 2003), p. 161.
55. H. Wainwright, *Labour: A Tale of Two Parties* (London: Hogarth Press, 1987), p. 17.
56. Freeman, *The Benn Heresy*, p. 112.
57. Medhurst, *That Option No Longer Exists*, p. 121.
58. Tom Sawyer from NUPE is quoted by Wainwright as saying that 'the Social Contract was a deal struck between leaders; the radical side of it did not have any roots among the people. For instance the argument for planning agreements had not really been put over to the people who worked in industries.' Wainwright, *Labour: A Tale of Two Parties*, p. 226.
59. Coates, *Labour in Power?*, pp. 39–40.
60. Meacher in Coates, *What Went Wrong*, p. 182.
61. Benn, *The Benn Diaries*, p. 380.
62. Interview with Tony Benn, 'On the True Power of Democracy', *Morning Star*, 24 October 2003.
63. Coates, *What Went Wrong*, pp. 10–12.
64. Cited in Medhurst, *That Option No Longer Exists*, p. 132.
65. V. Bogdanor, 'The IMF Crisis, 1976', from www.gresham.ac.uk/lectures-and-events/the-imf-crisis-1976.

Chapter Six

1. T. Benn, *Arguments for Socialism* (Harmondsworth: Penguin, 1980), p. 213.

2. Seyd, *The Rise and Fall of the Labour Left*, p. 116.

3. See J. Curran, J. Petley and I. Gaber, *Culture Wars: The Media and the British Left* (Edinburgh: Edinburgh University Press, 2005) for many hundreds of examples; for the historical context described see chapter 2.

4. Panitch and Leys, *The End of Parliamentary Socialism*, pp. 193–4.

5. Cited in Wainwright, *Labour: A Tale of Two Parties*, p. 229.

6. https://www.theguardian.com/commentisfree/2013/feb/22/defeat-in-bermondsey-defeat-for-left

7. 'Bermondsey By-election 1983: Homophobia, Hatred, Smears and Xenophobia', *Independent*, 24 February 2013.

8. K. Bean, *The New Politics of Sinn Féin* (Liverpool: Liverpool University Press, 2007), p. 76.

9. Ken Livingstone provocatively argued that 'I was struck by the similarity of what you might call the new radical left in the Labour Party and the radical left in Sinn Fein.' Cited in Bean, *The New Politics of Sinn Féin*, p. 77.

10. Bean, *The New Politics of Sinn Féin*, pp. 76–7.

11. Panitch in Coates, *Paving the Third Way*, pp. 207–8.

12. Freeman, *The Benn Heresy*, p. 116.

13. Benn, *The Benn Diaries*, p. 513.

14. Panitch and Leys, *The End of Parliamentary Socialism*, pp. 49–65.

15. M. Foot, *Loyalists and Loners* (London: Collins, 1986), p. 123.

16. J.D. Derbyshire and I. Derbyshire, *Politics in Britain: From Callaghan to Thatcher* (Edinburgh: Chambers, 1988), p. 100.

17. Benn, *The Benn Diaries*, p. 529.

18. Benn, *The Benn Diaries*, p. 529.

19. Wainwright, *Labour: A Tale of Two Parties*, p. 97.

20. Cited in P. Hain, *Back to the Future of Socialism* (Bristol: Policy Press, 2015), p. 148.

21. Thompson, *Political Economy and the Labour Party*, p. 227.

22. *In and Against the State*, published by Pluto Press in 1980, outlines these theories.

23. The Tories were on 27 per cent throughout 1981 and saw only a slight increase in 1982 before the 'Falklands Factor'. A. Nunns, *The Candidate* (London: OR, 2016), p. 277.

24. J. Adams, *Tony Benn: A Biography* (London: Biteback Publishing, 2011), pp. 412–13.

25. *Labour Weekly*, 18 February 1983.

26. R. Heffernan and M. Marqusee, *Defeat from the Jaws of Victory* (London: Verso, 1992), p. 28.

27. Heffernan and Marqusee, *Defeat from the Jaws of Victory*, p. 27.

28. Wainwright, *Labour: A Tale of Two Parties*.

29. J. Winterton and R. Winterton, *Coal, Crisis and Conflict: The 1984–5 Miners' Strike in Yorkshire* (Manchester: Manchester University Press, 1989), p. 113.
30. For more see S. Hannah, *Radical Lambeth* (London: Breviary Stuff, 2021).
31. Kinnock's tub-thumping, *Daily Mail* pleasing diatribe included: 'I'll tell you what happens with impossible promises. You start with far-fetched resolutions. They are then pickled into a rigid dogma, a code, and you go through the years sticking to that, out-dated, misplaced, irrelevant to the real needs, and you end in the grotesque chaos of a Labour council – a Labour council – hiring taxis to scuttle round a city handing out redundancy notices to its own workers.'
32. E. Shaw, *The Labour Party Since 1979* (New York: Taylor and Francis, 2002), p. 259.
33. Cited in Heffernan and Marqusee, *Defeat from the Jaws of Victory*, p. 172.
34. Heffernan and Marqusee, *Defeat from the Jaws of Victory*, pp. 125–6.
35. Heffernan and Marqusee, *Defeat from the Jaws of Victory*, pp. 66–9.
36. Shaw, *The Labour Party Since 1979*, p. 40.
37. Panitch and Leys, *The End of Parliamentary Socialism*, p. 222.
38. Wainwright, *Labour: A Tale of Two Parties*, p. 184.
39. Wainwright, *Labour: A Tale of Two Parties*, p. 186.
40. M. Wadsworth, 'Celebrating Black Sections', *Guardian*, 6 October 2008.
41. Heffernan and Marqusee, *Defeat from the Jaws of Victory*, p. 77.
42. Wadsworth, 'Celebrating Black Sections'.
43. D. Howe, *Black Sections in the Labour Party* (Race Today Collective, 1985), p. 15.
44. J. Golding, *Hammer of the Left: The Battle for the Soul of the Labour Party* (London: Biteback Publishing, 2016), p. 361.
45. Golding, *Hammer of the Left*, p. 364.
46. P. Taaffe and T. Mulhearn, *Liverpool – The City That Dared to Fight* (Liverpool: Fortress Books, 1988), pp. 368–9.
47. For more see S. Hannah, *Can't Pay, Won't Pay: The Fight to Stop the Poll Tax* (London: Pluto 2020).
48. P. Gould, *The Unfinished Revolution: How Modernisers Saved the Labour Party* (London: Little, Brown and Company, 1998), p. 158.

Chapter Seven

1. From his leadership statement 1994, published in T. Blair, *New Britain: My Vision of a Young Country* (London: Fourth Estate, 1996), p. 3.
2. P. Mandelson, *The Third Man* (London: Harper Press, 2011), p. 63.

3. Cited in A. Seldon, *Blair's Britain, 1997–2007* (Cambridge: Cambridge University Press, 2007), p. 26.
4. A. Campbell, *The Blair Years* (London: Hutchinson, 2007), p. 78, cited in M. Pugh, *Speak for Britain* (London: Vintage, 2011), p. 394.
5. D. Tanner and P. Thane (eds), *Labour's First Century* (Cambridge: Cambridge University Press, 2000), p. 368.
6. Golding, *Hammer of the Left*, p. 395.
7. A term coined by French intellectuals – the 'single thought'.
8. T. Blair, *The Third Way: New Politics for the New Century* (London: Fabian Society, 1998), p. 1.
9. G.R. Taylor, *Labour's Renewal? The Policy Review and Beyond* (Basingstoke: Macmillan, 1997), p. 176.
10. Beech and Hickson, *The Struggle for Labour's Soul*, p. 17.
11. T. Blair, *Let Us Face the Future* (London: Fabian Society, 1995), p. 7.
12. Cited in 'Blair's War on Enemies of Ambition', *Guardian*, 29 September 1999.
13. For more see Tom Mills' article 'It Was a Fantasy: Centrist Political Commentators in the Age of Corbynism', *New Socialist*, June 2017, at https://newsocialist.org.uk/it-was-a-fantasy.
14. Alan Simpson, 'Inside New Labour's Rolling Coup: The Blair Supremacy', *Red Pepper*, 1 December 2014, www.redpepper.org.uk/inside-new-labours-rolling-coup-the-blair-supremacy.
15. R. McKibbon, 'Defeatism, Defeatism, Defeatism', *London Review of Books*, 22 March 2007.
16. L. Minkin, *The Blair Supremacy: A Study in the Politics of the Labour's Party Management* (Manchester: Manchester University Press, 2014), p. 128.
17. Minkin, *The Blair Supremacy*, pp. 82–3.
18. *The Road to the Manifesto*, Labour Party, 1996.
19. Tony Blair knighted him in 1999.
20. M. Marqusee, 'New Labour and its Discontents', *New Left Review*, July–August 1997, p. 133.
21. Marqusee, 'New Labour and its Discontents', p. 130.
22. For a full blow-by-blow account see Davies, *Through the Looking Glass*.
23. 'Labour List, Cuts, Class War and a Left-wing Superstar', *LRC Conference Review*, 17 January 2011.
24. N. Lawson, 'Without the Soft Left, Labour is Doomed to Splinter', *Guardian*, 24 July 2015.
25. Davies, *Through the Looking Glass*, pp. 131–45, see also Ken Livingstone's memoir *You Can't Say That!* (London: Faber and Faber, 2011).

26. N. Dempsey, 'Two Classes, Two Responses to the Crisis', 1 June 2012, http://www.socialistaction.net/Economics/Two-classes-two-responses-to-the-crisis.html.
27. 'Unions Force Defeat on Hospitals', *Guardian*, 2 October 2003.
28. Cited in Minkin, *The Blair Supremacy*, p. 346.
29. 'Labour Party Membership Falls to Lowest Level Since it Was Founded in 1900', *Daily Telegraph*, 30 June 2008.
30. T. Benn, *More Time for Politics* (London: Hutchinson, 2008), p. 305.
31. Tom Nairn, writing about Labour in the early 1970s, said that the difference between Labour and the Tories was only half an inch, 'but it is in that half inch we survive'.

Chapter Eight

1. O. Reyes, Interview with Michael Meacher and John McDonnell, *Red Pepper*, 11 May 2007.
2. Martin Wicks, Labour Representation Committee conference, 21 November 2007, https://martinwicks.wordpress.com/2007/11/21/labour-representation-committee-conference.
3. J. McDonnell, 'Turning a Crisis into an Opportunity', *Guardian*, 13 October 2008.
4. R. Seymour, *Corbyn: The Strange Rebirth of Radical Politics* (London: Verso, 2016), p. 174.
5. *One Nation Labour*, edited by J. Cruddas (2013), at http://labourlist.org/wp-content/uploads/2013/01/One-Nation-Labour-debating-the-future.pdf.
6. O. Jones, 'Ed Balls' Surrender is a Political Disaster', *New Statesman*, 15 January 2012.
7. N. Watt and R. Syal, 'Ed Miliband to Review Labour's Link with Trade Unions', *Guardian*, 5 July 2013.
8. Nunns, *The Candidate*, pp. 59–60.
9. 'In Labour's Leadership Race, Yvette Cooper is the One to Beat', *Guardian*, 23 June 2015.
10. 'Jeremy Corbyn and his Acolytes are Simply in Denial', *Telegraph*, 5 June 2015.
11. Nunns, *The Candidate*, p. 15.
12. Nunns, *The Candidate*, p. 15.
13. Nunns, *The Candidate*, p. 10.
14. A phrase from David Hare's *The Absence of War*, a play that also deals with a beleaguered Labour leader.

15. P. Wintour and N. Watts, 'Corbyn: The Long Read', *Guardian*, 25 September 2015.

16. C. Lewis, 'Meet Momentum: The Next Step in the Transformation of our Politics', *New Statesman*, 8 October 2015.

17. D. Hodges, 'The Age of Jeremy Corbyn is Here. Now the Civil War', *Telegraph*, 30 September 2015.

18. This tactic had been tried by the Brownites against Blair in 2006.

19. Nunns, *The Candidate*, p. 314.

20. Nunns, *The Candidate*, p. 316.

21. 'Corbyn Tells Labour Councils to Hold Back on Illegal Budget-setting', *Guardian*, 18 December 2015.

22. R. Mason and J. Elgot, 'Peter Mandelson: I Try to Undermine Jeremy Corbyn "every single day"', *Guardian*, 21 February 2017.

23. 'Furness MP Apologises for Doubting Labour Leader Jeremy Corbyn After "Incredible Achievement" in General Election', *Westmorland Gazette*, 17 June 2017.

24. A. Chakelian, 'Winners and Losers of the General Election 2017', *New Statesman*, 9 June 2017.

25. Tony Blair, Speech to Progress, 22 July 2015.

Chapter Nine

1. For instance, leading left figures like Graham Bash from the LRC were expelled, and the ten pledges to continue Corbyn's politics that Starmer stood on lasted barely a few months before being completely abandoned.

2. Cited in L. Panitch and C. Leys, *Searching for Socialism: The Project of the Labour New Left from Benn to Corbyn* (London: Verso, 2020), p. 237.

3. 'Labour: 673 Anti-Semitism Complaints in 10 Months', BBC News, 11 February 2019, https://www.bbc.co.uk/news/uk-politics-47203397.

4. Labour General Secretary Jennie Formby said: 'I totally reject the suggestion that the existence of anti-Semitism in our party is a smear. I have seen hard evidence of it and that is why I have been so determined to do whatever is possible to eliminate it from the party.' Quoted in 'Labour: 673 Anti-Semitism Complaints in 10 Months', BBC News.

5. P. Oborne, J. Schlosberg and R. Sanders, 'Were Labour's Antisemitism Failures Really Corbyn's Fault?', *Open Democracy*, 26 June 2020, https://www.opendemocracy.net/en/opendemocracyuk/were-labours-antisemitism-failures-really-corbyns-fault.

6. 'British Army "could stage mutiny under Corbyn", Says Senior Serving General', *The Independent*, 20 September 2015. (Curiously the original *Sunday Times* article appears to have vanished.)

7. R. Dearlove, 'Jeremy Corbyn is a Danger to This Nation. At MI6, which I once led, he wouldn't clear the security vetting', *Telegraph*, 7 June 2017.

8. For comprehensive account see 'How the UK Military and Intelligence Establishment is Working to Stop Jeremy Corbyn Becoming Prime Minister', *Daily Maverick*, 4 December 2019.

9. 'Labour's Power Struggle Goes Further Than Just Momentum versus Unite', *Guardian*, 2 March 2018.

10. 'Jon Lansman Pulls Out of Labour General Secretary Contest', *Guardian*, 11 March 2018.

11. 'Len McCluskey: Accusing Unite of "Machine Politics" Undermines Jeremy Corbyn', *Labour List*, 26 September 2018.

12. 'Labour Remains Committed to Work Visa System – Not Free Movement', *Labour List*, 26 September 2019. Though Abbott had previously backed free movement and urged the left to defend it, for instance: 'Diane Abbott Calls on Left to Back Free Movement as Workers' Right', *Guardian*, 28 March 2017.

13. Jones, *This Land: The Story of a Movement*, pp. 282–90.

14. P. Wintour, 'To Corbyn's Dismay, the Story of the US-UK Dossier Has Mostly Been Its Origin', *Guardian*, 3 August 2020.

15. R. Seymour, 'No False Consolations', *Novara Media*, 13 December 2019.

16. 'In Their Own Words: Why Voters Abandoned Labour', *YouGov*, 23 December 2019, https://yougov.co.uk/topics/politics/articles-reports/2019/12/23/their-own-words-why-voters-abandoned-labour

17. 'Who Labour Lost in 2019 – and Why', *Labour List*, 19 June 2020, https://labourlist.org/2020/06/who-labour-lost-in-2019-and-why.

18. Lord Ashcroft, 'Diagnosis of Defeat: Labour's Turn to Smell the Coffee', 10 February 2020, https://lordashcroftpolls.com/2020/02/diagnosis-of-defeat-labours-turn-to-smell-the-coffee.

19. For instance, in the final days before the election, fake tweets purporting to be from Corbyn praising the terrorist attack on London Bridge on 29 November 2019 were circulated through countless WhatsApp groups.

20. 'How Fake Jeremy Corbyn Tweet About London Bridge Spread Like Wildfire In Minutes', *Huffington Post*, 9 December 2019.

21. Tweet on 20 January 2020.

22. For instance, the row over Long-Bailey's comments about nepotism, which were seen by some in Unite as a veiled criticism. 'Labour Leadership Contest: Rebecca Long-Bailey Causes "massive Row" over Claims of Nepotism', *Sky News*, 4 February 2020.

23. 'Labour Even MORE Radical? Sir Keir Starmer Pledges to Build on Corbyn's "Foundation"', *Daily Express*, 11 January 2020.

24. See, for instance, P. Collins, 'Time to Root Out Corbynites Once and For All', *The Times*, 23 July 2020, and A. Epstein, 'Keir Starmer Must Go Further to Axe Corbyn from Labour over Anti-Semitism Shame', *Telegraph*, 29 October 2020.

25. See above pages 24–25.

26. 'Jeremy Corbyn Says Labour Not "Wedded To Freedom Of Movement" in Relaunch Speech', *Huffington Post*, 9 January 2017.

27. The traditional Marxist approach is that the capitalist state exists to defend capitalist property relations, therefore the police are an instrument of capitalist rule and cannot be transformed into a force to aid working-class emancipation.

28. U. March, 'Momentum's Refounding Convention – Not the Process We Need', *Red Flag/Workers Power*, 28 June 2021.

29. By comparison, the SWP claimed to have 10,000 members in 2003 and helped lead a mass anti-war movement of over a million people.

30. 'Kinnock Warns Labour against "Perpetual Demonstration"', BBC News, 17 August 2015, https://www.bbc.co.uk/news/uk-politics-33959130.

31. Writing in *Renewal*, Paul Thompson makes the social democratic argument that it is wrong to confuse party and social movement, that a party necessarily must appeal to non-activists with a range of views, and cannot act as a vanguard organisation. Of course this is true of an electoralist party that seeks to win power through parliamentary elections, but not of a revolutionary party. See 'Corbynism Isn't a Social Movement, and Labour Shouldn't Be One', *Renewal*, 24 August 2016.

Conclusion

1. Corbyn made a statement about his handling of antisemitism during his time as leader that contradicted the official Labour line from Keir Starmer, which is what led to the disciplinary action.

2. 'Internal Report Lays Bare Poor Handling of Complaints by Labour', *Labour List*, 12 April 2020.

3. J. Ryle, 'I Saw from the Inside How Labour Staff Worked to Prevent a Labour Government', *Open Democracy*, 7 August 2020.

4. 'Opposition to Jeremy Corbyn "Hindered" Anti-Semitism Action, Claims Report', BBC News, 13 April 2020, https://www.bbc.co.uk/news/uk-politics-52271317.

5. 'Corbyn Supporters Attack Labour Moderates for "using targeted Facebook ads to trick him about own general election campaign"', *The Independent*, 15 July 2018.

6. R. Williams, *May Day Manifesto 1968* (London: Verso, 2018), p. 190.

7. From Roman Polanski's film *Chinatown* (1974), referencing the impossibility of fighting injustice.

8. *Second Congress of the Communist International Minutes of the Proceedings*, Volumes 1–2 (London: New Park Publications, 1977), p. 183.

9. L. Trotsky, *Writings on Britain Volume 2: Problems of the British Revolution* (London: New Park Publications, 1972), p. 12.

10. K. Marx and F. Engels, 'The Peasant War in Germany, Addendum to the Preface', *Selected Works*, Vol. I (Moscow, 1958), pp. 652–4.

11. See above page 45.

12. The Scottish National Party has largely replaced Labour as the left-wing party for workers in Scotland, but this is a left nationalist not a more socialist direction.

13. Panitch and Leys, *Searching for Socialism*, p. 254.

14. Panitch and Leys, *Searching for Socialism*, p. 255.

Index

Thanks to our Patreon subscribers:

Andrew Perry
Ciaran Kane

Who have shown generosity and comradeship in support of our publishing.

Check out the other perks you get by subscribing to our Patreon – visit patreon.com/plutopress.

Subscriptions start from £3 a month.

The Pluto Press Newsletter

Hello friend of Pluto!

Want to stay on top of the best radical books
we publish?

Then sign up to be the first to hear about our
new books, as well as special events,
podcasts and videos.

You'll also get 50% off your first order with us
when you sign up.

Come and join us!

Go to bit.ly/PlutoNewsletter

Made in United States
Orlando, FL
30 November 2023

39693038R00161